The Most Beautiful Job in the World

The Most Beautiful Job in the World

Lifting the Veil on the Fashion Industry

Giulia Mensitieri

Translated by Natasha Lehrer

BLOOMSBURY VISUAL ARTS
LONDON · NEW YORK · OXFORD · NEW DELHI · SYDNEY

BLOOMSBURY VISUAL ARTS
Bloomsbury Publishing Plc
50 Bedford Square, London, WC1B 3DP, UK
1385 Broadway, New York, NY 10018, USA

BLOOMSBURY, BLOOMSBURY VISUAL ARTS and the Diana logo
are trademarks of Bloomsbury Publishing Plc

First published in France, under the title *Le plus beau métier du monde*

© Editions LA DECOUVERTE, Paris, France, 2018

First published in English by Bloomsbury Visual Arts
Translation © Natasha Lehrer, 2020
Financial support for the translation work
was provided by CNL

CNL CENTRE
NATIONAL
DU LIVRE

Giulia Mensitieri has asserted her right under the Copyright, Designs
and Patents Act, 1988, to be identified as Author of this work.

Cover design by Philippe Rouy
Cover image © Christopher Anderson/Magnum Photos

A catalogue record for this book is available from the British Library.

Library of Congress Cataloging-in-Publication Data
Names: Mensitieri, Giulia, author. | Lehrer, Natasha, translator.
Title: The most beautiful job in the world : lifting the veil on the
fashion industry / Giulia Mensitieri.
Other titles: Plus beau métier du monde. English
Description: London, UK ; New York, NY, USA : Bloomsbury Visual Arts,
Bloomsbury Publishing PLo, 2020. | Translation of: "Le plus beau métier du
monde." | Includes bibliographical references and index.
Identifiers: LCCN 2019049091 | ISBN 9781350110137 (HB) |
ISBN 9781350110168 (PB) | ISBN 9781350110144 (ePDF) |
ISBN 9781350110151 (eBook)
Subjects: LCSH: Fashion merchandising. | Clothing trade. | Fashion design. |
Exploitation. | Social responsibility of business.
Classification: LCC HD9940.A2 M4613 2018 | DDC 338.4/774692–dc23
LC record available at https://lccn.loc.gov/2019049091

ISBN: HB: 978-1-3501-1013-7
       PB: 978-1-3501-1016-8
       ePDF: 978-1-3501-1014-4
       eBook: 978-1-3501-1015-1

Typeset by RefineCatch, Limited, Bungay, Suffolk
Printed and bound in India

To find out more about our authors and books visit www.bloomsbury.com
and sign up for our newsletters.

To my uncle, Giancarlo Coretti

Contents

Preface

Paris, April 2012

I was meeting Mia[1] in Paris's 10th arrondissement, at a bar called Chez Jeannette, popular with the fashion crowd. She was having a drink with Sebastien, the editor of a cutting-edge independent fashion magazine. When I arrived, Sebastien, who was wearing an unusual, sculptural black outfit, looked me critically up and down. Mia was in jeans, a hoodie, and a pair of Chanel pumps. Her Prada handbag hung from the back of her chair. She was very upset. 'I cried all weekend. Thursday I did a shoot for Derloge[2] and it was super intense. When I got home it was like total emptiness, the flat needed cleaning, I didn't have money for the rent, I'm owed money and I'm in debt. I don't even have the money to buy myself a drink.' She asked Sebastien if he would get her a beer. 'When it's up it's very up, when it's down it's very down. I can see results in what I do, but they're not financial.' Her Blackberry rang; she glanced at the screen but didn't answer. 'It's Bouygues, they're hassling me for 273 euros I owe them. They're going to cut me off soon.'

In October 2015, Alber Elbaz, artistic director of the celebrated French fashion house Lanvin, was let go after fourteen years at the label. In a statement he said: 'We began our careers as designers, we had dreams, ideas, emotions ... And then the job description changed. We became "artistic directors". Then it changed again, and we became people who created images. Now our job is to make sure that our designs look good on a screen. We have to make the screen explode, those are the new rules.'[3]

---

[1]   All names have been changed.
[2]   The fictional name of a well-known chain of hair salons in France.
[3]   'Alber Elbaz et Lanvin, la rupture?' 3 November 2015, http://blog.dailyshopwindow.com/alber-elbaz-et-lanvin-la-rupture.

Elbaz's words highlight the tensions brought about by evolutions in the fashion industry, whose profit motive is damaging the creative work it depends on. A week before Elbaz was let go, the same incompatibility between productivity and creativity led to the departure of Raf Simons from Dior, where he had been artistic director for the previous four years. In his statement to the media, Simons said that he wanted to focus on his own interests and passions. In response to Simon's departure from Dior, fashion journalist Suzy Menkes remarked in British *Vogue*: 'Like that bird in a gilded cage, creative people at the major fashion houses have everything: a circle of assistants, drivers, first class travel, access to elegant homes and celebrity clients. Everything, but time.'[4]

Menkes explained that Raf Simons left Dior because, despite all the money and prestige, the obligation to produce ten collections a year left him no time to find inspiration. But is it true that *all* fashion creatives are living in a gilded cage? Menkes' words are interesting – both for what they say and for what they don't. Raf Simons offers an interesting example. For his first Dior show, he covered the walls of a splendid '*hotel particulier*' in one of the most expensive neighbourhoods in Paris with millions of roses, lilies and orchids, at a cost to Dior of several hundred thousand euros, to create a stunning backdrop against which to show his collection. The event was covered by the world's media, who beamed across the world photos and videos of models garbed in gorgeous, eye-wateringly expensive clothes, striding confidently across ballrooms whose walls cascaded with flowers. But other aspects of the event are rather less well known. Many of the catwalk models were working for free. The Dior seamstresses, whose job it was to transform Raf Simons's ideas into actual clothes, were probably paid barely more than the statutory minimum wage.[5]

---

4   S. Menkes, 'Why Fashion is Crashing', vogue.co.uk, 23 October 2015.
5   Data from ethnographic survey.

That is the other side of the fashion world, and it is that world that is at the heart of this book: a world that creates luxury and beauty while paying minimal salaries and often expecting people to work for free. The fashion world I encountered is Mia, a stylist, who sleeps in the living room of a rented one-bedroom flat in a working-class Parisian neighbourhood, and the next day flies to Hong Kong to produce private fashion shows for Chinese millionaires in a sumptuous hotel. The fashion world is a journalist like Sebastien who, because he edits a cutting-edge magazine, gets away with not paying the photographers, the lighting assistants, the models, the stylists, the interns, the studio assistants, the retouchers, the makeup artists, the hairdressers and the manicurists who create the images he publishes. The fashion world is the woman who models for Chanel and is paid in lipstick. The fashion world is the photographer who has to finance a photo shoot in a hotel in Deauville for Italian *Vogue* himself, and doesn't pay any of the people who take part. The fashion world is clothes that cost 30,000 euros, made by seamstresses and embroiderers on the minimum wage, who are exploited by designer labels that make a huge profit on their work. The fashion world is handbags that cost 10,000 euros each, because they have a label that says 'made in Italy' even though they are actually made in China. The fashion world is all of that, and much more besides, and it's that world of fashion, where job and financial precariousness is concealed behind the shiny façade of capitalism, that this book focuses on.

Fashion and the dream

'Every day is a white page that I must fill with a dream', wrote the designer Alber Elbaz in a book about his work.[6] 'Fashion is a dream',

---

[6]   *Lanvin, I love you*, Milan, Rizzoli, 2014.

Ludo, a young photographer, told me. *Adorned in Dreams* is the title of a book by the fashion historian Elizabeth Wilson.[7] People who create fashion, people who study it and people who sell it all describe fashion as a world of dreams. It's not hard to understand why: it's a world of fantasy, made up of images that combine beauty, luxury, ostentation, creativity, excess, power and money, displayed on screens, in boutique windows and on the pages of glossy magazines.

One might think that the dream that fashion creates is a utopia, an ideal. But fashion is also an industry, a reality, the hard fact of skilled workers, factories, ateliers, bodies, fabrics, spaces, objects. How to understand this coexistence of the idea of the dream, which became strongly apparent during the course of my research, with the materiality of the system that creates these dreams and fantasies? The concept of a 'heterotopia'[8] is a way of resolving this question, of bringing together the immaterial, dreamlike dimension of fashion with its material, tangible dimension. Heterotopias are 'places which are beyond place, even though they can in fact be localized';[9] they are 'other spaces', which can take the form of 'imaginary places', of 'parallel worlds',[10] yet which nonetheless do exist somewhere. If fashion is a dream, this dream is a heterotopia: it extends over the very areas where it is produced and staged.

Yet this fantasy world of luxury and beauty, which circulates globally on television and cinema screens, on the pages of glossy magazines and via the Internet and the advertising hoardings that are omnipresent in urban space, kindling desire and encouraging consumption in all four corners of the globe, is a place where all these fantasy elements exist alongside financial and job instability,

---

[7] Elizabeth Wilson, *Adorned in Dreams: Fashion and Modernity*, London, I.B. Tauris, 2003.
[8] Michel Foucault, *Le Corps utopique, les hétérotopies*, Paris, Lignes, 2009.
[9] M. Agier, 'Le campement urbain comme heterotopie et comme refuge, Vers un paysage mondial des espaces précaires', *Brésil(s). Sciences humaines et sociales*, no. 3, May 2013, p. 11.
[10] *Ibid.*

exploitation, domination and the quest for power. This dream, this 'other space', displays in other words all the characteristics of capitalism. This might seem surprising: how can a world of dreams be founded on a system of exploitation? And how can it be governed by rules that also govern the world that it exists outside of?

In fact, heterotopias have a specific social function: by creating these 'counter-sites',[11] circumscribed sites of 'deviation'[12] and otherness, they work to define, by opposition, the norm. Fashion as a heterotopia also plays the role of decoy, which, thanks to its display of fantasy, makes it possible to normalize the exception. Fashion is simultaneously a dream displayed on catwalks, advertising hoardings and in shop windows, and a global industry that generates excessive consumption, massive profits and multiple kinds of exploitation. Mia and the other people I met doing fieldwork for this book all work in this heterotopia. In spite of the apparatus of fantasy that distinguishes it from the 'normal order of things', fashion is lodged deep within the heart of contemporary capitalism. It is this simultaneous occupation of fairytale and fantasy and economic and professional reality that makes it an 'other space', a heterotopia. By considering it through this perspective I have set out to analyse the fantasy dimension, the social restructuring, the different ways of working and the economic instability that characterize contemporary capitalism.

---

[11] M. Foucault, *Le Corps utopique, les hétérotopies, op. cit.*, p. 24.
[12] *Ibid.*, p. 26.

Introduction

When Fashion Becomes a System

In spite of being an intrinsic part of society since early modern times,[1] fashion was not always so widespread, nor has it always had the same role within the capitalist system. As it evolved over the centuries, the industry around it also changed and evolved. It changed most dramatically over the course of the twentieth century, in terms of direction, scale and financial value, and now occupies a central position in the desires, representations and economies of contemporary capitalism. In 2008, for example, the fashion industry represented '6% of global consumption over all sectors, with a net worth of 1,400 billion euros'.[2] It was over the course of the twentieth century, particularly during the 1960s with the massive expansion of the ready-to-wear market,[3] that the

---

[1] The historian Sarah-Grace Heller points out that is impossible to establish the precise point at which 'fashion' came into being, since every historian has their own definition of the phenomenon. The most widely favoured position, however, dates it to the Renaissance period. See S.-G. Heller, *Fashion in Medieval France*, Cambridge/Rochester, D. S. Brewer, 2007. See also F. Braudel, *Civilisation matérielle, économie et capitalisme, xve–xviiie siècle* (Book 1), Paris, Le Livre de Poche, 1993, and P. C. Campbell, *The Romantic Ethic and the Spirit of Modern Consumerism*, WritersPrintShop, 1987.

[2] F. Godart, *Sociologie de la mode*, Paris, La Découverte, 2010, p. 6.

[3] 'Prêt à porter' is defined as clothes that are not made to measure. It emerged with the passage from artisanal couture and made-to-measure clothing to the standardization of sizes that enabled mass production. Originating in the United States as 'ready-to-wear', it was exported to France in the 1950s, but it was only during the 1960s that it became popular.

industry was transformed into a global system,[4] also called the fashion system.[5]

Up until the 1960s fashion products were divided – both in terms of production and symbolically – into two hermetically distinct categories: haute couture was defined by its luxury and its craftsmanship and was purchased by the social elite, while industrial and semi-industrial production was destined for the rest of the population. The post-war boom revolutionized the structure of society, with the emergence of a middle class whose economic and social power rapidly grew, becoming, from the 1970s onwards, intrinsic to the success of ready-to-wear fashion. This was also the period when fashion began to branch out and become multipolar: Milan became part of a new triumvirate of global fashion capitals, preceded by Paris (which lost its hegemony) and London. Luxury was beginning to democratize; the middle classes were now dressing in *prêt à porter*, or ready-to-wear fashion, and the working classes were also now able to access a certain level of quality and style.

The 1980s: 'Dress for success'

But the transformations that most marked the world of fashion, leading to its emergence as the economic and symbolic colossus that it is today, did not take place until the 1980s. This was the period when fashion became dominant in popular culture, thanks to the hegemony of the culture of the image. A fundamental transformation took place:

---

[4] 'Global system' is defined here as a political and historical global economy with cultural and symbolic dimensions. See Jonathan Friedman and Kasja Ekholm-Friedman, *Historical Transformations: The Anthropology of Global Systems*, Lanham, Altamira Press, 2008.

[5] Following Nello Barile, by fashion system I mean both the globalized industry with all its ramifications, the symbolic fantasy world produced by this industry, as well as the social world of those who work in the sector. See N. Barile, *Sistema moda: Oggetti, strategie e simboli: dall'iperlusso alla societ low cost*, Milan, Egea, 2011.

fashion was no longer understood as being a vessel, in other words merely a form, empty of meaning, and became content – appearance became a bearer of meaning in itself. This paradigm shift dovetailed with a new public recognition of those who worked in fashion. Television was the privileged medium for the celebration of these new divinities, the models and fashion designers who soon began to attain the status of stars. The 1980s were the years during which financial capital triumphed and neoliberalism began, with the elite classes reasserting their power and earning huge salaries, businesses being listed on the stock exchange, the introduction of free trade and the free movement of capital at a global level, a new discipline imposed on both bosses and employees, and economic policies entirely dedicated to this new order.

Neoliberalism was embodied by the figure of the yuppie, widely portrayed in both film and literature.[6] Yuppies were young, dynamic, ambitious professionals, obsessed with finding a way to present an image that indicated their social ascent, which they found in fashion, thanks to its distinctive immediacy that was the perfect means of signalling the dazzling change in status bestowed on them by the financial economy. In general terms, luxury items – not just fashion – allowed the new financial elites to distinguish themselves and endow themselves with recognizable and symbolic hegemony. The catchphrase that sums up the era, 'dress for success',[7] perfectly encapsulates the relationship between fashion and power. This was the period that reinforced the importance of the 'brand' – the idea that a label has value in and of itself, independent of the quality and design of the article of clothing. It was also the period when the fashion

---

[6] The archetype of the yuppie was brilliantly drawn by Bret Easton Ellis in his novel *American Psycho* (1991), and more recently in the film *The Wolf of Wall Street*, directed by Martin Scorsese (2013).

[7] The phrase comes from the eponymous book by John T. Molloy, published in 1975, in which he analyses the effect of clothing on personal success and introduces the notion of 'power dressing'.

industry began to delocalize and expand, selling licences for accessories to be emblazoned with the name of the brand. Designers like Ralph Lauren, Armani and Versace launched designer accessories lines, and these labels became omnipresent in all areas of everyday life, assuming a central role in popular culture.

This was the era that saw fashion become spectacle, and models and designers elevated to the rank of stars of popular culture, taking the place that had been occupied until then by singers and actors. Fashion moulded itself to the capitalist dream, with its combination of beauty, power and money, and the idea of working in fashion became more and more attractive to young people.

The 1990s: The 'imperialization' of fashion

The 1990s also played an important role in this evolution. Structural changes dating back a decade – the opening up of international markets – transformed the dominant culture: brands became globalized and were transformed into extraterritorial financial powerhouses. At the same time, the media was devoting much space to enthusing over the opening up of markets, new commercial flows, cross-cultural fertilization, and the increasing prominence of fashion celebrities. The 1990s was the decade that confirmed the fashion system and its takeover by financial capital, which, with the birth of luxury conglomerates, led to a concentration of brands. In this new neoliberal economy, fashion products – clothing, fantasy and dreams – began circulating around the world.

Between 1980 and 1990, fashion began the process of imperialization, 'characterized by a development that was both organizational, with the emergence of luxury fashion conglomerates, and societal, with the extension of a dynamic that originated in fashion into different spheres of activity'.[8] The reference to the imperialist dimension of fashion is not a metaphor. With the increase in power of the luxury holdings, fashion increased its symbolic power by fabricating a dream that was specific to this new consumer society, at the same time as its economic power was growing thanks to its geographical and financial expansion.

The most emblematic of these fashion empires is without question the LVMH group, the most powerful holding in the sector, listed on the Paris stock exchange. Since it was founded in 1987, the group has acquired many high fashion labels including Fendi, Berluti, Givenchy, Marc Jacobs, Kenzo, Emilio Pucci, Céline, Donna Karan and Loro Piana.[9] It also owns several cosmetics and perfume brands, and shops or franchises including Sephora, La Samaritaine, Le Bon Marché and the Grande Epicerie, as well as jewellery and watchmaking marques including Chaumet, De Beers and Dior Watches. This list is far from exhaustive. In 2013 the group owned 867 subsidiaries all over the world and a network of over 3,000 boutiques. In spite of the symbolic hegemony of high fashion and luxury goods within the group, the fashion and leather goods part of the group represented only 35 per cent of its turnover in 2014.[10] This makes it the biggest part of the group, but it is far from representing the majority of its revenues. The same year, 30 per cent of its turnover was in Europe, 30 per cent in Asia (excluding Japan) and 30 per cent in Japan.

[8]   F. Godart, *Sociologie de la mode*, pp. 97–8.

[9]   LVMH was created in 1987 from the merger of the companies Moët Hennessy (which itself was the result of the merger between the champagne label Moët et Chandon and Hennessy cognac) and leather goods label Louis Vuitton. In 1990, Bernard Arnaud became head of the group and its major shareholder. Since the group was founded, it has bought up many cosmetics, jewellery, fashion, leather goods and wine and spirits brands, as well as upmarket retail chains, making it currently the most financially valuable luxury conglomerate in the world.

[10] This information is taken from the LVMH website and its 2014 financial declaration (lvmh.fr/wp-content/uploads/2015/02/lvmh-documents-financiers-2014.pdf).

The astronomical turnover of the industry is evidence that, in spite of the financial crisis, fashion continues to sell, thanks to its 'desirability', as Bernard Arnaud put it in 2014 – in other words, the dream disseminated by its products. All that is made possible by its 'entrepreneurial spirit',[11] which is to say its absolute adhesion to the neoliberal model. The data shows how globalized these empires are, with both production and distribution spread all over the world. Fashion is now a global system that has, since the 1990s, converted more and more followers to its cult.

The New Economy and the cult of creativity

The 1990s were marked by major structural and social changes that were determining factors in the generalized expansion of contemporary capitalism. While fashion was becoming imperial, the West was beginning to move into a new era, the era of the New Economy,[12] based on communication and services. As industrial production was increasingly delocalized, Europe began to place service industries at the heart of its economy. Communication, culture, creativity and information became the buzzwords of this new mode of production. The role and significance of work, as well as its organization, were similarly transformed, rendering the traditional salaried employee a retrograde and restrictive model, and privileging the notion of flexibility, a term constantly hyped up by people with political and social influence. A new way of working was developing – creative, casual and unshackled – which, particularly in English-speaking countries, was promoted by a number of writers,[13] who

[11] Ibid.
[12] C. Leadbeater, *Living on Thin Air: The New Economy*, London, Penguin Books, 2000.
[13] The emblematic figure of the literature of the New Economy, frequently cited by public and political figures, is Richard Florida. See Richard L. Florida, *The Rise of the Creative Class*, New York, Basic Books, 2002.

argued that the end of a salaried society signalled a form of emancipation, permitting an individualistic and satisfying working life, based on a person's skills and capacity for independence.

It was in this context of deindustrialization, and the decline of the society of salaried employees and the promotion of new ways of working,[14] that fashion schools began to proliferate. Fashion was no longer just a dream concocted through the media looking-glass – it was developing into a new professionalized industry. The fashion industry combined all the ingredients of the neoliberal dream: competitiveness, creativity, beauty, power and money. But the proliferation of degree courses and the consequent increase in the number of professionals rapidly came up against the lack of jobs, leading, inevitably, to an increase in workers without stable jobs.[15]

While I was doing my fieldwork, I was able to observe the mechanisms and the impact of this 'overproduction of dream creators' in the course of the many interviews I conducted with teachers and former students of a Brussels school of art, fashion and design, whose fashion department is considered one of the best in the world. Its graduates are in great demand at the large Parisian fashion houses and luxury labels. As Jacques, a teacher and former student at the school, told me, 'fashion is fashionable . . . When I applied there were about sixty applicants, nowadays between 160 and 180 people apply every year.'

The institutionalization of fashion work effected by these schools leads inevitably to the institutionalization and normalization of types of exploitation specific to the industry, as their degrees prepare

---

[14] One of the best books documenting this paradigm shift is Luc Boltanski and Eve Chiappello's *Le Nouvel Esprit du capitalisme*, Paris, Gallimard, 1999.

[15] The UK was a pioneer in the legitimatization of fashion as a profession and opened several fashion departments in art schools during this period. The British sociologist Angela McRobbie was one of the first to recognize the link between the New Economy, the proliferation of fashion schools, and increased social precariousness. See A. McRobbie, *British Fashion Design: Rag Trade or Image Industry?* London/New York, Routledge, 1998.

students for the 'rhythm of the large fashion houses', in the words of
another former student of the school. Fourteen-hour days and
working through the night are the norm, in complete contravention
of EU labour law. By financing this pedagogical model in public
universities, the state is participating in the production of workers
who will never demand their social rights, because they don't even
know what they are. The 'new spirit of capitalism',[16] in which the
normalization of job instability and the cult of self-expression through
creativity coexist, can be seen in the world of fashion in almost its
purest state. The fashion system is a privileged arena for the study of
capitalism, both in its global dynamics and its dimension of fantasy, in
the manner in which labour is organized, and in the subjectivities and
strategies of subjugation it creates.

I deliberately chose not to include in my research an entire swathe
of this industry – factory workers, specifically – and to focus only on
those who work on fashion's immaterial production,[17] in order to deal
more broadly with the category in the industry known as 'cultural and
creative'.[18] The book begins by looking at the economic and political
role of the dream element of fashion, and the different forms of
globalization that structure it (in other words, the global circulation
of desirable dreams, and the delocalization of production in order to
bring costs down). This is followed by an analysis of the logic by which

[16] L. Boltanski, E. Chiapello, *Le Nouvel Esprit du capitalisme.*
[17] Antonella Corsani, Maurizio Lazzarato and Antonio Negri, *Le Bassin de travail
       immatériel (BTI) dans la métropole parisienne,* Paris, L'Harmattan, 1996.
[18] Though each expression refers to the same domain, that is to say 'how cultural goods are
       produced and disseminated in modern economies and societies' (D. Hesmondhalgh,
       'Cultural and Creative Industries', J. Frow, T. Bennett (eds), *The SAGE Handbook of
       Cultural Analysis,* SAGE, 2008), the concepts of the 'cultural industry' and the 'creative
       industry' are not equivalent, for both political and theoretical reasons. The two concepts
       have had a paradoxical trajectory. The first was explored in the writings of the Frankfurt
       School (see M. Horkheimer, T. W. Adorno, *Dialectic of Enlightenment,* 1947), and
       subsequently became a descriptive and analytical notion. The second became
       widespread thanks to explorations of the New Economy, Richard Florida's in particular,
       which argue that those who work in the creative industries are the pioneers of the future
       way of working. However, these ideas soon acquired a critical dimension.

the economic and symbolic values that regulate the fashion world[19] are attributed, leading to the paradox that the more prestigious the occupation, the less well-paid it is; an exploration of the variety of fashion jobs which make up this world; and an analysis of the precariousness specific to these different professionals. Finally, I interrogate the forms of subjugation and subjectification (understood here as the process of creating subjects) specific to fashion, by focusing on the role of emotions within the hierarchies of this professional world, the injunctions to conform and to appear to conform to a specific professional role, and the methods and strategies that those who work in fashion use to enable them to cope with rampant inequalities and different kinds of domination.

Anonymity

The purpose of this book is not to denounce but to observe, describe, understand and analyse. Paradoxically, fashion products and dreams are highly visible and widely available, while what goes on behind the scenes remains extremely opaque and difficult to access, which leads one inevitably to consider issues of disclosure. I have tried throughout to remain descriptive and my principal objective when writing up my research has been to guarantee the anonymity of my interviewees, in order to avoid any risk of damaging their careers. For this reason, all names have been changed and I have omitted some elements of sociological description and altered others. Occasionally I changed or combined physical details and locations. For the same reason, all the names of magazines have been changed (with the exception of *Vogue*,

---

[19] 'Fashion world' refers to a specifically defined social world that I encountered during my research, an entity composed of individuals, relationships, networks, situations, economies and exchanges. It does not refer to a fiction or an 'objectivizing' construction.

which publishes so many fashion stories that it would be difficult to identify those I write about in the book).

The names of companies have similarly been modified in cases where there was any risk of making employees who participated in my research recognizable. Nonetheless, this book is concerned with deconstructing the fantasies created by fashion, an industry that is rich and powerful and yet predicated on inequality. It seemed important to name some of the largest companies, while taking care to avoid any correlation that could be established between the circumstances, the individuals and the companies described.

Part One

Fashion and Capitalism: A System for Producing the Dream

I originally met Mia long before I started researching this book; she was renting an apartment in Paris with Jaime, an old friend of mine. Mia was thirty at the time, and had come to France in the wake of a romantic breakup, keen to both establish a new personal life and develop her career. After gaining a degree from an Italian fashion school, she worked as a journalist for a fashion magazine in Milan and then as a consultant for several ready-to-wear labels. In Paris she began freelancing as a stylist for photo shoots. Her work as a stylist consists of overseeing all the different elements of a shoot, whether a story for a magazine or an advertising campaign for a brand: she chooses the inspiration, theme, location, clothes, accessories, background and models. Sometimes she also recruits the people working behind the scenes: photographer, hairdresser, makeup artist and photo retoucher. She basically directs the shoot, working alongside the photographer. She has a strong personality: authoritative, charismatic and incisive. She cheerfully acknowledges that she can be a 'prima donna' or a 'drama queen'. She has a gravelly voice, and often wears bright red lipstick. Her style is an eclectic blend of sophisticated and bold, sometimes casual but never predictable, mixing up luxury labels with high street brands. It was thanks to Mia that I was able to gain an introduction to people who work in fashion.

1

Fabricating Desire: Press and Advertising

The *Heidi* shoot

During one of our many Skype conversations, Mia told me that she was doing a fashion shoot the following week with a couple of supermodels.[1] It was going to be 'a really professional, high level thing', and the way she talked about it, it was clear that it was something I shouldn't miss. It was a shoot for *Heidi*,[2] a Swiss women's magazine, that was going to run both online and in print. As Mia didn't have the precise time of the shoot yet, I decided to stay over the night before at her apartment, in La Chapelle, an ethnically mixed, largely working-class neighbourhood in Paris. Around ten o'clock that evening she received an email from her agent telling her to be at the studio at 8.15 the following morning. That night we shared a bed in the kitchen-living room of the apartment she rented with her friend Jaime, who had the bedroom.

The press offices of the labels whose clothes were appearing in the story had sent over the pieces that Mia had selected directly to the studio in the 14th arrondissement, which meant that we weren't going to have to haul bags full of clothes with us. At 7.30 the next morning, at the height of the rush hour, we found a taxi; but the traffic moved

---

[1] The term 'supermodel' is generally used to refer to a highly paid model with a worldwide reputation. The term remains relatively vague, however, as there are no precise criteria for applying it. For further discussion of the term, see H. Quick, *Défilés de mode: Une histoire de mannequin*, Courbevoie, Soline, 1997, and H. Koda and K. Yohannan, *The Model as Muse: Embodying Fashion*, New York/New Haven, Metropolitan Museum of Art, 2009.

[2] Fictitious title.

so slowly that Mia began arguing with the driver, telling him he had taken the wrong route. Luciana, an Italian photographer with whom Mia often collaborates, called her to let her know that she was late and that everyone else had already arrived. The people with the most power on a shoot are the photographer and the stylist. It's often the case that a magazine will choose a photographer and then let them decide which stylist they want to work with (or vice versa), and inevitably they often ask the people they're used to working with. Mia and Luciana had already worked together several times. I realized from Luciana's patronizing demeanour towards Mia that on this occasion she had been selected to be the photographer, and it was she who had invited Mia to collaborate on the shoot.

When we eventually arrived at the studio, a young man, who couldn't have been more than twenty, welcomed us with a shy smile. Blushing, he led us onto the set. Even though we were only about twenty minutes late, most things had already been set up. The space was organized over two levels: a large area which served simultaneously as set, dressing room and seating area, and the mezzanine level reserved for makeup and hair. Mirjana, the model cast to appear in the video, was upstairs with the Austrian makeup artist and the French hairdresser. Downstairs, in the wardrobe area near the stairs, Mia's assistant Annie had already emptied all the bags and hung up the clothes, which she'd sorted according to colour, and probably other criteria that I wasn't aware of. Beneath the mezzanine there was a large black leather sofa and a smoked glass coffee table on which sat a plate with a solitary croissant, presumably all that was left over from the morning's pastries. Everywhere we looked there were things to remind us that we'd arrived late.

I didn't know a soul, and it soon became apparent how stressed Mia was in this professional environment. I introduced myself in French to Annie, who answered me in Italian. She told me she was half-French and half-Italian, and she used to live in Rome, like the assistant photographer Riccardo and Luciana herself, the photographer, who seemed irritated by my presence. Everyone was in black – jeans and tops – including Mia, who was also wearing a voluminous black fur headband. It made her look a little eccentric, which suited her personality. She was rifling through the clothes on the rack, selecting items to put together into outfits for the models to wear. Along with the hair and makeup, these would create what are called 'looks'.

I made myself a coffee at the Nespresso machine then sat down on the sofa. In front of me a huge black sheet lay on the floor, taking up half the space and blending in with the black wall at the back. This was the set, the backdrop against which the models were going to be photographed, a decor that would later be retouched by the photographer and her assistant. Laid on the ground under the black cloth were several thick cables connecting the generator and the lights – all the paraphernalia that was required to fabricate the dream and make it as alluring as possible. The assistant photographer, Riccardo, aided by the young man who had let us in, was positioning the lights and adjusting their intensity. The set was ready.

A few minutes later Mirjana came downstairs from the mezzanine. It was my first sight of her, but the evening before Mia had described her to me in admiring detail: she kept saying how beautiful she was, and what a lovely person, how much money she earned, what a stunning apartment she owned in the elegant 17th arrondissement. From my position on the sofa, the first thing I saw of her as she descended the staircase was her feet – she was wearing a pair of those white towelling slippers you find in the bathrooms of luxury hotels – and then the hem of her long white bathrobe. She came down and greeted Mia warmly, '*Amore!*' I was no more than a metre away from her but without even glancing at me she turned her back to confer with Mia. The photographer reminded everyone sharply that we were running late. Mia asked Annie to hand Mirjana her first outfit – in spite of the fact that it was right in front of her and Annie was on the other side of the room.

Mirjana took off her robe with no evidence of shyness or hesitation and stood there, almost completely naked. It occurred to me later that she did this so naturally that I didn't even have the reflex to turn away in respect for her privacy. The atmosphere was such that I felt entitled to look at her as if in some sense her body was there expressly to be stared at. She wore a flesh-coloured thong that was barely visible against her skin, from which dangled a tampon string, and a pair of compression socks that were also flesh-coloured. The sight of her skeletal frame, with the hint of medical problems at calf level and the lack of sophistication that was reinforced by the tampon string, contrasted strongly with the image of the supermodel that Mia had described to me the previous evening.

I had mixed feelings: I understood that in this situation the model's nudity was completely ordinary, and that looking at her body was simply part of the rules of the game, but at the same I time I felt somehow assaulted by the excess of information about this person to whom I had never even spoken. Seeing her nearly naked body I could tell that she had her period and suffered from circulation problems. This negotiation between reserve and intimacy, which I hadn't experienced before, gave me the impression that her body was first and foremost a work tool that she made available for the creation of images. Mirjana put on the outfit that Annie handed to her: a sheer flesh-coloured body with the faintest touch of grey, and a pair of wide beige palazzo pants in a subtly iridescent diaphanous pleated silk. The 'look' they were shooting was nude, Mia said. Mirjana went and stood under the lights. Mia, Annie, the hairdresser and the makeup artist stood around her for a final touch-up. This was the first time I had seen her face properly. She was wearing a huge amount of makeup. She had fine features and glacial grey eyes. Something about her manner was extremely cold, but I couldn't tell if that was because of all the makeup she was wearing. After she was touched up the hairdresser dragged over a huge fan to blow gusts of air into the trousers and

Mirjana's luxuriant mane, which was made of her own hair woven with false hairpieces. Luciana moved into position with her large camera.

Mirjana began to sway sensually, her hair rippling in the artificial breeze. Her grey eyes stared straight at the camera, casting seductive glances as she caressed her breasts and opened her mouth, painted an intense deep red, then closed her eyes and mimed little moans of pleasure. Luciana was down on the ground lying on her stomach, her legs wide, snapping her from below. Behind her, Mia, Annie, Riccardo, the hairdresser and the makeup artist were watching the performance, scrutinizing the young woman while keeping up a running commentary on her appearance. 'She's absolutely stunning', said Mia. The makeup artist, with a grave, knowing frown, injected a note of doubt: 'Yes, but she's definitely put on a couple of kilos. She needs to lose a bit, and she knows it.'

At Mirjana's request, someone put on some music with a pulsating beat. She began to dance in front of the camera, swaying and squatting with her legs apart. She stayed a few seconds in that position, watching the camera with an arch expression, then she stood back up and began caressing her inner thighs. Even though her movements were explicitly sexual, I noted no surprise in the people around me; it was clear that this corresponded to the codes of the assignment.

When Luciana decided she had taken enough pictures, Mirjana returned to the dressing area. Mia had selected a gauzy white tulle skirt, like a ballerina's tutu, hemmed with lace and with two deep splits on either side that exposed the model's thighs. Luciana said that she thought it was hideous, and she didn't want to photograph Mirjana in it. Mia explained that it was a piece by one of the advertisers[3] and that the magazine's editor insisted that it had to be featured in at least

---

[3]   In other words, these are labels that buy advertising space in a magazine and are then featured in fashion stories in the same publication.

one of the images. Luciana tried to persuade Mia to choose another piece, but Mia said that the entire collection was utterly hideous, and this was the least ugly piece she could find. The two women decided that Mirjana would hitch up the skirt so that it would be barely visible. The hairdresser removed Mirjana's hairpieces and restyled her hair, and the makeup artist touched up her face. Mirjana took off the palazzo pants, put on the skirt and asked what she was to wear on top. She was told to keep the body on, and that she would take it off later. She returned to the set and tried out various poses, but Luciana thought that the skirt was still too visible and that it ruined the pictures. Mirjana sat down on the floor with her legs folded beneath her. She lifted the skirt right up and began caressing her breast as she gazed at the camera. Luciana was very enthusiastic about this idea and asked her to pull down the body down on one side to reveal a breast. She shot multiple photos until she decided she had enough images.

Meanwhile another model, Crotoy, had arrived at the studio. She sat down alongside me on the sofa without greeting me, her eyes focused on her Blackberry. Unlike the mostly still-teenage models I had previously encountered, Mirjana and Crotoy were distant and cold, barely interacting with the other people present, unless they absolutely had to. They were already sufficiently famous that they had no need to please anyone or do any networking. Crotoy, in particular, emanated an intimidating hauteur; I didn't introduce myself to her or try to cross the symbolic barrier that she'd erected between her half of the sofa and mine. She was very thin, her skinny legs on display in a little pair of shorts. She had fine hair, dark rings under her eyes, and yellowing teeth, which suggested that she might be anorexic or bulimic. Once Luciana had finished the shoot with Mirjana, it was Crotoy's turn to be made up and have her hair done. As she stood up I saw from the discreet logos on her sneakers, shorts and dark top that she was wearing head-to-toe Chanel. This was in striking contrast to the other models I'd come across, who tended to wear much less expensive clothes. I was struck by Crotoy's fragile, unhealthy appearance, in contrast to Mirjana's – even though I didn't know what Mirjana really looked like without all the makeup.

By now it was lunchtime and the studio assistant was going round asking people what kind of sandwich they wanted him to pick up from the bakery round the corner. He carefully wrote down everyone's request, but when the two models ordered salad he reddened and looked slightly panicked; they had an agreement with the bakery to provide sandwiches and pastries, not salad. The models insisted, however, and he assured them he would sort it out and they would have their salad. Half an hour later he was back. I found him in the toilets washing lettuce leaves from a supermarket bag. He told me he had bought salad and plastic plates and forks for the models' lunch. He seemed so inexperienced, so young and beleaguered, I wondered if he was an intern. He told me he was, and had only recently started. I asked if his internship was paid; he shook his head and said he'd bought the salad with his own money.

Everyone ate quickly. The models barely touched their salads. Crotoy was in a robe with her hair in rollers. After having her makeup done, she took off the robe and put on the outfit that Mia had prepared for her: white shirt, straight red and black skirt and a pair of high heels. She went and stood under the lights. Just as with Mirjana, her outfit and the effect of the lights immediately transformed the image I had of her. She suddenly looked stunning. The mechanism of fascination had been set in motion and I fell for it completely. It was like a magic trick engineered by the lighting. Once they were all done up and positioned under the artificial lights, the bodies of these two young women, which I thought were far too thin, unhealthy, almost viscerally raw, became suddenly attractive. I wondered what it was that made them now so gorgeous and alluring. These bodies, whose fragility had made me feel protective, concerned, appalled, even revolted, now seemed to evoke something entirely different. Under the lights they gave out a sense of being almost supernatural, unattainable, superhuman. Utterly hypnotic. Like everyone else in the room, I couldn't take my eyes off the two women. I stared avidly at them, with a kind of irrepressible desire. I wanted to scrutinize every inch of their bodies, and it felt as if I had been given permission to do so, to judge them, evaluate them, take them apart. Enthralled by the spectacle, I felt like a cannibal who wanted to possess what I saw, an ephemeral sophistication that had something corrupting about it. The physiological fact of these bodies, with their tampons, compression socks and yellowing teeth, had been transformed into aesthetically beautiful bodies, dressed up and optimized under the lights, to be frozen forever on glossy paper or screens. This is how the dream is confected.

Fashion photography: The link between production and consumption

In print, online and broadcast media, as well as in the public arena, we are constantly confronted with fashion images. Yet at the same time we have no idea how a fashion story is put together, nor about the commercial recompense that will result from it. The shoot described above was, like many of the situations described in this study,[4] for a women's fashion magazine. The role of these magazines is fundamental to the fashion system, and functions on several different levels. Without these magazines, fashion products would have little or no

---

[4]   According to Michel Agier, the methodology of the situational approach abstains from bringing into play the structural/institutional nature of what is being observed. It is the detailed observation and analysis of phenomena at the interactional scale that makes it possible to identify the real constraints of the encompassing social order. (*Esquisses d'une anthropologie de la ville: Lieux, situations, mouvements*, Paris, Academia-Bruylant, 2009, p. 41). This approach has its origins in the Manchester School. The work of Max Gluckman and Clyde Mitchell in the UK and of Georges Balandier and Gérard Althabe in France is fundamental to this approach.

visibility, and would reap no profit from their symbolic, social and commercial value. Magazines create and circulate the fantasies and dreams that fashion needs to sell its products. On a display mannequin in a boutique, a black cardigan is a black cardigan. But this black cardigan, or one very similar to it, can cost anything from fifty to five hundred to two thousand euros. What on earth can justify such a huge variation in price? What makes some consumers ready to invest in the most expensive version? It is virtually the same quality as the others, so what additional value are they actually acquiring? What they are buying is a designer label,[5] in other words a brand selling, above all else, an imaginary world.[6] These imaginary worlds are carefully constructed and conveyed using a variety of different communication and commercial strategies: catwalk shows, advertising campaigns, editorial content in magazines, celebrity endorsements. These different commercial strategies are given increased visibility thanks to magazines. For this reason, the function of magazines within the fashion system is worth examining.

Plenty of newspapers and magazines have fashion sections or run fashion content. Leaving aside for a moment actual advertising, magazines often devote several pages to models sporting fashion items. Such editorial content is made up of several pages of fashion with an accompanying text. The photos are taken in a studio or on location (beach, restaurant, museum, city). In general, the choice of clothes and designers is made by the section editors and stylists, according to criteria that take into account not only their personal tastes but also commercial demands. In her job as a stylist, Mia chooses pieces from various collections and combines them to create

---

5 Y. Delsaut, P. Bourdieu, 'Le couturier et sa griffe: Contribution à une théorie de la magie', *Actes de la recherché en sciences sociales*, vol. 1, no. 1, 1975.
6 By 'imaginary world' I mean a world of projections and images, with its own rules, aesthetic and values. For deeper analysis of this idea, see F. Cusset, T. Labica and V. Rauline (dir.), *Imaginaires du néolibéralisme*, Paris, La Dispute, 2016.

both a feature and pages of shopping suggestions. She describes her job thus:

> I deal with the press offices at all the fashion houses. In the organizational hierarchy of a fashion business, the press office deals with every aspect of the house's communication strategy, including anything to do with celebrities. Houses basically do a deal with them, along the lines of 'I'll lend you so many clothes each season, and in return you have to wear one of my dresses to the Cannes Film Festival', so they can then say: 'So-and-so wore Prada at Cannes.' Every fashion house has a press officer, whose job is to make sure its clothes are featured in magazines, on websites, and on television. I watch all the fashion weeks and catwalk shows on dedicated websites. Every house has a collection of clothes for stylists and the press, in model sizes; it's all done by email or by phone or in meetings, and when they don't know you the magazine you work for writes a letter saying that you work for them and that they should lend you whatever you ask for.

I asked her why in fashion stories certain items of clothing are sometimes barely or even not at all visible, even though the captions refer to them. She explained that, depending on the magazine, particular labels have to be given prominence for commercial reasons. That was the case for the tulle skirt described above:

> All the magazines have advertisers. These are fashion houses that pay an annual or biannual fee to the magazine, for advertising. Brand X says: 'I want the two first pages in *Vanity Fair* and I'll give you 60,000 euros, but you have to promise me a certain number of appearances [either in fashion stories or on shopping pages where the label is mentioned] every six months.' If you don't feature the label at least five times during the season, the senior management of the fashion house may recommend not paying next season. So I make my selection, but I know I've got to feature one piece from such-and-such a label; and if it's something I really hate, I try and make sure it's a close-up, so that you can't really see it. But I do try to keep the magazine and the client happy as much as I can.

Mia, like other stylists, creates fashion stories; she is part of the production of these imaginary fashion worlds. As she herself acknowledges, she does it by cherry picking from the enormous range of the current collections, always constrained by the demands of the labels that have invested in advertising and consequently demand visibility. Even a magazine with a large circulation owes its economic survival to advertisers, rather than sales and subscriptions.

The labels that feature in fashion stories showing each season's collection are those that have paid to be seen. The entire process is a circular dynamic: what is seen in the magazines – not only in advertising but also in fashion stories and editorials – are the labels that have paid for the visibility. In other words, what is seen, and thus desired by consumers, are those labels that have paid to be seen and desired. Pedro, who works as a commercial agent for a French luxury label, emphasizes this point:

> When one talks about the image of fashion, the problem is the following: why is *that* thing cool? Because its image is cool. And who created the image? The same people who made the product. The image is linked to the product. In *Vogue*, the labels that pay for advertising are promoted as being the cool labels. You're cool because you pay, not because you make nice things.

Pedro is making an important point about the relationship between the economic power of labels, and the archetypes of beauty, social status and the dream that they conjure through their advertising. This dream, apparently forged by magic, is in reality a direct consequence of the economic power wielded by fashion labels. It is vital to understand this in order to recognize the pivotal role of the magazine within the fashion system. Without magazines, the products and the social positioning of fashion would function within a closed circuit. Magazines are the link, the means of communication between the producer/supplier (understood here as the labels which create fashion items) and the consumer.

Labels feature in magazines not only in traditional advertising, but also in editorial content. The purpose of this content is to illustrate – through images and with the help of stylists and photographers and makeup artists – current trends and contemporary glamour. The nature of magazines is thus dual: they are both a commercial and a cultural product.[7] This dual character is fundamental because it creates the conditions that transform fashion into a fashion system, both economically and symbolically; without the images of clothes in the magazines, fashion in the way that we understand it would not exist.

Essentially, magazines are the link between production and consumption, and by combining advertising with editorial content they determine not only what is in fashion but what fashion is. But they also have a role in confirming and consolidating fashion as a social world. They do not only address consumers; they are also a tool for those who work in fashion, who are dependent on the same media for remaining informed about what is current in the world of fashion and keeping abreast of the latest collections. According to Mia, 'Everyone in fashion reads *Vogue*, obviously, and Garance Doré's blog. There's a whole list of blogs and websites for news, to keep up with what's going on. In all jobs it's like that.' Pedro agrees: 'The blogs that are read in Japan, in the States, in France, *Vogue*, *L'Officiel*, they're like fashion bibles, everyone reads them. Every single professional, every single fashion victim.'

Fashion magazines are aimed at people all over the world who work in the industry, keeping them informed about current trends. But they also address them at another level. Magazines are the platform upon which fashion shapes itself and legitimizes itself as a social world. For several decades now, the fashion industry has been

---

[7]   B. Moeran, 'More than just a fashion magazine', *Current Sociology*, vol. 54, no. 5, 2006. For a deeper analysis of this point, see S. Plattner, *High Art Down Home: An Economic Ethnography of a Local Art Market*, Chicago, University of Chicago Press, 1996.

portrayed in magazines through articles on designers, models and hair stylists, alongside stories about galas and parties featuring celebrities wearing particular designers, or places where fashion people hang out. When they are featured in the pages of fashion magazines, the people who work in this world become part of an advertising campaign for the fashion industry itself, not simply for a fashion brand.[8] This process has a dual function: on the one hand, it renders this world both familiar and a fantasy for the consumer; on the other, it both produces and corroborates the notion of the 'world of fashion' in which those who work in the industry can situate themselves.

The dream of transformation

'Fashion is like trying to catch a fish with your bare hands; you grasp it for a second, a fraction of a second, and then it's gone. But you'll do anything for that second. That's what fashion is.' Ludo, a photographer, is explaining the disparity between the amount of time and work required to set up the scene in order to seize the fleeting instant it takes for an image to be shot. To these two time spans – the lengthy period of preparation, and the brief instant it takes to photograph it – must be added a third: the time it takes to produce the images, for the ephemeral moment is then to be fixed on glossy paper or broadcast on a screen in order to persuade people to purchase the dream. When you observe the process of creation, this dream frozen on the pages of a magazine is no more than ephemeral, fleeting instants and transformations. Effectively, as the aesthetic and symbolic metamorphosis of Mirjana and Crotoy shows, the dream that fashion

[8]   B. Moeran, 'More than just a fashion magazine'. Howard Becker describes an analogous dynamic in the art world; see Howard S. Becker, *Art Worlds*, Berkeley, LA, London, University of California Press, 1982.

creates through advertising and fashion stories is the dream of a transformation. The fashion industry creates the illusion of a transformation of nature and the status of things as much as people, and this dream is manufactured through the production of images.

In an essay on fashion, Pierre Bourdieu defines this process as 'the power of transmutation'.[9] The dream fabricated by fashion consists of the artifice of the 'transformation of the social nature of objects'[10] and of individuals. The fashion industry produces and sells its ability to transform the value of an object (through labels and brands) and the social status of individuals (through ownership of luxury branded articles), as well as the body (through cosmetics and clothes). Yet this dream of transformation, represented in these images as something fixed, is in practice unattainable, or ephemeral. Models are emblematic of this process: though they seem at first to be the very incarnation of the dream, all they do is lend their bodies to it for a brief instant, as they stand before the photographer's lens. Rather than embodying the dream perpetually, they 'perform' it;[11] and they only perform it once the artifice of the transformation has taken place, thanks to the products derived from the dream: cosmetics and clothes. In a similar dynamic, though on a different scale, consumers to whom these fashion images are addressed dream of their own transformation by purchasing the products of the dream that they can afford. But the dream is not attained through the purchase of certain items, for it exists in a different sphere: in the world where the objects come from

---

[9] Bourdieu writes: 'How else to explain, if not by faith in the magic of the signature, the ontological difference – which makes its mark economically – between the copy signed by the master himself, and the counterfeit or fake? We know the effect that a simple change of attribution can exercise over the economic and symbolic value of a painting.' See Y. Delsaut, P. Bourdieu, 'Le couturier et sa griffe', p. 21.

[10] P. Bourdieu, *Questions de sociologie*, Paris, Minuit, 2002, p. 204.

[11] E. Goffman, *The Presentation of Self in Everyday Life*, New York, Doubleday, 1956; *Behavior in Public Places: Notes on the Social Organization of Gatherings*, New York, The Free Press, 1963.

and which they symbolize. For those who work in fashion, the dream includes both a concrete dimension – it is the product of their work composing images and desirable fantasies – and a dimension of projection – the desire to belong to this social and highly desirable world.

2

Haute Couture: The Apotheosis
of the Dream

The *Abir* shoot

If fashion is an industry whose productions are both material and immaterial, haute couture is undoubtedly the category that is most emblematic of this overlap. The only direct contact I had with the world of haute couture during my fieldwork was the photo shoot of a selection of dresses for a women's magazine published in the United Arab Emirates. In spring 2012, as I was beginning my research, Mia called to invite me to join her for a day at work. It was the middle of haute couture fashion week in Paris. In the early afternoon I went to meet Mia at a studio in Bastille where the team had been setting up since the morning for a shoot for *Abir*,[1] a Dubai women's magazine, for a feature on dresses from the current haute couture collections. A young man, dressed like a Californian surfer, greeted me at the door with a kiss on the cheek and then led me onto the set.[2] Inside, silence reigned; Mia and the others were looking at the images from the earlier session on a computer screen while the model was getting

[1]   Not the real title of the magazine.
[2]   I discovered later that this was the studio assistant, in other words the studio's point of contact with the team renting it out. The studio assistant, who usually has several skills and is often a trained photographer, is there to learn and increase his or her skills through observation and collaboration with professional photographers. I realized, as a result of various interviews and my own observations, that the studio assistant generally has very little to do with the photo shoot itself: their job usually extends to shifting the set decoration and lighting, fetching food, making coffee, and so on. They are often unpaid or poorly paid interns.

changed. I looked for a place from which I could observe without getting in anyone's way, and found myself a spot by the table with the tea and coffee machines. The leftovers of the lunch buffet were astonishing: a huge plate piled high with colourful, expensive-looking pastries and cakes, a triumph of sugar art and calories, from which a single pistachio éclair appeared to have been taken, alongside several empty cans of Coke Zero, some aluminium containers containing a few limp leaves of undressed lettuce, and several sleeves of paracetamol and ibuprofen to which people had evidently already helped themselves, as though they were also on the lunch menu. The juxtaposition of all these different elements seemed to me to be a powerful metaphor: the extravagant pastries were a sort of status symbol, there to remind everyone that they were working in the world of luxury, but they remained untouched because of the widespread fashion injunction to remain thin. The pills and cans of Coke Zero were a reminder that this is a lifestyle that demands an intense work rhythm, where no one gets enough sleep and everyone feels as though they are constantly suffering from jetlag.

Opposite me, peering at the computer screen, sat Mia, Angelo, an Italian photographer based in Rome, Clio, his Italian-Chilean assistant, also based in Rome, Diego, an Italian retoucher who lives between Paris and Milan, Kevin, the Australian studio assistant recently arrived from Canada, and Giorgio, an Italian lighting assistant living in Paris. On the other side of the room, behind the spotlights, María, Mia's assistant, a Spaniard living in London, was getting the next outfit ready. In the dressing area, Carlotta, a French-Algerian model living in New York, was being prepared by Yves, a French hairdresser from Paris, and by Yoko, a Japanese makeup artist who had recently relocated to Paris.

Mia and the others moved away from the computer and preparations for the next session began. She came over and greeted me warmly, which led to other affectionate greetings, hugs and kisses, from her colleagues. No one actually introduced themselves in spite of the fact that this was the first time we'd met. I was rather embarrassed by the way one young woman greeted me, which felt to me both extreme and incongruous: while the others greeted me with big smiles – American smiles, as I called them in my fieldwork notes – and embraced me in a way that was as warm as it was unexpected, she gave a forced, shrieking laugh – hysterical, I wrote in my notes – and held me in a stiff extended embrace.[3]

Mia gestured for me to come into the dressing area where Carlotta was being dressed and made up by Yoko and María. 'This dress weighs twenty-five kilos and costs at least 30,000 euros',[4] she told me. Carlotta could barely walk in this Chanel extravaganza entirely covered in sequins. On the table, alongside all the makeup paraphernalia, the next outfit was waiting, a Margiela trouser suit covered in discs of blown glass. 'This one's even heavier!' said Mia with a gleeful grin. The jacket weighed as much as a coat of armour; it was impossible to imagine how anyone could walk or even move with so much glass dangling from their body. While Mia waited for María to roll her a cigarette, she explained to me that the dresses for the shoot had just been shown on the catwalk for the haute couture fashion week that was still going on. 'We've got Dior, Valentino, Armani Privé, Chanel, Margiela, nothing but things that no one can afford. It's for the Arabs, for an Arab magazine.'

The lighting was changed. Carlotta was now wearing the next outfit, and her makeup and hair had been redone to go with the new dress. She took her place on the white sheet that made up the set,

---

[3] This was Yoko, the Japanese makeup artist who had only recently arrived in Paris. From my point of view this inappropriate reaction must have been due to the fact that she was not yet able to distinguish between the different codes of interaction in this type of situation.

[4] Later on, once I acquired more knowledge about haute couture, I realized that the dress in question – entirely covered with sequins – cost at least three times the price quoted by Mia. The prices of haute couture clothes are so cloaked in mystery that even those who work in the industry have no idea what they are.

where everyone was waiting for the next session. As soon as she emerged from the dressing area where she had been for the last forty minutes, she was surrounded by Yoko, Yves, Mia and María, everyone fiddling with her appearance: her nose was powdered, her face patted with a sponge, an invisible hair removed from her shoulder, her dress adjusted a few millimetres. Mia, feeling that the atmosphere was a bit lifeless, asked Diego to put on some music. He chose some electro, and as soon as the music came on it was as if a party had started, a stark contrast with the visible exhaustion and physiological limpness of everyone's post-lunch state. As Mia began to sway to the beat, someone whooped with enthusiasm. The model stood aloof, and Angelo grabbed his camera. 'Arrogant Carlotta, sexy, beautiful Carlotta, I love it, so sophisticated, *j'adore!*' cried Mia, as Carlotta swayed in time to the camera clicks.

A little further away, near the entrance to the studio, I noticed two women, one of whom particularly caught my attention. From the way they stood it was clear that they weren't involved in the shoot. Watching them, I could see how their clothes and appearance indicated their economic status. I focused on the one I had noticed first: though the studio was well heated, over her black outfit she wore an unbuttoned long, dark, fur coat with a relaxed cut. The hem of the coat just grazed the gold Gucci logo on her heeled ankle boots. On the table by her iPad sat a Hermès handbag. A Vuitton suitcase stood alongside. She wore large diamond ear studs, framed by her glossy hair, which was neatly tied back from her face. Her outfit must have cost several thousand euros, yet it was in striking contrast to the aesthetic codes of the fashion 'creatives' working on the shoot. I asked María who she was. She told me she was the editor-in-chief of the Emirates-based magazine, who had come to Paris with her assistant to see the collections and oversee the production of this fashion story for a readership that is particularly interested in haute couture.

Several outfits later I left, after arranging another meeting with Mia. We met up two days later in a bar on the Rue du Faubourg-Saint-Martin. When I arrived she was on the phone, gesticulating dramatically. I sat down and listened, realizing after a moment that she was in the midst of a heated discussion with Angelo, the photographer, about the fee for her work on the shoot for *Abir*, the Emirates magazine. Furious, she ended the conversation. Without even saying hallo, she said: 'The mean bitch is offering me fifty euros a page, while she struts around with a Hermès Kelly bag that cost 8,000 euros.' She was clearly referring to the editor-in-chief of the magazine. She was equally disappointed with Angelo, a longstanding friend and colleague, who hadn't supported her when the editor proposed this derisory fee, considering that she usually charged three times more than that. I asked her to explain who would be paid for their work on the shoot. María earned a symbolic fee from Mia, but she had come over especially from London at her own expense. According to Mia the photographer was well paid, the assistants had their expenses paid, the makeup artists and hairdressers were paid, and the model was not. Mia was disgusted by the outcome of this experience, which had involved a full day of preparation followed by a long day on the shoot itself – from 8.00 am to 11.00 pm – and for which she would be paid 250 euros.

What is haute couture?

One day Mia told me about the black market in invitations for catwalk shows: 'People are mad, some pay 1,000 euros or more to see a show. There's a whole black market in invitations.' Haute couture shows are like the Vatican mass of fashion. During fifteen minutes of spectacle all the most startling contradictions of the industry converge: the production of the dream and its astronomical costs, in a market that essentially produces at a loss. Then there are the different ways for haute couture clients, the genuine global elite, to participate in the dream, and for those who create it, the people who are paid a pittance to make these eye-wateringly expensive clothes.

Haute couture is a system of producing and selling that has changed little since the eighteenth century; while it is today the tip of the fashion iceberg, it is the origin of a contemporary industry that has grown to be tentacular and global. It is impossible to understand fashion from a symbolic perspective without understanding haute couture, which creates the image of prestige and uniqueness that fashion disseminates and uses to sell its products. It is an extremely small sector, with just a dozen or so designers in the entire world and no more than a few thousand clients, but its media resonance and commercial repercussions are huge. To understand the stakes of this very specific area of fashion production it is necessary to consider the origin of the term itself.

Although it is now a quintessentially French concept, the origins of haute couture can actually be traced back to an English immigrant to Paris, Charles Frederick Worth. Worth was a dressmaker who found success in Second Empire Paris – at the time an imperial capital exemplified by a style of gaudy ostentation – where the demand for luxury goods was concentrated. He was soon taken up by Napoleon III's wife, and counted among his clientele members of Parisian high society and the international aristocracy. Worth is an iconic figure in the history of fashion: it was thanks to him that the status of the dressmaker changed to that of artist. Worth was the first to inverse the couturier–client relationship, imposing his taste on his clients, who trusted him implicitly, where previously it was the client who expected the dressmaker to make dresses according to their instructions. Worth also came up with the idea of the label, the show and the collection. He was the first to produce and show designs in advance of each season, to attach labels with his name inside his creations, to choose a theme for each collection and to make up dresses in different styles according to this theme; he was the first to use living models to show his creations, and the first to sell 'patterns'[5] for the production of multiple versions of a dress, enabling him to maintain his rights to a design and prevent imitations. He was the first to order specially designed fabrics from factories in Lyon for his creations. Fashion, thanks to Worth, was transformed into a spectacle, evolving into both a creative industry and a publicity machine.

In order to crystallize these changes and to eliminate the blurred boundary that existed at the time between couture and dressmaking, in 1968 Worth founded the *Chambre syndicale de la couture et de la confection pour dames et fillettes* (The Guild of Couture and Dressmaking for Women and Girls). In 1911 the association became the *Chambre syndicale de la couture parisienne* (The Guild of Parisian Couture) and then the *Chambre syndicale de la haute couture* (The Guild of Haute Couture), incorporated since 1973 into the broader *Fédération française de la couture, du prêt-à-porter, des couturiers et des créateurs de mode* (French Federation of Couture, Ready-to-Wear, Couturiers and Designers). As the website of the Federation says:

> The Guild of Haute Couture is an organization to which fashion houses belong in order to benefit from the haute couture label, a label that is legally protected and can only be applied to businesses on a list that is approved each year by a committee from the Ministry of Industry and which is subject to ministerial decree.[6]

Haute couture is clearly a strictly regulated, serious business. There are stringent criteria to which designers aspiring to be permitted to take part in haute couture fashion week must subscribe: they must

---

[5]   These are full-size paper versions of each element of a piece of clothing for cutting out the piece in fabric, enabling the reproduction of multiple versions and sizes.
[6]   M. Zijlstra, 'Interview: Didier Grumbach remonte aux origines de la haute couture', Puretrend.com, 23 July 2012 (http://urlz.fr/5WE9).

have at least two design ateliers in Paris,[7] at least twenty employees,[8] present two collections a year with at least twenty-five unique pieces entirely made by hand (originally it was seventy-five pieces; in the 1990s this was reduced to fifty and more recently to twenty-five). The establishment of such precise criteria goes back to the Second World War, when fabric was rationed. The president of the Guild at the time, Monsieur Lelong, managed to negotiate with the Germans that haute couture be exempted from fabric rationing. Because of this agreement it was imperative that the criteria be defined precisely, in order to establish who could benefit from this exemption. Monsieur Lelong sent a survey to all the Guild's members, and since 1942 its results have been used to define haute couture.

Today the haute couture guild is a true elite, with only thirteen permanent members, six 'corresponding members'[9] and guest members invited each season. Unlike everything else – the vast media coverage of the haute couture shows, and their symbolic and commercial role in the fashion industry, as well as in the image of France and of Paris in particular – the criteria and the means of production of haute couture pieces have not changed since the 1940s. Haute couture shows take place twice a year. Until the 1960s, these shows took place away from the gaze of the mass media, in the exclusive atmosphere of private showrooms where women of the

---

[7]   Even foreign designers are obliged to respect this rule. It is interesting to note that even in a globalized market like the fashion industry, haute couture is subject to strict state jurisdiction (French), and is geographically restricted to within the perimeter of a single city (Paris).
[8]   This regulation has been somewhat loosened in the last few years in order to allow young designers to participate in haute couture fashion week.
[9]   The creation of the title 'corresponding member' goes back to 1997. The title 'guest member' is granted to a designer following a vote by the committee of the *Chambre syndicale de la haute couture Parisienne* permitting a designer to join the inner circle of the fashion elite. 'Guest members' are not allowed to use the label 'haute couture', but may use the term 'couture'. Their eventual passage to full membership is not based solely on seniority, for even when they fulfil all the necessary conditions it requires at least two years of being a 'guest' before being allowed to apply to become a permanent member.

aristocracy and the haute bourgeoisie occupied a few dozen chairs lining the catwalk down which models paraded in silence. The clients jotted down in their notebooks the numbers of the items they liked, which they would then look closely at later on with a view to ordering them in their size. Nowadays the haute couture shows are spectacular events produced down to the last detail, and covered by the media from all over the world. But the spectacular dimension of the dream produced by the haute couture houses can be read in several different ways. Haute couture is equally spectacular in terms of the detail and the precision of the work involved in making the garments. This level of the spectacle is far more selective because it is the exclusive privilege of insiders, namely haute couture clients. These garments are unique pieces made entirely by hand, demanding dozens, hundreds, even thousands of hours of labour and requiring a wide variety of extremely specific skills.

The story of an haute couture dress

How is an haute couture dress made? What is it made of? What is its story? Whose hands have touched it? On average, from an initial sketch to the catwalk, it takes around four months to make. To start with, the theme of the collection is chosen by the 'grand couturier' (the title used in haute couture to indicate the artistic director of a fashion house, the designer at the head of the design team), a theme for which all the design personnel are required to do research, in order for the designer to then sketch out his or her designs. Each grand couturier has his or her own style, not only in terms of the actual designs but also in the way they sketch out their ideas. Some produce very detailed drawings, while others express their ideas in rough silhouettes. These *croquis*, or sketches, are then presented by the head designer to a key figure in the process, who is both central to the process and almost invisible in the media: the atelier head,[10] the only person who works directly with the 'grand couturier' to translate the sketch into three dimensions. The prestige of haute couture is also the result of the fact that it is the 'grand couturier' who personally conceives these pieces. Unlike ready-to-wear, where the designs are often delegated to in-house designers, haute couture dresses are usually made using the *croquis* of the designer, who often follows its creation up until the client receives the garment. But the differences between haute couture and ready-to-wear are not only symbolic, they are also material: unlike ready-to-wear, haute couture garments are made without a flat construction, without a pattern, but with a '*moulage*'. This is made in '*toile beige*', an off-white cotton fabric, at this stage in the three-dimensional creation – it is not until the shape and the proportions of the dress are finally decided on that it is made up in the final fabric – and cut directly on a wooden mannequin. Patterns are used for making multiple models of a garment; since haute couture garments are unique pieces, they are made to order and to measure without a pattern.

The creation of these intricate jewels of craftsmanship requires many hands. According to the criteria required to merit the official haute couture label, a house is required to employ a minimum of twenty seamstresses in its atelier. In fact, in the large houses like Dior and Chanel, at least twice as many are employed as fashion week approaches. The atelier head coordinates the team with the help of the assistant head, who manages the seamstresses. While in the tailoring section the seamstresses are working to realize the designer's sketches, in other parts of the atelier are those who work to source, propose, design and have made the fabrics that will see the designer's vision brought to life. Once the dress has been created in *toile beige*, it is

---

[10]   In the large fashion houses, the material side of production is very segmented and hierarchical; each job has its own specific tasks. The atelier head (usually a woman) is both a manager and a seamstress.

shown to the designer, who agrees – or not – to proceed to the next stage: the creation of the dress in its final fabric. During the three or four months of the creative process the work schedule becomes increasingly intense as fashion week approaches: twenty-four hours a day, with three teams working eight hours a day each. Embroidery, pleating, buttons, fabric flowers, feathers and jewellery – all major elements in haute couture – are outsourced to specialist ateliers,[11] which in turn regularly employ the services of part-time workers. An haute couture dress requires several hundred hours of labour, and dresses that are embroidered or covered in sequins are the most time-consuming of all. Every tiny piece is hand-sewn by the skilled hands of these workers, who are known as *'petites mains'*, or little hands, and have the same status as factory workers.

What astonished me when I first saw Loïc Prigent's documentaries about what goes on behind the scenes of the catwalk shows was the environment in which these dresses are created. Dozens of women work in almost religious silence, peering through their glasses to focus on the tiny details of their creations. Sometimes up to ten women, occasionally even more, work on a single dress, hunched over the exquisite fabric. These workers (as they describe themselves in the documentaries) wear white tunics. Many have blond highlights in their hair; they are often overweight and wear cheap jewellery. When they take a break, they drink coffee and smoke out of the window of the small staff room, eat sandwiches and yoghurts that they brought from home, speak colloquial French, and have hands that show the evidence of years of manual work. They store their coats and bags in lockers and

---

[11] Chanel has bought up the largest Parisian ateliers that work with haute couture houses: a shoe atelier, a feather atelier, a jewellery atelier, an embroidery atelier and a fabric flower atelier. Every year Chanel organizes a special show where these skilled women and men show items designed by Karl Lagerfeld and fabricated in these ateliers. As an example, in the main Chanel atelier there is, I was told, a button area, where two designers are responsible for designing the buttons that are then fabricated in the dedicated atelier.

have to clock in when they arrive and out when they leave. With hindsight, my initial surprise was clearly naïve, and demonstrates my lack of critical distance: I had believed in the image of exclusivity that the fashion world seeks to convey and imagined that its aestheticism and glamour would infuse its every aspect. And yet, far from the bright lights, in the places where the material production takes place, in the actual sites of haute couture's infrastructure, fashion reveals itself for what it is, namely an industry ruled by profit, where production is undertaken by skilled workers who make luxury items while retaining the lowly status of factory workers within the social structure.

I conducted a long interview with Marie-Sophie, who worked as an embroiderer for one of these outsourcing ateliers for several years, first as an employee and later on as a temporary worker. My first contact with her was via her beautifully designed website through which she offers her services. I went to meet her in March 2012, in the first six months of my fieldwork, in a hipster café in Brussels, where she had been living for a year. The website, the café where we met, and the formality of our email exchanges had given me an idea of what kind of person to expect: a confident, cool, elegant Parisian woman. In fact, right from our first meeting, I was struck by the sense of both emotional and social vulnerability that she conveyed. At the time we met, Marie-Sophie was living on benefits with her child, and trying to find work. Apart from a brief stint as a part-time sales assistant, she had been working undeclared for a designer who paid her two euros an hour. She'd made an effort to look good for our meeting; she wore a stylish long black skirt and heels that she told me she had picked up in a second-hand store. But she couldn't hide the traces of what appeared to be a difficult existence; her expression was sad, she had bags under her eyes, tobacco-stained teeth, a slight shake in her hands and voice, burst capillaries on the side of her nose. She seemed caught between two worlds: the one she wanted to inhabit, that of the hip café and the image she projected on her website, and the world she lived in, where she experienced exploitation, financial stress and alarming precariousness.

Marie-Sophie was the first person who explained to me the process of making an haute couture garment, describing in detail how the work was outsourced to different ateliers. She had started out as a costume designer in a regional theatre, before moving to Paris to develop her career. One weekend, thanks to a tip from an acquaintance, she found herself filling in as extra help on an Yves Saint Laurent haute couture garment.

> It was an embroidery atelier, but in we were a team putting together a pile of small pieces of fabric. It was at this girl's place in Paris, an amazing house, and there were, I don't know, about thirty of us working in shifts on a coat. After that I started working at the atelier doing embroidery, and they took me on to make samples for haute couture houses. I was taken on, but as an outworker. I'd make four or five samples a month for them. The atelier had its own embroiderers, but I worked completely on my own. Then they asked me to make another coat identical to the one that thirty people had worked on, but this time I made it on my own in a fortnight in the atelier.

I asked her what she was paid and what the garment cost.

Marie-Sophie   Because I'd worked on the prototype for the show, I made the dress myself, by hand, with invisible thread. I spent days and days sewing silk chiffon. I earned about 800 euros. It took me, I don't know, about ten days. All I did was sew it by hand all day long, and the dress was sold for at least 30,000 euros.[12]

Giulia   And what do you think about this disparity?

Marie-Sophie   It's slave labour! But we were all working for the same label. My final year working in haute couture, it was at this

---

[12] A suit by Chanel or Yves Saint Laurent with no embroidery or embellishment costs at least 30,000 euros. Evening dresses cost several tens of thousands of euros, and sometimes cost over 100,000 euros. It is highly likely that this dress was sold for a good deal more than 30,000 euros.

toiliste's house[13] working for Christian Lacroix ... We were only allowed by law to work 35 hours a week, so we worked in teams. She had a day team and a night team. We worked literally nonstop. We were paid 1,500 euros a month. This was ten years ago. Because it was all made by hand, it took a really long time. There'd be six or seven of us on an eight-hour shift. We did everything, put the pieces together, did the embroidery. And then it went to Lacroix for fittings.

I asked her if once the dresses were finished she and her colleagues were invited to the shows, and generally if she took part in fashion events of any kind, if they were part of it all. 'Oh no, I've never been to a fashion show. It's very rare to be invited. I think only the people who actually worked directly for Lacroix were invited, and even then. Same thing for the other houses, only full-time employees go to the shows.'

My question was certainly naïve and wrong-headed, a result of the preconceived ideas I held about fashion, which at the time I believed to be different to other industries. A few television documentaries confirm what Marie-Sophie told me.[14] Only the head and assistant head of the ateliers are allowed backstage during the shows to deal with last-minute alterations. Sometimes they sew the dresses directly onto the models, literally in the last seconds before they take to the catwalk.

But to return to the process of production of haute couture dresses: once the dresses have been made up in *toile beige* they are then made up in the final fabric, and fitted to a wooden mannequin. After this, more fittings take place on living models, and because they are often thinner than standard wooden models the dresses usually need to be

---

[13]   This is where the three-dimensional version of the designer's sketch is made up in off-white cotton. In ready-to-wear, a flat paper pattern is made in order to be able to recreate the model in different sizes and proportions for mass production. In haute couture, because these are unique pieces, there is no pattern. Each piece is made to measure.

[14]   See in particular *Signé Chanel* and *Le Jour d'avant*, Loïc Prigent, 2005 and 2009.

adjusted. Often the designer insists on significant modifications at the last minute, and a dress might even be excluded from the final collection a few hours – or even minutes! – before the show begins. At no point are any of the skilled workers invited to see the results of their labour. At Chanel there is a small, sparsely furnished side room with a catwalk down the middle where the models parade after the official show in front of an audience made up of the people who made the dresses they are wearing.

An extreme social divide prevails in the fashion industry. On the one hand, the manufacturing of the clothes, the manual work, is the very basis of haute couture and is what gives it its uniqueness; on the other, those who actually do this work, and who have the skills to make concrete the artistic vision of the designer, have no place in fashion's social hierarchy. In haute couture those who materially produce the glamour are simultaneously excluded from it. They do not participate in the social and symbolic construction of fashion. Everything takes place as if, in a certain way, the osmosis between the glamour of these objects produced by fashion and the glamour and prestige of those who work in fashion ends at the spheres that are called 'creative'.

The clientele

What happens at the end of fashion week, after the world's media has finished photographing the young models displaying these luxury garments? What happens to the clothes themselves? Who buys them? And how?

Anna Wintour, editor-in-chief of American *Vogue* – not only the most powerful woman in the world of fashion but, according to *Forbes*, one of the seven most powerful women in the world, and the model for the central character in the novel and film *The Devil Wears*

Prada – is always to be seen in the front row of the fashion shows, alongside other important fashion journalists from all over the world, and celebrities from the worlds of cinema and music, all seated according to a precise geopolitical protocol. These people are the focus of an enormous amount of media attention and an intrinsic part of the spectacle; many sponsor the labels, in that they are paid by them to be seen in outfits from the collection before they are available in boutiques. These fashion celebrities are photographed at least as often as the models themselves. In the background, far from the flash of the cameras, sit a few women, usually sporting black sunglasses and dressed in elegant but sober outfits. These women are either haute couture clients or the buyers who represent them. A designer dress never costs less than 15,000 euros, and the cost of the most elaborately embellished pieces can go up to several hundred thousand euros. It's hard to know who actually pays these prices because the fashion houses carefully preserve the anonymity of their clients, as Karl Lagerfeld explained in an eloquent BBC documentary, *The Secret World of Haute Couture* (2007):

> They don't want to be mentioned. You know there are many, many rich people today that the public have no idea who they are ... They don't want people to know how they look, and who they are, and where their money comes from. So don't ask me too many questions in that area, because it's like a doctor, there is a medical secret.

Indeed, very little is known about them, and all the evidence suggests that these women number no more than a couple of thousand, only a handful of whom actually attend fashion week or visit the fashion houses in person.[15] They are film stars, pop stars, princesses,

---

[15]   After Paris, the fashion houses put on fashion shows in other cities for their international clients. After the shows the fashion houses send out DVDs and catalogues produced in-house, which are sent out to clients accompanied by detailed descriptions of the garments, the fabrics used and the production process. The designers also send out sketches and fabric samples to clients who live far from Paris.

the offspring of the world's wealthiest families, wives of international leaders and bankers. The largest number are women whose fortunes come from countries in the developing world, from the Arab world, China, Russia and, more recently, Brazil.

The purchase of an haute couture dress is a process that takes place in several different stages, all of which confirm at every step the client's ultra-privileged status, of which her wardrobe is the material proof. Haute couture is destined for the true economic global elite, who wish to remain private, anonymous, far from the focus of magazines and the media spotlight in general. Owning an haute couture dress has a precise social signification which only initiates are able to understand: 'I think that haute couture does change you, from the point of view that you enter into another world, a really refined world, a rarefied world, that has become increasingly smaller', explains Susan Gutfreund, the widow of John Gutfreund, once known for being the highest-paid executive on Wall Street, who appears in the BBC documentary.[16] 'It's something ... I feel very privileged to be a part of it, it's a different dimension', another women tells Margy Kinmonth, the film's director.

Kinmonth describes haute couture clients as being members of a 'secret club'. It is not enough to have money to become a client; people need to be accepted socially into this exclusive inner circle. In the film this phenomenon is vividly illustrated by Becca Cason Thrash, who was born into a working-class family and married an immensely wealthy Texan oil tycoon. Cason Thrash describes how, although like all the other haute couture clients she too stayed at the Ritz when she was in Paris, she nonetheless felt excluded at the shows, where she was

---

[16] Margy Kinmouth, who made *The Secret World of Haute Couture*, recalls in the film how hard it was to find haute couture clients who were prepared to talk to her. She received dozens of refusals; in the end only four women agreed to talk to her, three of whom were American rather than from European 'old money'. As these women explained, the purchase of haute couture is akin to acquiring a specific social status.

always given a seat at the back and generally ignored. It was not until she raised 450,000 euros for the Society of the Friends of the Louvre that she began to be seated in the front row and acknowledged by the other front row clients as being one of them. At last she was received at the private showrooms of the labels according to protocol when she went to order clothes.

After the shows, clients make appointments to be received at the private showrooms of the haute couture houses, where an employee, traditionally known – despite her social and cultural capital and her highly developed managerial skills – as a '*vendeuse*', or 'sales director', receives them individually, sometimes in the presence of the designer and the atelier head. Often the sales director, who is responsible for the entire sales process, is already acquainted with the client and her tastes. She will show her the models she thinks she will be interested in, worn by '*mannequins de cabine*' or 'fitting models'.[17] But the majority of clients do not come to Paris to see the collections. Private fashion shows are organized in the USA, Asia, Brazil and in various Arab countries. Chanel organizes up to six fashion shows a year in the USA for its best clients.

Once the client has chosen an outfit, she makes her order. She might want some modifications to be made to the design, as long as it remains true to the designer's vision: she might ask for it to be made a little longer in the sleeve or for the depth of the décolleté to be modified, for example. These alterations will be more or less substantial or significant depending on where she lives: according to Marie-Sophie, who used to do these kinds of alterations, because women from Arab countries are now major haute couture clients, significant modifications to dresses are increasingly being requested, because

---

[17]   Every haute couture house employs 'fitting models', who work outside fashion week, on whom dresses are altered to fit, as well as for showing clients current pieces from the collection.

diaphanous fabric and showing skin are not permitted in many social contexts in these countries:

> After the shows, they order what they want in their size. In general these houses keep a bust in the client's size that they use to make the first version of the dress in *toile*. How mad is that? I used to work for Chanel, not for very long, whenever they needed to take on extra workers to make clothes for the clients, all Arab women. It was always embroidered things. It was crazy, there was all this embroidered lace, and because you could see through it we had to line the dresses in flesh-coloured jersey. It still had to be transparent so that you could see the lace. It was bonkers, and I don't think it looked very nice, to be honest. The dresses became really thick and heavy, they lost all their charm . . . And they'd been designed for a size 32 or 34, while most of these clients were at least a 46.[18]

Because all the garments produced by these haute couture labels are made to measure, the houses keep busts of clients in order to cut the cloth to the exact size, down to the last millimetre. Once the order is made, it takes several months for the dress to be ready. In spite of the bust, fittings are necessary before the item is finished, because the client's morphology might have changed. In fact, the atelier head, often in the company of the sales director, travels all over the world for fittings, ensuring at least one for each client. In her film, Kinmouth shows dresses travelling first class, accompanied by the atelier head.

Apart from film stars, who wear these dresses at events such as the Oscars or the Cannes Film Festival, with their intense media focus, haute couture clients tend not to be seen in their dresses on public occasions. Haute couture functions completely differently to the dominant modes of consumption. The logic of exhibiting a logo as a status symbol, which consists of the wearer showing that they own a

---

[18] I frequently heard these kinds of negative judgements about the tastes and aesthetic codes that are prevalent in the Arab world, in spite of the fact that it is one of the leading markets for the luxury industry in the world.

certain luxury item so as to be associated with a particular social status, doesn't exist in the context of haute couture where there is nothing to prove. Unlike the dominant commercial dynamic, where people specifically want to wear the same clothes that celebrities wear, if an haute couture client sees the dress that she intends to order has been worn in public by a celebrity, the spell of the unique is shattered and she won't buy it. 'If I see something on a film star I don't want it any more, that's for sure. It's done', says Daphne Guinness in the BBC documentary. Since haute couture is all about exclusivity, the houses are duty bound to inform their clients if someone else has already ordered the same dress. It is vital to avoid a situation where two women are wearing the same dress at the same occasion. It is possible, for a price, to purchase a dress exclusively in order to guarantee that no one else anywhere in the world will wear it. The construction of privilege also takes place through the establishment of a personal relationship between the house and its clientele that takes place outside fashion week. The sales directors and designers themselves regularly call their clients for news about them and their families, or to extend an invitation for lunch or to a gala reception. From the point of view of the clientele, haute couture is more of a process of constructing and confirming being part of the global elite than a matter of beautiful dresses.

Is haute couture a viable business?

There are perhaps two thousand women all over the world who purchase these fairytale garments, whose cost, in terms of production (exceptionally expensive materials and hundreds of hours of work) and media coverage (each fashion show costs many hundreds of thousands of euros to put on), is astronomical. Even if the entire collection gets sold, the house will not make a profit: haute couture never covers its costs in spite of the prohibitive prices. From a strictly economic perspective, it always functions at a loss. It continues to exist only because it is the incarnation of the dream that fashion transmits to the middle classes through the media. Haute couture constructs the image of the labels that in reality make their profits from the merchandise and accessories sold by their commercial arms. In the no-nonsense words of Bernard Arnault, president of LVMH, 'Haute couture is a fantastic tool to demonstrate the prestige of the house. Its impact on all the other lines – clothes, accessories, and cosmetics – is enormous. Obviously it's very costly but it's not our intention to cover the cost through sales.'[19] The designer and business magnate Giorgio Armani said the same thing in an interview with an Italian magazine:

> Of course couture has nothing to do with the profits of a fashion house. Film stars don't pay – on the contrary, they're often paid to wear a garment on the red carpet. With royalty it's different: Paola de Liège or Queen Rania of Jordan do pay, maybe they get a reduction, which is fair enough. What I mean is, buyers exist, but even so, haute couture can't follow the normal logic of business. Its fantasy element and the power it has to tap into people's desires serve to increase the status of the label better than any publicity campaign ever could.[20]

Haute couture is the industry of the dream that is displayed on the catwalk and on the film stars who wear it. Images of these dresses are circulated in the press, on the internet and on television, fabricating desire in women all over the world who can't possibly afford such garments and so instead buy themselves a lipstick, a handbag, a pair of glasses or a perfume sold by the label. They're buying themselves a tiny fragment of the dream that they can afford.

---

[19] Mark Tungate, *Fashion Brands: Branding Style from Armani to Zara,* London, Kogan Page, 2005, p.139.

[20] As quoted in an article by Antonella Matarresse in the Italian weekly *Panorama.* See http://urlz.fr/5WFC.

Haute couture: Fabricating an image of France and Paris all over the world

The role played by haute couture doesn't stop with commercial business strategies. If the industry continues to exist and to be protected, in spite of its anachronisms and financial realities, it's because it has a weighty role in the symbolic and financial economies of the city of Paris, in the first instance, and by extension that of France, for the image that this sector of the fashion industry creates is propagated nationally and internationally. It is an intrinsic part of the image of France and its capital as the cradle of luxury, elegance and sophistication.

Financially vulnerable, haute couture is above all else an industry of symbolic production, fabricating a fantasy that the media and other institutions that display it call the 'dream'. This dream is materially linked to the creation of the most exquisite garments imaginable, and its production is structurally linked to the city of Paris, because the designers who want to benefit from the haute couture label are obliged to locate their ateliers in the city. Because of this, haute couture cannot exist outside Paris (the same kind of production in Italy is called *alta moda*).

Like an interlocking structure, the couture houses, Paris and France at once produce and benefit from these confections of lace, sequins, beauty and craftsmanship, constructing an image of luxury and prestige that is of enormous value to their individual economies. A useful document on the website of the French Federation of Couture, Ready-to-Wear, Couturiers and Designers, promoting the objectives of the Federation, formulates it thus: 'The economic importance of designer labels in France: visible in the world's media and present in over 1,500 own-brand boutiques and more than 5,000 multimark boutiques, they promote an image of excellence and constitute active ambassadors for French products.'[21] A few paragraphs further down,

---

[21] Official website of the *Fédération française de la couture, du prêt-à-porter, des couturiers et des créateurs de mode* – https://fhcm.paris.

the document cites figures for haute couture professionals who come to the various fashion weeks: 'Every March and November the Federation sets up an International Press and Information Centre. This centre enables 800 buyers, 2,000 journalists, 400 photographers and all other fashion professionals to access information.'[22] To these official press figures must be added the models, makeup artists, hairdressers, assistants in all areas, and above all non-official journalists, including bloggers, as well as clients and interested members of the public. It is not only the commercial profits strictly linked to the sales of products that are 'made in France' that makes fashion weeks a highly profitable financial resource for Paris.

But the capital's image of luxury and opulence, which is created through fashion and haute couture in particular, extends well beyond the four fashion weeks that take place each year. The image of Paris as the fashion, luxury and haute couture capital of the world makes the city an attractive destination for anyone who dreams of making their career in fashion, and a key objective in the career of anyone who is already working in fashion but who wants to move up in their career. The city teems with interns, assistants, fashion students and creatives who don't have high incomes but nonetheless participate, through their aesthetic, cultural and social capital as well as through their work, in maintaining the city's image as well as its economy. Parisian luxury is a sort of smokescreen for what is a mass of low-income workers with unstable jobs; in the words of Annie, Mia's Italian-born assistant, 'In Rome there's no Dior or Chanel, there's no haute couture or fashion week, but here you've got all of that. You see all this money and luxury and you want to be part of it as well, it seems to be within reach, it's right here.'

[22] Ibid.

Fashion workers or those who aspire to work in fashion are attracted by the world of Parisian luxury. Some make economic sacrifices to be in Paris, to consume in Paris and to experience Parisian glamour. The manufacturing of haute couture dreams has major repercussions from an economic perspective, on a variety of spatial and temporal levels.

The different types of dream

A focus on the different stages of the production and sale of haute couture offers a way of exploring the way the dream, apparently homogenous, in fact has different meanings depending on who is speaking. For those who work at the lowest rung in the industry, who are excluded from the social prestige that other fashion workers enjoy, the dream element is reduced, consisting primarily of the sense of being part of a business. These workers' labour does not fit in with the notion of the dream, because it is concrete, based on their highly skilled craftsmanship. They don't create the dream, because the dream, as we have seen, is produced by imagery not things. What they produce, through their skilled work, is the raw ingredients of the dream, in other words the garments themselves. Once they have finished their work and the dresses are no longer physically within reach, having left the ateliers to be displayed on the catwalk, the clothes definitively change status and essence to create the dream.

For couture houses, understood here as businesses dedicated to profit, the dream is a commercial strategy: its purpose is to sell other products, namely leather goods, accessories, perfumes and cosmetics, the only items that are truly profit-making. The dream that the haute couture houses produce during a show is actually directed primarily towards the middle classes. The fundamental logic of consumer society makes them, via the media, the intended spectators of these images and of the dream of luxury and beauty, which they in turn identify with by purchasing affordable products, thus generating the most significant part of the fashion industry's revenue.

For haute couture clients, meanwhile, the dream means something entirely different. For those who come from so-called emerging economies, the purchase of designer dresses has the principal purpose of demonstrating the economic power and opulent lifestyle that has only recently become available to them. For older clients, who have been buying haute couture for many years, and younger women, born into a social context that is historically familiar with haute couture, it means something different again; it is about recognizing and valuing the traditional craftsmanship and skills of haute couture. The value of these garments does not inhere in what they might indicate *outside* these clients' social worlds, but rather in the fact that it confirms *within* them that they have an appreciation for the actual process of creation, the exquisite fabrics and craftsmanship that are not necessarily visible in the outward appearance of the final product.

For the people working on the shoot for the Emirates-based magazine, the dream has yet another meaning. For them it represents the possibility of participating in the creation of an ultimate vision of beauty, a sort of aesthetic perfection that exemplifies the style of a particular moment. The precise fitting of the dress on the model, the constant retouching of her hair and makeup, are testimony to a form of collective performance dedicated to this quest for absolute beauty. But the dream for them is above all about owning the knowledge and the aesthetic codes that give them the skills to create the images of the dream – both in the present and in the future – for ordinary people. These skills are both implemented during the production (hair, makeup, selection of clothes) and incorporated into the appearance (the style or look) of the shoot, and are thus integrated into the social world, becoming social and symbolic capital. The dream, for these people, is a process of distinction that places them at the top of the ladder of aesthetic authority and the fabrication of imaginary worlds. It is precisely Mia's awareness of this prestige that allows her to present herself as being both familiar with and blasé in the presence of haute couture, and to project a certain contempt towards the magazine's editor-in-chief, in spite of her lower status in the hierarchical and economic structure of the fashion world.

3

The Circulation of the Dream: Fashion and Globalization

Any research into the world of fashion is inevitably an anthropological investigation of globalization: fashion is a globalized industry that produces both merchandise and fantasies which circulate around the world and are kept alive by the people who work in it, who are frequently mobile and cosmopolitan. Globalization is not a new or modern phenomenon – the movement of people, merchandise and capital is an intrinsic part of human history. The fashion industry, preceded by manufacturing, including that of clothing, has always been part of global trade characterized by the importing of raw materials and the circulation of fashion and aesthetic repertoires. In the past and still today, fashion, in the form of fashion merchandise, workers and fantasies, circulates in multiple ways all over the world. Throughout my research I was confronted by a veritable 'globalization from below'[1], by situations in which individuals had to deal with issues related to globalization.

---

[1] I have borrowed this expression from the anthropologist Alain Tarrius (A. Tarrius, M. Wieviorka, *La Mondialisation par le bas: Les nouveaux nomads de l'économie souterraine*, Paris, Balland, 2002) but am using it to refer to something else. It has generally been employed to describe the informal economy, whereas I wanted to use it to highlight the discrepancy between a macro-phenomenon such as globalization and the ways in which it is experienced on an individual level. See also A. Gupta, *Anthropological Locations: Boundaries and Grounds of a Field Science*, Berkeley, University of California Press, 1997. Methodologically, I looked at globalization as a macro-economic phenomenon, through an ethnographic lens, in order to understand it as a composite of practices and situations that can be observed locally. (M. Agier, 'Le tournant contemporain de l'anthropologie,' *Socio*, no. 1, March 2013, p. 89).

Pedro and the curse of 'made in China'

If one were looking for a magic spell to give one the power to remove all the potential attractiveness of any given fashion product, it's right there in the phrase 'made in China'. The expression has entered common parlance and has, since the first news reports appeared about Chinese shoe factories began to appear in the 1990s,[2] indicated much more than merely where a product was made. In the popular imagination, as well as for many of those who work in the fashion business, this label is synonymous with poor-quality products whose manufacture depends on the exploitation of women and children. The reality is obviously more complicated. As we have seen, beginning in the 1970s, many manufacturing businesses have delocalized their production not only to China but also to many other Asian countries, including Bangladesh, South Korea, India, Vietnam, Thailand and Indonesia. Since the 1990s, with the rise of neoliberalism and the acceleration of deindustrialization in Europe, luxury labels, no longer able to support the cost of local labour, have followed this trend. Nowadays 'made in China' is a discrediting label indicating a symbolic rather than a material production. It is also the emblem of delocalization. The issue of 'made in China' was raised by Pedro, a sales representative for an upmarket French label. For a monthly salary of 6,000 euros, his job is to locate distribution channels and develop sales strategies at an international level, from department stores and independent boutiques to franchises. When I requested an interview with him, he suggested we meet in a bar on the Rue du Faubourg-Saint-Denis in Paris, which he calls his 'office'. Pedro's style is studied and cool: he wears silver rings, stylish clothes and unusual glasses. During our interview, I asked him about how fashion and those who work in the industry are seen in wider society. He turned

---

[2] D. Thomas, *Deluxe: How Luxury Lost Its Luster*, New York, Penguin, 2008.

the conversation to the question of products that are 'made in China', a constant issue in his job, because the brand he works for manufactures in China. Without me even bringing up the subject, he talked about the impact on consumers of media campaigns against products 'made in China'. 'Opinions are changing fast at this level. It's been happening over the last year. Now people say, "It's made in China. I won't buy it then." And they give really stupid reasons.'

Pedro launched into a lengthy justification, almost systematically ignoring my questions. He began with a four-point explanation:

> First, there's the issue of cost. 'It's made in China, but it costs 100 euros, it's too expensive, I don't want it.' Then there's the ethical argument, which I really don't buy: 'It's child labour, I don't want anything to do with it.' And then there's the argument that says, 'Look, they've closed the factories in France and now they're manufacturing in China, it's disgusting.' There's an answer to all of that. And then there's the fourth argument, the worst one of all.

His way of arguing, the structured nature of his responses, made it clear that he has gone over all these points many times in his work. The 'made in China' issue is clearly a real problem for the brand, whose customer base no longer wants to buy its products after they've seen the label. Pedro has become adept at making his points to his clients, in order for them to subsequently make the same points to their customers. Nonetheless it was often ineffective. 'I love my job, but my clients all tell me, "Pedro, I promise you, even if we spend twenty minutes explaining this all to the customer, she isn't going to buy it if it's Chinese".' Pedro tries to convince them, emphasizing that:

> If we could make our T-shirts in France we would. No one does it any more. I used the example of a T-shirt, and maybe it's not true in that case, but for example knitted items can't be manufactured in France any more for a reasonable price. Everything is closing down. Producing things in France, and we're the first to say it – when we can do it, we do it.

The basic issue is that of the delocalization of manufacturing and widespread deindustrialization in Europe. Globalization has led to many European countries suffering from a dearth of local industry. Beyond the catastrophic impact on employment, this has led to a rise in the costs of local production and a considerable decline in supply. Only luxury labels – and even then, not in every case, as we shall see – can still afford to manufacture some of their goods in France and Italy without negatively impacting their profits. Upmarket brands, such as the one for which Pedro works, have no choice but to delocalize production and labour, which is, from a legal point of view, the main thing that distinguishes them from luxury labels.[3]

Pedro then moved on to the second point: 'The whole argument that "made in China" means child exploitation, that's just crap. If you buy a product that's labelled Armani or Dior, it's definitely made in China. We all work with companies that respect European directives, human directives. There's aren't many of them, but they're the ones we work with.' Pedro criticizes the way the media describe working conditions in China, in particular child labour. He insists that all fashion brands, including luxury labels, manufacture in China, and that the brand that he represents has chosen to work with the minority of producers who respect labour law. He explains the reasons for this choice:

> We can't afford the hassle, because we would be held responsible. I don't know if you know this, but legally we make that commitment to our clients, we commit to the guarantee that our products are made by adults, that there are regular checks, and so on. I don't know if it's true, but in any case we sign these guarantees, we have

---

3   According to a 2008 report from the French Economic and Social Council, 'Luxury goods: production and services', luxury goods are distinguished from upmarket goods because of their integrated local production (as opposed to being delocalized and outsourced), the small scale of production of items that are not subject to ever-changing trends, a pricing policy that almost always excludes sales, a selective and limited distribution policy, and a specific communication policy. Upmarket brands make similarly high-quality products, but production is delocalized (http://urlz.fr/5WFP). The report makes clear that it is becoming increasingly difficult to differentiate between the two.

to. I know that there aren't many factories like that in China but there are a few. So there are basically two Chinas.

The brand works with these ethical manufacturers for commercial rather than ethical reasons, because they 'have to'. It's interesting to note Pedro's evasion when he says 'I don't know if it's true', by which he reveals the truth at the heart of his argument, which is aimed at increasing sales, rather than being a genuine commitment to the principles of labour law and human rights. He brings up the idea of a dualist Janus-like China, with two faces, one that is morally and qualitatively debased and debasing (the China that his clients think of) and the other that is civilized and ethical, manufacturing quality merchandise for his brand.

Pedro then launched into his third point:

When, for example, we make something in in China, we send over Italian thread. So if it's an issue of quality for the buyers, the fact that it is made in China shouldn't be a problem, because with Italian thread the quality is guaranteed, and if it's not okay then you just go back to the shop to change it. That's a sensible way of looking at it. Try it and if you don't like it bring it back. I think that makes sense. A jumper that's made in China with Italian wool is considered to be 'made in China', which is fair enough except that the raw materials aren't Chinese, they're Italian, and the machines they use aren't Chinese either, they're German or Italian. So in the end it's made with European labour too, but it costs less to produce the final article in China. The product, the famous T-shirt we were talking about, would be the same if it were made in France except it's cheaper to make it in China and import it to France. For some items, like knitwear that's very difficult to make in France and very expensive, it costs less to make it in Italy, for example, but that's not a problem. In any case, it's really difficult to produce knitwear in France.

This brief extract from our conversation offers the opportunity to reflect on a fundamental aspect of globalization: the asymmetries that it creates are not simply economic but also symbolic. Pedro's argument hinges on an apparent contradiction: according to him, the products made for the brand that he represents should not be 'stigmatized' by being described as 'made in China' because they are the result of a globalized production process. On the other hand, products with the label 'made in France', which are, as we shall see, no less transnational, are highly valued. An item that is made in China with European materials and machines should be presented as being of the same quality as if it had been produced in France. 'Made in China' items would then be equivalent to French products, but cheaper for the company to produce. This would mean that the Chinese labour contribution would be rendered completely invisible in the production process. China seems to be, if not an 'accidental' part of the process, at best no more than the brand's production workshop. This argument re-establishes the imperialist map of the world in which 'centres' and their products (in this case France) are intrinsically superior to peripheral countries.

One final question, however, remains unexplored, which is fundamental to understanding the issues facing labels regarding provenance and symbolic geographies. Pedro pointed out quite correctly that even clothes labelled 'made in Italy' or 'made in France' are the result of transnational production. How is it, then, that some brands are allowed to label their clothes attractively while others have to insert the stigmatizing label 'made in China'? Pedro's fourth point is a response to this question:

> The fourth argument is the least legitimate. If we take the example of an Italian company, I won't name it because I don't need the hassle, it's a very cool independent company that makes nylon bags. We both use the same Chinese factory. If you went to Galeries Lafayette tomorrow you'd see this company's stand, then you'd go to our stand, you'd look inside the bags and on theirs it's written 'made in Italy' and on ours it says 'made in China'. It's legal! This is actually legal! It's globalization that makes it legal. It's possible

because that's the law. Or some buttons on a shirt, that's an easier example. It's enough to show the authorities in Italy or France that the button cost three euros even though the shirt only cost two euros and you can label it 'made in France' or 'made in Italy'. The button needs to cost more than 30% of the overall cost of the shirt. And by the way, we know that company used to have its shoes manufactured in China and they put 'made in Italy' on them, illegally, but they did it anyway.[4]

The attribution of labels is regulated by the European Union customs code that brings together the rules, regimes and procedures applicable to merchandise traded within the European Economic Area and with third countries.[5] In article 24 of the code ratified by the European Union, it is stated that any merchandise during the production of which two or more countries are involved is considered to come from the country where the last transformation or processing was done, assuming it is economically justified, in a company equipped for that purpose, and having either manufactured a new product or contributed to a significant stage in the production.[6] This legalistic language confirms Pedro's point: paradoxically, a label stating where a garment was made does not in fact testify to the actual origins of the product. What does it attest to? Above all, it attests to an imagined world of luxury, in the case of Italy or France, or its opposite, in the case of almost every other country in the world. If, concretely, the majority of fashion items, including luxury labels, are produced in this globalized process, labels are nothing less than a marketing operation that do not indicate – or at least do not always indicate[7] –

---

4   The law regarding label attribution is complicated and subject to issues of interpretation. Generally speaking, products of which 45 per cent of their overall value was manufactured in France can be labelled 'made in France'. http://www.economie.gouv.fr/cedef/fabrique-en-france

5   https://ec.europa.eu/taxation_customs/business/calculation-customs-duties/rules-origin/nonpreferential-origin/introduction_en

6   http://urlz.fr/5WFW. [link doesn't work]

7   Only in the highly regulated sector of haute couture, with its production based on French skills and craftsmanship, is each unique piece completely made in France.

that something was really made where it claims to have been. A label that states that something was made in France or Italy does, however, confer a certain status, or symbolic value, on the item. Extranational regulations allow brands that are inclined to invest – even partially – in local production to benefit from such prestige. Again, this about selling a dream of distinction via an imaginary idea of those countries whose names are printed on these labels. Buying something that is 'made in France' or 'made in Italy' does not offer the guarantee that a product has been manufactured locally and in respect of labour laws, but it does allow the consumer a small share in the notion of elegance associated with France and Italy.

In this global cartography of luxury, France and Italy are the places that evoke a history and tradition of elegance, quality and sophistication, while China and other countries where so many clothes are manufactured are places that have become invisible, stigmata that have to be erased. French regulations actually create this differentiation of status, because France severely punishes companies that falsely label their goods to indicate that they have been made in France or are of French origin,[8] while also benefiting from the European Union's extranational regulatory framework that makes the concealment of delocalized production entirely legal. But the images of the different countries described above also plays out in the opposite sense: if China is synonymous with exploitation in the collective imagination and in the media, the multiple forms of exploitation that take place in the symbolic centres of luxury often remain invisible, as Pedro points out:

[8]   Article 39 of the customs code forbids the importing of products from abroad that are labelled in any way that might indicate that they were made in France or of French origin; if any such label is found on the product it must be removed or corrected before it is authorized for import. Article L. 121, and those following, of the consumer code (which simply transposes into French legislation the European directive D 2005/29 relative to dishonest commercial practices) defines as dishonest any commercial practice with allegations, indications or presentations that could result in inaccuracy regarding its origin; such an infraction (article L. 121–6) is punishable by a jail sentence of up to two years and a maximum fine of 3,500 euros, up to 50 per cent of which can be borne by the expenditure of the practice constituting the offence.

This argument [about child labour and worker's rights] is just as valid for Prato or Naples, and for the Sentier [Paris's clothing district]. Two hundred metres from here there are Chinese people working in windowless basements. If today I had to choose an upmarket item, I really would choose something 'made in China' over one that is 'made in France', manufactured in these conditions [he points towards the Sentier], because I make sure they work in certain conditions in China. Over there [in the Sentier] they are treated like shit, they're slaves. I'm not saying that in China they aren't slaves, you know. I'm just saying that all over the world there are people who do awful things and people who don't. So I'm not defending anything, any equivalence between different countries, imports, exports, I'm just showing you the lack of information. And this ignorance is fed by the media, which says, 'China is shit, H&M is shit' ... It's true sometimes, but there are people who work in decent conditions in China. They're not stupider than we are. That's all.

It's true that one need only walk through the Sentier area of Paris or around the outskirts of Naples, where I was born, to recognize that products made in Italy or in France are often based on exploiting workers. All over European cities there are workshops in which migrant workers as well as local people work in the most miserable conditions. And, arguably even worse, such exploitation also takes place in the artistic and creative centre of the fashion world, in the very heart of the luxury fashion business. This latter phenomenon is totally invisible, to the point that Pedro does not allude to it at all, despite the fact that this is his world.

Corinne against China

China is much more than the image of the label 'made in China' conveys. It is the second-largest economy in the world, and its arrival at the global hegemonic centre is undoubtedly one of the most significant aspects of contemporary globalization. Since the 1970s it has been a key region for industrial manufacturing. Today China is a rising power, and the growth of its middle class as well as the emergence of a wealthy economic elite means that it has also become an important upscale fashion market. This means that China plays a double role in the fashion industry: it is both a favoured location for manufacturing and one of the largest markets for luxury goods produced by that market. Corinne's experience with the Chinese illustrates the way that an individual must accommodate themselves not only to the rules of a globalized fashion market, but also to those of the Chinese state. It also shows, at a granular level, the issues facing a small independent fashion label keen to enter the international market.

Corinne was born and grew up in Belgium, where she trained as a ballet dancer. She went on to study choreography and then fashion design, after which she set up a business as a lingerie designer. At the time we met she was on her fourth collection.[9] We met in Paris, in a café on Rue Charlot. She had come to Paris to show her collection to a buyer at a famous Parisian boutique who had invited her to the meeting after perusing her website. When I arrived, Corinne had just come out of the interview. She looked angry and disappointed. She told me that when she arrived for the interview the buyer told her, without any explanation or warning, that she had changed her mind and refused to let Corinne show her the contents of the leather case she had brought with her: 'That doesn't interest us, our customers aren't interested in that kind of thing.' Corinne had barely finished telling me about her career path when she announced that she wanted to give up fashion. She was living on benefits and had never made more than 100 euros profit from her work, in spite of the fact that her collections had sold relatively well; the overall cost of production was

---

[9]   It is generally held that a young designer needs to produce four collections over a period of two years to gauge their success in their specific sector of the market.

so high that she couldn't turn a profit. She'd discovered that, contrary to what she initially imagined, the creative aspect of her work was minimal compared to the rest of what she had to do to keep the business afloat. She told me about the disparity between the financial investment that she needed to set up the business and the minimal profit she was making: 'For example, I spent 200 euros on the train ticket and hotel to come for this interview and they didn't even look at my work, it didn't last five minutes. I've just thrown two hundred euros out of the window.'

Corinne went on to admit that her disenchantment with her career had dawned after 'what happened with the Chinese'. In autumn 2011, during Paris Fashion Week, she was given the opportunity to show her work in a showroom in the Marais where young designers, sponsored by a Belgian government export agency, were showing their work to international journalists and buyers.[10] Corinne was approached by some Chinese buyers – who are increasingly present at such events, as entering the Chinese market has become increasingly important commercially – who appeared to be very interested in purchasing pieces from her collection. The buyers spoke to her in an English that she found impossible to understand. They asked for her postal address and told her they would send her a written proposal. A few weeks later Corinne received a 700-page document written entirely in Chinese, of which the only elements she could make out were the places she was supposed to sign. Completely bewildered, and having failed to communicate by email with the people who had sent her the contract, she paid a translator, who explained to her that the contract was not for the purchase of pieces from the collection, but for the purchase of her name, her logo, her brand (which used both her first and last names) and all

---

[10]   These are professional buyers who order a set number of pieces from designers and brands from the collections for department stores and boutiques.

her prototypes, with the purpose of launching the brand on the Chinese market. The contract specified that she would lose all rights over the use of her own name as well as over all future collections. Horrified, Corinne asked the translator to help her do some online research. She discovered that a patent had already been filed in China to trademark a brand using her name and logo. She turned to a lawyer specializing in international commercial law, who told her that according to Chinese law only a Chinese citizen or a foreigner who owns a business in China is allowed to file a complaint against a Chinese business. She looked both utterly incredulous and defeated as she related this story. 'The whole thing, between paying the translator and the lawyer, cost me 7,000 euros. All my savings.' The lawyer told her that the Chinese market, and indeed probably the entire Asian market, was definitively closed to her now. They advised her to file her trademark for the rest of the international market as quickly as possible. Corinne spent another several thousand euros in order to guarantee access to the North American, Brazilian, Australian and Saudi Arabian markets.

This episode is extremely revealing: it shows an individual, Corinne, not a brand, as in Pedro's story, coming up against an entity with an entirely different scale of operations, in this case the Chinese state and its jurisdiction. It's an interesting example of an image of China that is very far away not only geographically but culturally, a place that is reified and demonized, contrary to Pedro's narrative in which it has been excluded and rendered invisible. China appears to be a sort of a blurred, symbolic entity emblematic of all the constraints that the fashion system has to deal with: a sinister, abstract emblem of globalization, the dark side of fashion. Corinne's experience demonstrates that global circulation is not fluid, and nor is it simply a process of rebalancing power: the hegemonic rule of law meant that Corinne could do nothing in the face of the Chinese legal system.

Local people versus citizens of the world: Chloé, Micaela and the ancestral charm of delocalized workers

As well as the delocalization of manufacturing and the free movement of both capital and individuals, contemporary globalization also manufactures global fantasies[11] and its own social categories. This is the aspect that differentiates it from the earlier phases of the expansion of capitalism. If human beings, goods and capital have always circulated, our era is characterized by telecommunication and the speed of transfer, which have created a diffuse awareness of the world, in other words a sense that we all inhabit the same world. But in spite of this, globalization is not within the reach of everyone; access to it is based on social class and status. Millions of unwanted refugees[12] move around the globe yet do not manage to integrate the globalized landscape that produces a particular discourse about globalization.[13]

The anthropologist Jonathan Friedman[14] illustrates this difference in an analysis of the dialectic between the notions of the 'indigenous' and the 'cosmopolitan', and defines, within these terms, the category of the 'cosmopolitan elite'. This category has been central to my research, because it best expresses the identity of many of those I met, both because of their mobility and their identification with the transnational dimension of fashion. The following two situations testify to this cosmopolitan discourse. Both reveal a different and complementary aspect of the discourse within which class, and the symbolic and concrete domination brought about thanks to globalization, are both visible and blurred.

---

[11] A. Appadurai, M. Abélès, F. Bouillot, *Après le colonialisme: Les consequences culturelles de la globalisation*, Paris, Payot, 2005.

[12] M. Agier, *Gérer les indésirables: Des camps de réfugiés au gouvernement humanitaire*, Paris, Flammarion, 2008.

[13] A. Appadurai, *Après le colonialisme*.

[14] J. Friedman, 'From roots to routes: Tropes for trippers', in *Anthropological Theory*, vol. 2, no. 1, March 2002; J. Friedman, 'Indigenous struggles and the discreet charm of the bourgeoisie,' *The Australian Journal of Anthropology*, vol. 10, no. 1, 1999.

Chloé

I met Chloé in Paris at a salon for independent designers who produce work using traditional craftsmanship. The event takes place once a year in a showroom near the Canal Saint-Martin. Chloé was showing her brightly coloured leather bags. She approached me thinking I was a potential customer, and talked to me about her products and her sources of inspiration: 'The style is ethnic because that's what I love. The Masai, Indian ceremonial guards, they all have these super-cool patterns and colour contrasts, I love all that.' When I asked her if she made the bags herself, she answered me with a knowing smile: 'I have a set-up in Shanghai, a cousin who lives there and deals with the production side of things, it's so much cheaper, it costs almost nothing.' Chloé is a perfect example of the cosmopolitan elite. Parisian by birth, in spite of her youth she has already lived in Shanghai, Argentina and London. She explains she came back to Paris for the fashion, which she says is 'in her blood'; her mother is a designer and her sister makes jewellery. But in fact she's bored because she 'doesn't recognize the city any more', she thinks it has become terribly provincial and segregated, and she says with relief that she can always escape the city to stay in various friends' country houses at the weekend. It's clear from what she says that she thinks of herself as a citizen of the world: she no longer identifies with the place where she was born, which she doesn't like precisely because it has too many borders and is too 'local', which corresponds perfectly with Jonathan Friedman's description of the cosmopolitan elite.[15] For Friedman, cosmopolitanism implies, from an ideological perspective, the capacity to move away from one's birthplace. For the cosmopolitan elite, national and international cultural affinities do not define a sense of belonging. Cultural diversity is consumed as a product – food or music, for example – and is

---

[15] Ibid., p. 114.

appropriated aesthetically through fashion and furnishings that are loosely called 'ethnic'. The imaginary world of the cosmopolitan elite is denuded of the demarcations between local affiliation, geographical location and social class. By contrast, locality is appreciated when it is situated somewhere else, when one's home is not an actual place but a social class and a type of space;[16] this 'elsewhere' is an 'otherness', sometimes spatial but more often social and cultural, indistinct; it is an immense aesthetic repertory from which inspiration can be drawn, within which the Masai and Indian ceremonial guards are merely elements of the same ethnic ensemble, where the only differences that matter are pattern and colour.

Micaela

Micaela is another example of the way the cosmopolitan elite's discourse conceals the class differences and structural asymmetries that are vital to capitalism. In March 2012, I joined the delegation of the Wallonie–Brussels Design and Fashion Federation on a visit to Paris, where I worked as a volunteer at the showroom for Belgian designers during fashion week. One evening, as the showroom was closing, Giorgia, one of the directors of the federation, offered to show me around the dozens of stalls scattered throughout the Marais neighbourhood where the designers were exhibiting their work. This was where I met Micaela, an Italian jewellery designer. Because we shared a common native language, Italian, it was easy for us to communicate, and we began talking. I asked her to tell me about her work. She makes large pieces of silver jewellery whose complex forms are the result of long and painstaking work. Micaela emphasized that

---

[16]   Here I am referring to globalized neighbourhoods or communities of expatriates that can be found in many cities around the world.

everything was done by hand. She had worked in Milan for several years as a designer for Dolce e Gabbana, but had left her job there because the pressure and the working conditions were inversely proportional to her meagre salary. She decided to set up her own business, but quickly discovered that in order to create her capsule collection[17] she was going to have to invest several tens of thousands of euros. She explained that the advantage of making jewellery is that it does not have to be made in different sizes, and it also releases her from seasonal requirements and collections. Above all, the production costs are considerably lower. When I asked her if she made the pieces herself, she explained that she didn't have the skills, but she spent several months a year in Indonesia working with local artisans to bring her designs into being. With a dreamy and nostalgic expression, she told me:

> There are whole families who do this, they make everything by hand, it's like the Middle Ages. We have so much to learn from them, from their philosophy of life. I spend four months a year there. I show them my sketches and whole families work on them all day long, from the grandfather to the grandson, everyone together, while I spend the day at the beach. They work so hard, they're always smiling, they're like little smiling worker ants.

In practical terms, Chloé and Micaela do the same thing: each runs her own business and both have their designs made up elsewhere in order to benefit from cheap labour. Their practices are entirely unexceptional: the delocalization of production to the world's peripheries is a distinctive characteristic of neoliberalism and a common practice in the fashion world. Nonetheless, their aesthetic practices and discourses are quite different: Chloé draws on ethnic

---

[17] A capsule collection is a collection of prototypes in a limited number of pieces, made by a designer who is at the beginning of their career. Such a collection requires an initial investment of at least 30,000 euros.

designs for her creations and avoids drawing attention to the fact that their production is delocalized. The way in which she talks about herself makes clear that she doesn't consider herself to have roots anywhere. Micaela meanwhile designs minimalist silver jewellery with no ethnic influence, but her discourse is tinged with a racist notion of the exotic, in which the people creating her jewellery are described as being both backwards and charming. In a sentimental tone that is both exoticizing and evolutionist, her words also point to structural inequalities and differentiated access to modernity that she exploits to her advantage. The perspectives of the two women are different expressions of the same phenomenon of cultural globalization that creates different oppositions between cosmopolitans and locals.

Private fashion shows and global inequality

Mia's lifestyle is peripatetic. In May 2012, for example, she worked in Milan, Singapore, Hong Kong, London and New York. She lets me know about her travels in text messages or via Facebook. During a brief period that month when she was in Paris we met up in a café and she told me about her recent trip to Asia, a trip which she'd casually let drop in a text message a few weeks previously. We were chatting on the terrace of a bistro on a street off the Rue du Faubourg-Saint-Martin. I noticed that she seemed to alter her manner when the waiter approached our table: she'd start talking loudly and her gestures became more mannered, as if she was hoping to be seen. She certainly stood out, in a pair of large designer sunglasses, bright red lipstick and expensive handbag that sat on the table in front of her.

Curious, I asked her to tell me about the project, which she insisted was under wraps. She told me she had been asked by a prominent Italian brand to work as a stylist and producer of a series of private fashion shows. An increasing number of luxury and haute couture labels now organize private fashion shows all over the world; the ones that Mia worked on were specifically for showing furs to Asian millionaires. She looked very serious as she told me that the label did not want the story to get out. Private fashion shows held in these new economic powerhouses are purely commercial operations: they bring in a lot of profit for luxury labels, but divulging information about them could have a negative impact on their image. The representatives of the label invited Mia to Milan to show her the collection and discuss the project. Together they selected the pieces from the ready-to-wear collection that would be shown alongside the furs. They also showed her the hair and makeup designs so that she could give instructions to the local team. The trip was scheduled to last two weeks, or possibly three if a third stop in Russia was confirmed. The label booked an outbound flight in first class for Mia, who was travelling alone, while the clothes were sent over separately. In Singapore, her first destination, Mia was agreeably surprised by the fast-paced rhythm and modernity of the city, and by the politeness of the people: 'I arrived and got straight into a taxi, there's such an amazing energy, everyone's smiling, it's all "Welcome, enjoy". It was incredible, such a good vibe.' She arrived at the Ritz-Carlton, where she would be living and working for the week, and met the hairdressers, makeup artists and representatives of the model agencies. She was in charge of casting the models for the shows. I asked if because it was in Singapore the models were Asian. 'There are loads and loads of European girls. I'm supposed to use Europeans, bloody Russians, I really loathe the Russians, and local girls too, Asians, Chinese. I only used three of them in the end.' Mia wasn't impressed by the local girls, explaining that because Singapore isn't a fashion capital, the models there 'are either "new faces"[18] or second choice'. Once the models had been cast, she had to decide who was going to wear what, in preparation

---

[18] 'New faces' are girls who are just starting out in modelling.

for the first fashion show at the hotel the following day: there were six a day, for up to six clients at a time, and they took place in one of the hotel's suites. Mia was in charge of everything behind the scenes, but she didn't interact with the clients. They were greeted upon their arrival by the local buyers, who already knew them personally. The buyers also dealt with taking orders.

The hotel is a huge skyscraper overlooking Singapore's Marina Bay, and all the suites are above the twentieth floor. Mia was blown away by the view of the skyline. The hotel is a luxurious, minimalist fantasy that perfectly suited the label's image. The salon of the suite was set up with plasma screens showing videos of fashion shows. The clients were welcomed one by one by the local representatives of the label and invited to take a seat. The models paraded the clothes under the spotlights, with music backing. Once the show was over the clients put in their orders and then helped themselves from the buffet. 'The whole thing took place in this suite, on I don't know what floor, there were screens, visual merchandising, no more than five or six clients at a time, champagne, petits fours.'

I could barely begin to imagine how such an expensive setup for such a tiny audience could be profitable. When I said this to Mia, she explained that the shows are organized by local oligarchs: 'That's where all the money is, you have no idea.' I asked her to tell me a bit more about the clients.

They were so horrible, I've never seen people spend money like that. They're all kept by their husbands. Every single one spent like 100,000 euros on dresses and furs. When you think that a crocodile skin handbag costs 40,000 euros ... that's how much you pay for a house where I come from. But these prices ... you cannot imagine. Everything's the absolute height of luxury. One woman in Singapore spent 190,000 euros. They're all married to men who work in finance, CEOs. They spend staggering amounts of money like this every month.

The daily routine of the fashion shows at the Ritz meant that Mia didn't have time to even leave the hotel to visit the city. As soon as it was over she flew to Hong Kong to begin all over again, casting models and organizing shows in another five-star hotel. The positive impression she had when she arrived in Singapore was not replicated in Hong Kong. On the flight she had a moment of panic, which increased the following day, the only day off she had planned during the entire trip.

> I didn't feel good on the plane, I felt lonely, a bit stressed, my heart was beating really fast. I just felt really down, I don't know why. I got to Hong Kong in the evening and the next day was a day off, but I'd had to do some work for Vincent for a New York–London thing, so I was exhausted. I had a million things to do, and suddenly I'm in Hong Kong, with the humidity and shitty weather, I hated everybody. I decided to go out and get something to eat, but I freaked out when I left the hotel, and went straight back to my room and got into bed. I had a massive panic attack, you can't imagine. I took an aspirin, went to bed, thought I was going to die, it was awful. Later I Skyped some friends which calmed me down a bit. They told me I had to breathe deeply, it was just the climate. I was scared, I called a friend who's a cardiologist, he told me not to worry, it was just stress, coffee, Coca Cola, the heat, the latitude. Everything was more difficult in Hong Kong, the castings, the girls were ugly, I didn't like any of them, I was a stressed. It was harder but I did it. They're so insanely rich in Hong Kong, it's crazy.

I asked her how much she was paid for the job. 'Quite a lot', she told me. 'I'm not sure exactly, but for a couple of weeks work it was between five and six thousand euros. I didn't give a damn about any of it, I was the boss, with a cigarette hanging out of my mouth.' She laughed. 'I really acted like a star, like in a film, in my heels, it's reassuring wearing heels for a shoot, now I always wear them. Everyone loved me, everyone wanted to have their picture taken with me. One of the models asked me for my autograph, they all liked me so much it was unbelievable. The guy from the label said to me: "Who wouldn't love you?"'

The waiter brought us a bowl of peanuts. As he put them on the table he noticed my tape recorder and asked us about it. Mia told him: 'She's interviewing me because I'm famous! Giulia's an anthropologist and she's writing a book about me. She comes to shoots, watches me at work. I've just got back from Asia and I was telling her all about it.'

Local elites, global elites

Private fashion shows expose a different side of globalization. They testify first to the fact that a giant European luxury label must physically transport its dream machine if it wants to meet these new economic elites, who are today the number one consumers of luxury goods in the world. For centuries, until the 1960s, the global elites came to Paris to have their clothes made. With the arrival of neoliberalism, the financial and symbolic hegemonic poles have multiplied and relocated and the hierarchies have changed, obliging the producers of luxury goods to travel to their clients, rather than the clients travelling to them. Unlike in the past, the process has to remain secret, as Mia says, because in spite of economic realities, emerging economies are not yet on the world map of luxury. The dream must remain symbolically anchored in the fashion capitals, it must remain unattainable and exclusive. If it came out that high fashion labels travel across the world to sell to people who do not correspond to this image of sophistication their image would be damaged. This situation bears witness to the encounter between the two different elites that globalization has produced: the cosmopolitan elite, exemplified by Mia, and the economic elite, exemplified by the Asian clientele.

Mia's life is one of constant travel around the world. She rubs shoulders with people from the same professional milieu, who have the same lifestyle: an international group of people who are constantly on the move and think of themselves as cosmopolitan. This is certainly an elite, who own and create highly valued symbolic capital: they manufacture the dream of capitalism, embody the very idea of modernity, and have highly desirable jobs, in spite of a certain financial instability. The clients, meanwhile, belong to another category, that of a local financial elite: they embody literal economic power and represent through their staggering consumption the structural inequalities of capitalism.

These two categories meet in a luxury context, which for Mia is her work environment and for the clients their everyday life. The labels put in place a sales process that for Mia is a professional situation but also allows her to access the dream. This dream resides in her own occasional experience of luxury, wealth and power. For the clients it is a situation of consumption and status confirmation: the dream is not located in the context itself but in the access to elegance and distinction that the labels are selling to them.

The way Mia talked about herself that day it was as if she were a member of the economic elite and a 'star', drawing on elements from the world of her clients and celebrities: flying first class, staying in a suite in a five-star hotel, taking taxis, being asked for her autograph or being photographed, the slew of compliments she received. She moves in a world of luxury without belonging to it in a material sense. As we have seen, she shares a small flat in a scruffy neighbourhood and has periods of financial precariousness. That doesn't stop her identifying sometimes with the world of the dream in which she works. But the way she talks about it is ambivalent, because the glamour she describes is contradicted by other elements: panic attacks provoked by overwork, the feeling of isolation, loneliness and disorientation, as well as the uncertainty linked to this condition, a consequence of the fact that she never knows how long a job will last, or how much and when she will be paid. This is, in a sense, the price she must pay for belonging to the cosmopolitan elite.

Fashion in the world

Whatever the universalist and inclusive claims that are so often made for it,[19] globalization in fact establishes a huge number of frontiers. These frontiers are both material and symbolic, as amply illustrated by the kilometres of walls constructed all around the world, vast economic disparities between nations and citizens, and inequality of access to free movement. The kinds of situations described in this chapter are useful for understanding how globalization and its frontiers function at the scale of this study. Pedro's discourse illustrates what Arjun Appadurai calls 'technoscapes',[20] industries with businesses that operate at a global level both economically and symbolically (such as, for example, fashion), thus leading to a hierarchy of merchandise as well as of workers and states. According to the anthropologist Lynda Dematteo, 'corporations are transnational entities that contribute to the redefinition of place'.[21] In a globalized world, certain supranational economic realities create places, and this in turn creates frontiers. In the fashion system, globalization's influence works simultaneously on a material and a symbolic level: in the global fashion market, not every country has the same value, either in terms of infrastructure or in terms of fantasy. In the geography of luxury, the symbolic value of a country becomes commercial. This means that globalization is far from being fluid and homogenous: the gap between different national jurisdictions and supranational regulations (the European Union, in the case of fashion) is clearly demonstrated by the issue of labelling. What we have seen of the different images of China shows that even though fashion is completely dependent on countries

---

[19]   In *La Condition cosmopolite*, Michel Agier notes that 'the universalist injunction often becomes a mode of exclusion'; M. Agier, *La Condition cosmopolite*, Paris, La Découverte, 2013, p. 95.

[20]   A. Appadurai, *Après le colonialisme*.

[21]   L. Dematteo, *La Ruée vers la Roumanie des entrepreneurs italiens*, Paris, Notre Europe, 2009 p. 98.

outside Europe in terms of both production and consumption, Europe is not keen on being 'provincialized',[22] in other words downgrading its position in the world. The Old Continent is no longer economically hegemonic, as the private fashion shows in Asia make plain. And yet, Europe is doing all it can to preserve its symbolic power, a power that is lucrative precisely because the luxury industry makes a profit thanks to its trade in a particular hegemonic ideal of elegance and sophistication. In fact, the process of globalization does not always lead to the coinciding of economic hegemonies with symbolic hegemonies, and this disparity of status brings about the construction of new frontiers: a bag doesn't have the same value if it is made in China or in Italy, and a fashion show doesn't have the same value if it takes place in Paris or in Hong Kong. But symbolic frontiers – in other words, these disparities of status – do not only concern countries and products, they also concern social categories and individuals, as exemplified in the words of Chloé and Micaela, who essentialize and culturalize Indonesian craft workers, or an outfit that is supposedly 'ethnic'. Apparently anecdotal, they in fact reveal a representation of the world that is very widespread among those in dominant social categories, a representation according to which they are cosmopolitan, modern and mobile, while subordinate classes are either positively or negatively 'local', in some way backwards, producers of fantasies and 'cultures' whose sole function is to be consumed by the cosmopolitan elite. Access to cultural globalization is resolutely differentiated, and cosmopolitanism is the exclusive privilege of the elite.

The fashion industry exploits these different strata of globalization[23] in order to maintain its profits. The interlocking representations and frontiers, at once social, economic and symbolic, are jointly produced and appropriated by the fashion industry and its actors in order to

[22] Dipesh Chakrabarty *Provincializing Europe – Postcolonial Thought and Historical Difference,* Princeton, Princeton University Press, 2000.
[23] J. Assayag, *La Mondialisation vue d'ailleurs. L'Inde désorientée,* Paris, Le Seuil, 2005.

guarantee productivity and profitability. Fashion, as both an industry and a social world, thus actively participates in maintaining these asymmetries at a global level and remains a major influence on the economy and the fantasies of contemporary capitalism.

*

The dream is the engine of fashion. A dream one leans towards, one desires, and which, in order to attain it, one consumes – or is consumed by – in order to get closer to it. The young people who dream of a job in fashion are dreaming of entering a socio-professional world and attaining a coveted economic status, while those who are actually working in fashion dream of attaining a sophistication that they only intermittently have access to. Haute couture workers dream of the opulent world of the clientele, while the clientele, in spite of their ultra-privileged economic situation, dream of a condition that is also out of their reach, the world of celebrity or, for the nouveau riche,[24] the sophisticated world of the old bourgeoisie. Clients also dream of attaining the inaccessible beauty of the models that fashion sells to them; meanwhile, models offer up their bodies for the brief moments during which they 'perform' the dream. Even for the models this condition is only transitory, and the result of artifice. On a global and globalized level, the dream is a geographical and symbolic 'elsewhere', in terms both of the transformation of the status of objects and of countries.

But the fashion system does not only manufacture the dream and the objects of consumption, it also produces types of work, lifestyles, and its own range of subjectivities.

---

[24] In a chapter on haute couture, Bourdieu defines '*parvenus*', or the nouveau riche, as people who lack much specific capital. These people have financial capital, but they lack the capital of elegance and sophistication of the traditional bourgeois class. See P. Bourdieu, *Questions de sociologie,* p. 197.

Part Two

Working in Fashion, or 'Lucky to Be There'

I made my way to a studio in Saint-Denis, on the outskirts of Paris, where I was going to observe a fashion shoot for a label that Mia said was 'shit, not real fashion'.[1] The photos were for a clothing catalogue.[2] The studio was in a large concrete tower lit throughout with neon, which cast a sallow light on the proceedings and gave the building the atmosphere of a Soviet-era administration building rather than a place where glamour was being created. There was a different studio on every floor. I finally reached the right place. Mia was in the dressing area with the makeup artist, Dominique, who was setting out her tools. On the table in front of the mirror she had lined up an incredible array of lipsticks and eyeshadows in all imaginable colours and shades, brushes, cotton wool balls, tweezers, creams and mascaras. Most bore the Chanel logo, for whom Dominique frequently worked as a freelancer. She had beautiful skin, and wore little makeup, and was aged somewhere between forty and fifty. A few minutes later the model came in to the dressing area. She was seven, blue eyed, with long, straight, blond hair. Pointing at each of us in turn – Mia, Dominique and me – she asked: 'Who chose me? Did you choose me? Or did you?' Dominique and Mia told her that someone else had

---

[1]   'Lucky to be there': Working in fashion: Between glamour and precariousness is the title of the doctoral thesis on which this book is based.
[2]   Mia was paid 350 euros off the books for this job. Because it was so lacking in prestige it risked being bad for her career, so she did it under an assumed name.

chosen her, but that she was very pretty and they were very happy it was her. She sat down in front of the mirror and Dominique began to put on makeup and plait her hair, as we continued our conversation about Dominique's career and her work. Suddenly the little girl interrupted us: 'I love being a model because I love putting on makeup and dressing up.' Mia asked her what she wanted to do when she grew up and she said: 'I want to be a model and earn lots of money. I've got more money than any of my friends. I've got five figures more than anyone else in my bank account, that's what my mum told me. I want to do more castings and make more money.' Mia, Dominique and I looked at one another in silence. Mia got the girl dressed in the outfit she'd selected and we went out into the main space. The little girl ran to take her place under the lights and immediately began a series of smiles, nodding her head from side to side, then flicking her hair, though Mia and the photographer weren't ready to start the session. Once the session began, Mia whispered to me that it was no good, the child was much too thin and it would all have to be retouched on the computer. The girl carried on mechanically smiling. Once enough photos had been taken, we returned to the dressing room to change the little model's outfit.

Mia Are you going to have something to eat? You have to eat something, you know.

Child I don't like to eat very much.

Mia That's not healthy.

Child Because I don't want to get fat!

Dominique But you aren't fat at all!

Mia You're really quite thin.

Child I weigh eighteen kilos.

Dominique Who told you you shouldn't eat too much in case you get fat?

Child My mum says I mustn't get fat.

She put on the next outfit. Mia twisted her hair into a knot, and we went back into the main room. In the corner at the back a woman was sitting in the shadows. I greeted her, and she answered with her mouth full. It was the little girl's mother. She was eating a hamburger and chips balanced on her lap on top of a brown paper McDonald's bag. On a chair next to her was a litre cup of Coca-Cola. She must have been in her late forties. She was overweight and had grey roots showing in her dyed brown hair. She wore a purple tracksuit. The contrast between her and her perfectly turned out little girl was striking; it was as if she had invested in her daughter a sort of social and economic revenge based on appearance.

After the photo session ended we went back to the dressing room. The little girl got changed and she and her mother left. Dominique and Mia were still talking about how shockingly thin she was, that it wasn't normal, and that the agency that represents her needs to keep an eye on her weight. Someone suggested getting in touch with the agency, but no one actually proposed doing it; this kind of 'anomaly' was presumably in fact completely 'normalized', and perhaps the two women were talking about it only for my benefit.

While she was doing the little girl's hair Dominique told me more about her work:

Dominique   Nowadays no one says, 'What else do you do?' But when I trained as a makeup artist twenty years ago, people would be like, 'What are you going to do for money?' Nowadays everyone gets it, so when you say, 'I'm a professional makeup artist', they're like 'Oh, wow, cool!' [she makes a comically exaggerated expression of excitement with her mouth and eyes] You know, there's absolutely nothing artistic about this job, you're in the fashion world, sure, but it's not the dream that people think it is.

Giulia   What do you think it is about it that makes people dream?

Dominique   When you see the magazines, it's all just so mind-boggling. It's amazing, all the celebrities. People are much more drawn to the dream than they used to be, they really want to touch it, because it seems like it's right there, like anyone can reach it, even though that's not really true at all. I do a lot of work for Chanel, and people have crazy fantasies about what that's like. I do really like working for Chanel. I never dreamed I'd ever have clients like that.

The way Dominique talked about her work highlights how people who work in fashion benefit from the exposure and glamour of the profession. This is even more true nowadays, when jobs in fashion have branched out to include not only skilled work, but other coveted jobs. This desire, and the glamour that goes with it, is born out of the manufacture of the dream: the fantasies of luxury, prestige and elegance that fashion produces in order to market itself to consumers.

Nonetheless, the reality of working in the industry does not always correspond to how outsiders might imagine the dream. It's not just *bright lights*, fashion is *overexposed*. In photography, overexposure means there is too much light, so that the nuances, shadows and contours are blurred, imprecise and sometimes rendered invisible. The metaphor of 'overexposure' is a way of pointing both to the attractiveness of the dream, a result of its constant exposure, but also its opacity, the way it's impossible to detect the reality beneath the fantasies, rendered invisible precisely by what is 'too visible'. Fashion is a system that is simultaneously overexposed and opaque. Overexposed by the omnipresence in the media of desire and consumption, and opaque because it is so difficult to see what is really happening behind the images and the fantasies that it manufactures. In fashion everything happens as though the overexposure to light makes the realities and the internal rules of production impenetrable, obscure, unknowable, and sometimes intentionally concealed. But overexposure also leads to a projection of the dream onto the workers themselves, the reflection of fashion's beam conferring on them a coveted social status. Mayra, a designer, told me: 'When you tell people you work in fashion, suddenly people want to talk to you, because everyone identifies in a way with fashion. I think that's what makes people dream.' People who work in fashion themselves kindle that desire because they are perceived as being intermediaries through whom other people can brush up against the dream. When I asked Iris, who trains personnel for an upmarket brand, the kinds of images fashion work generate, she said:

> I think what it is, you feel like you're part of the elite. It's different things: most people, when they see fashion magazines or adverts, or fashion week on the television, don't know where it all comes from, it's this great mystery. And when you work in fashion you know all about it! It's not a mystery any more, you're on the inside. Maybe that's also because people really want a lot of stuff. It's a strong desire that is created when you're surrounded by all this fashion. It's the models, or the products, or the look, or ... I don't know, it doesn't really matter what it is, it's so ... it just makes people crave, and you're a part of it, and you feel, maybe you feel a bit different to other people ... You're so close to it all, it's like some divine thing, because people get so excited. They're attracted by success, it's a kind of ... Not everyone who works in fashion is famous, but you're close to things that people idolize, you feel like you're part of it.

Charlotte, a fashion journalist, confirms this notion of an elite produced by the media focus on working in fashion, an elite founded on the fabrication of desire. Without going into a psychoanalytical analysis of the principal, it is interesting to consider the social and economic dimensions – desire as a force, an energy, a motor that capitalism has appropriated.[3] Capitalism produces both the merchandise and the desire for the merchandise. In terms of fashion, this desire is not just about merchandise and consumers; it extends to those who work in fashion, who are both the envied and the enviers. In this sense, people

---

3   F. Lordon, *Capitalisme, désir et servitude: Marx et Spinoza*, Paris, La Fabrique, 2010.

who work in fashion are the elite of desire.[4] Elsa, a stylist, confirms this idea of a social structure based on desire triggered by visibility:

> It's all the glitter, you know, people think it's awesome, and sometimes you meet actual celebrities . . . It used to be for the upper classes, now it's all about celebrity. It's a star system with castes, there are the reality TV stars, they're at the bottom, then the real stars, red carpet royalty, at the top.

Fashion's overexposure produces and maintains this desire; the media only focuses on the fantasy and prestige, and keeps invisible and opaque the conditions of production. But the people who work in fashion also appropriate some of the overexposure and desire that it creates. Ludo, a fashion photographer, told me that 'luxury is the dream', and acknowledged that when people find out he works in fashion, 'they're super-impressed. I don't think they really understand, and they're kind of intimidated too because it's a world that makes people dream more than if you say "I'm a banker".'

The dream is composed both of a desire for glamour and the prestige that comes from doing a job that is not mundane. According to Ludo, fashion's prestige inheres in the fact that those who work in fashion are the emissaries of a dream, of a fantasy that the idea of working in a bank doesn't generate. Such a dichotomy results in the transformation of the value and the role of labour brought about by capitalism during the last fifty years. This becomes clear when investigating the different jobs available in fashion, beyond the distorting effects of overexposure.

---

4   It's probably more appropriate to say that some of those who work in fashion are part of an elite, but I prefer here not to get into this level of distinction. This is a generalized representation. Regarding the notion of the elite, it is useful to recall the sociologist Nathalie Heinich's reflections on the elite of visibility (N. Heinich, *De la visibilité: Excellence et singularité en régime médiatique*, Paris, Gallimard, 2012). According to Heinich, because of the influence of the media, contemporary societies have created a new kind of 'aristocracy', no longer based on class privilege, but on a privileged media presence. Using Heinich's analysis, rather than questioning the idea of celebrity being predicated on visibility, I am interested in the desire that is linked to this visibility. On the notion of the elite, see also A.-C. Wagner, *Les Nouvelles Élites de la mondialisation: Une immigration dorée en France*, Paris, PUF, 1998.

4

On the Threshold of the Dream: The Salespeople

When I asked Annie why she had left her stable job as a costume designer for an unpaid job in fashion, she answered:

> Because since I started working in fashion, I've eaten at the Ritz, which I never got to do before. Since I started working in fashion, everyone wants to talk to me about my job, everyone's curious, interested, impressed. When I was working in the theatre, even if I was working on some big production, no one ever asked me anything about my job.

The fact of working in fashion has transformed Annie's symbolic capital; now she triggers desire, despite the fact that she is unpaid. The interlocking of gazes and images that are put onto and created by those who work in fashion is a necessary element for understanding the phenomena of overexposure and opacity. Apart from the fascination for bright lights, overexposure is also the dream in the expression of the other when it lands on those who work in fashion, for in order for overexposure to function, it needs 'spectators', who look and who desire, and are situated outside the circle of bright lights. The elite of desire can only exist in this condition.

But who really has a coveted position in this social world? It's hard to say; fashion is such a tentacular system, and it produces a heterogeneous professional milieu. It's almost impossible to state objectively who is within it and who is outside it, because the inclusions are relational and situational, and the world of fashion is strictly structured and predicated on exclusion. Rather than define membership, it is more interesting to describe and decrypt how status is expressed, hierarchized, confirmed and contested, and to observe how, in spite of these symbolic inner hierarchies, people who work in different areas of fashion, who are closer or further away from this world, manage to appropriate this overexposure.

The job that best elucidates these mysteries is that of the salesperson for luxury goods. This figure embodies the threshold, the fluid border between those who are inside and those who are outside. They are the final link in the chain of the production of the dream, the people who operate the transaction between production and consumption, who put into the hands of the purchaser both the material goods and the dream that accompanies them, fabricated by the media. Because they are on the margins of this world,[1] those who sell luxury goods are pivotal figures who make it possible to understand the way in which attractiveness in this milieu functions, and what type of work it gives rise to.

Gilbert and the dream of luxury

Gilbert is a twenty-six-year-old law student. I initially met him through Jaime, and we subsequently met up again several times. At our first meeting, he told me that although he had signed up for a law degree, his real interest was fashion. He was working full-time at H&M and in spite of his plan to study, his dream was to find a job with a luxury brand. Encouraged by friends and family, he decided to pursue his dream and to look for a job in fashion. He signed up with a temping agency and assiduously checked out job offers on the internet. He sent his first application to Chanel and then applied to Lucceto,[2] who were looking for a salesperson. Lucceto replied, and

---

[1]   The salespersons interviewed considered themselves to be part of the fashion world, while other fashion workers insisted that they are not.

[2]   A fictional brand name.

Gilbert had several interviews, during which he was asked questions about Lucceto's history and fashion lines, as well as his own motivation, in great detail. The recruitment process involved three interviews,[3] at the end of which he was offered the job. During one of our conversations, he explained that the fact that he was a law student had worked in his favour, because 'brands like the people who work for them to have a certain level of education'. He was very excited at the prospect of working for a luxury label, and thrilled at the perks of the job: wearing a specially designed Lucceto suit for work, and benefiting from a 20 per cent reduction on all the brand's goods.

He was taken on initially for a three-month trial period, which would be followed, if all went well, by a permanent contract. His initial delight at working for a luxury brand was rapidly tarnished, however, by his new working conditions. He had thought he was being taken on to work in one of the flagship boutiques, but instead he found himself on a small stand in the department store Galeries Lafayette. This was a disappointment, because in the spatial hierarchy of luxury sales, this corner is right at the bottom. Within Galeries Lafayette, Lucceto was located on two different levels – the principal stand with all the collections and another 15-square-metre stand on the lower ground floor, where handbags were sold. Gilbert was the cashier on the handbag stand. He spent the day in a tiny space by the wall by the till. His job was not, as he had envisaged, giving advice to customers, but taking payments. On top of that, the customers were not sophisticated Parisians, because the stand 'was positioned strategically to target

---

[3] Under the heading 'Retail, fashion and luxury: What salary can you expect?' on the employment website cadremploi.fr, candidates are told that they may have up to five interviews during which they will have to demonstrate that they understand the 'codes' of the world of luxury goods (have a good sense of customer service, discretion) and that they have some knowledge of fashion (flagship products of the brand, competitors). In addition, the candidate must demonstrate reliability, commitment and past experience.

coaches of Chinese and Japanese tourists who came into the department store and didn't have time to go to the upper floors'.

Over the course of my meetings with Gilbert, I was able to follow the evolution of his relationship to his job, from his initial excitement and enthusiasm to his apprehension and disappointment. Instead of forging relationships with his customers, as he had imagined, he was faced with hordes of 'loud, rude and badly dressed Asian tourists', who sometimes bought five or eight handbags at a time. The cheapest Lucceto handbag costs 1,800 euros. One day Gilbert sold 250,000 euros worth of handbags. The stand he worked on had a turnover of three million euros a month. After his three-month trial period was up, the brand decided to keep him on, but went back on its promise of a permanent contract and instead signed him for another three months. However disappointed he was with his work, Gilbert accepted, both because he needed to work and because he hoped he would be promoted, but in the end he was disappointed in this as well: he discovered through a colleague that he had been taken on to cover someone's maternity leave and the company never intended to give him a permanent contract. He was earning 1,800 euros a month, the equivalent of what he had been paid at H&M.[4] When I pointed this out to him, he replied that working for H&M and working for Lucceto were not the same thing. Why not? For the same salary, what is the added value of working for a luxury brand?

Selling the dream: David and the brand ambassadors

David, in his mid-forties, is head of recruitment and training for all the French boutiques of a well-known French luxury label. I asked him what the criteria were for employing salespeople:

[4]   At H&M he worked nights shelving merchandise, for which he was paid more than the other salespeople.

They're people who understand luxury codes. What does it mean to say someone understands the codes? They're not people who necessarily buy luxury goods, because after all a luxury item might cost several times their monthly salary, but they're people who speak a foreign language, who are comfortable talking to people from other countries, who have a strong cultural background. Knowing the codes means a certain code of ethics, a certain civility, a kind of international social understanding.

The profile of the ideal salesperson sketched by David is that of someone who straddles different worlds: a member of an elite that possesses strong cultural capital and interpersonal skills, in which salespeople are in some sense at the same social level as the customers, yet whose economic situation has nothing in common with luxury consumers. David went on: 'When you interview someone, you pick up signals. My job is to detect and interpret these signals. The signals I am looking for are those that indicate chic, sophistication, an understanding of that language.'

In other words, David's job consists in detecting symbolic and cultural capital[5] in potential salespeople, which is then employed in the sales process: 'We are looking for salespeople whose main characteristic is not selling, in fact, but welcoming, receiving, introducing, we're looking for what we call brand ambassadors. We are recruiting ambassadors.' In other words, the salespeople have to embody the dream and the fantasy of the brand's goods in order to transmit and sell them to the customer. Their role as ambassador is vital, because the dream has to be orchestrated right up to the last minute – in other words, at the moment of the sale:

> When you go into one of our stores, even outside France, the idea is that it should be a cultural experience, sophisticated, welcoming. The idea is for the customers to be made to feel comfortable. It's supposed

[5]   P. Bourdieu, *La Distinction: Critique sociale du jugement*, Paris, Minuit, 1979.

to be a special moment, and then they leave with something that they're proud of owning, which is a way of expressing their status or their wealth.

The role of salespeople is central to the fashion economy, and shows once again how fantasy and material dimensions are intertwined in the industry. Consumers are not only consuming objects, they are having an experience, through the ritualizing of the acquisition of a luxury product by the salespeople, who depict the fantasy element of the brand and bring it into existence in the sales situation. The brand ambassador's job is to sell products by selling a dream of distinction and of being part of an elite:

> The idea is to welcome everyone the same way, with the same respect, and to offer the same special experience. It's called the 'ware experience'. You're supposed to enter the boutique and immediately you're welcomed, 'How are you, can I help you?' You're treated like a VIP. The salesperson's job is more to make you feel this than to sell you something. Selling is not the thing that interests us most. It's collateral damage.

'Selling is collateral damage.' And yet fashion is an industry dedicated to profit, and the brand David works for has the highest turnover of any high fashion brand in France, perhaps in the world. Which means that this ritualizing, that consists of making everyone who walks through the door of these temples to luxury feel like a VIP, is presumably profitable. The salespeople are the high priests of the experience. But to become the emissaries of the dream, they themselves must be genuinely enchanted by it. For them to serve the cause, they must be committed to it. David acknowledges this, telling me that during the recruitment process, the aspiring salespeople must already be in love with the brand:

> First of all, we're lucky, and I think this is true for luxury labels in general, to be very attractive to job candidates. We represent, as I said,

a universe that's very strong in terms of quality, history, innovation, modernity, it's very 'fashion', and that's attractive to a lot of people. We have people working for us who really love the brand, and we enhance this through the brand's universe, especially during their training. We want our salespeople to share this world with our customers.

During our conversation, David rarely mentions the quality or the material properties of the products. He uses words like 'experience', 'ambassador', 'the world of the brand' – a lexicon that focuses on the brand's symbolic dimension, the dream that it conveys. This dream is primarily created for the salespeople within the company structure, through reproduction, in the context of the training process, of what David calls the communication of 'core values' – in other words, the basic values that are to be transmitted to the customer. From the point of view of these 'brand ambassadors', being included in the symbolic dimension of luxury is the greatest reward they can hope for, for as David says, 'Just because you work for a luxury brand doesn't mean you earn a lavish salary'. The salespeople offer the company their aesthetic,[6] social and cultural capital, and become the means by which the company depicts and sells the dream. The reward for their services is not primarily material; those at the bottom of the ladder can barely live decently on their salaries. The maximum salary is 4,000 euros a month for the manager of a boutique, while the minimum is around 1,800 euros for a cashier,[7] the lowest position on the shop floor, superior only to those who work in the warehouses. On a salary like this, the salespeople cannot afford to buy the products they sell: the cheapest woman's handbag sold by the brand David works for costs around 700 euros, and they go up to 40,000 euros. Yet according to David, the salespeople are also consumers:

---

[6]   C. Warhurst and D. Nickson, 'Employee experience of aesthetic labour in retail and hospitality', *Work, Employment and Society*, vol. 21, no. 1, March 2007.

[7]   These figures are approximate, and represent an average. They are taken from various online sources.

> Our salespeople, our staff, adore the brand and they make sacrifices to be able to buy our products. The brand recognizes their commitment and they make it possible for them to afford our products. We hold staff sales, always very chic, very classy, and our employees always flock to them, myself included.

The products are still extremely expensive, even with the maximum 20 per cent staff reduction. The salespeople might love a particular label, or luxury goods in general, but they can only express it in the disparity between their coveted material status and their actual material status. Like many customers, when they purchase a product they are purchasing a fragment of the dream. They are, in a way, failed consumers, aspiring consumers, lacking the economic capital that would allow them to properly access the material dimension of luxury, bringing into play their immaterial capital in order to share in its symbolic dimension. The transaction between the company and the salespeople is not solely based on economics, but also on their occasional participation in an 'experience' of luxury, identical to the one they offer to their customers. The salespeople bring into play their subjectivity, in other words their relational capacity, their cultural, economic and aesthetic capital,[8] with the aim of attaining the luxury that they sell or produce, or within which they develop. Desire thus circulates among the salespeople, the customers, and the people who work higher up in the hierarchy, like David, who claims to be very happy that he can afford his company's products: 'I buy a lot because I know it's a privilege, because I know that when I wear this stuff it gives me status.'

Those who work in fashion profit from the overexposure of the brands that employ them which gives them 'status'. Their proximity to objects of desire adds value to their work. To work for a luxury brand means to be part of the dream, and to profit, even just a little, from its glow.

---

[8]   B. Urciuoli, 'Skills and selves in the new workplace,' *American Ethnologist*, vol. 35, no. 2, May 2008.

5

The Greater the Prestige, the Lower the Pay: The Rules of the Game for Fashion Workers

The *Mena* shoot

In December 2012 I accompanied Mia to a fashion shoot for *Mena*,[1] according to Mia a very prestigious independent British magazine. The shoot was taking place in a loft in the south of Paris that belonged to a young Italian painter. Because the magazine didn't have a budget for the story, the team couldn't hire a real studio. The shoot began at 8.00 am, though I only arrived around midday, when everyone was in the middle of lunch. Apart from Mia and María, her assistant, I didn't know anyone. Sitting around the table in the corner of the loft's kitchen area were Adèle, the French photographer, Carmelo, the Italian hairdresser, Eleonora, the Franco-Italian makeup artist, and the assistant photographer whose name I didn't catch. They were all in their forties, except for Vanja, the Hungarian model, and the French manicurist, both of whom were twenty-four. Sitting in a chair slightly away from the table was a young French girl, the assistant photography intern, and the lighting assistant, a young Eastern European man. Everyone was eating sushi from a nearby takeaway restaurant. Mia invited me to join them at the table between her and Vanja. Vanja, in a white dressing gown and a pair of hotel slippers, was made up spectacularly, with turquoise eye shadow and orange nail varnish. She

---

[1] Not the magazine's real title.

was wearing a wig – a black bob – that I never saw her without, because I ended up leaving at 7.00 pm, long before the shoot was over. Mia introduced me according to the usual formula, explaining that I was an anthropologist writing a book about fashion and about Mia herself. Once the introductions were over, Vanja began talking. She talked a lot and seemed to take up a lot of space, in spite of her ethereal, almost disembodied presence: she had fine, pale skin, pale blue almond-shaped eyes, a neat little turned-up nose, and plump lips. She was very thin. She looked like a porcelain doll. I noticed that she picked off only three pieces from her tiny portion of maki sushi. Mia had told me with a touch of pride that there would be several well-known people at the shoot. Vanja, a supermodel, had done ad campaigns for perfume and luxury brands, as well as fashion shows for several top designers. By now I was beginning to get to know the fashion world, and I knew without being told that she was a supermodel, simply from the way she monopolized the conversation. Expressing her subjectivity is part of the supermodel's job, because it confirms the difference in her status to that of less successful models, who have to be as discreet as possible on a job. Another clue: she didn't hide her age. In the world of modelling, by the age of twenty-four a model is either a supermodel or she's too old to be cast in shoots for 'non-commercial' or artistic jobs. In a low, confident voice, she launched into a long monologue about her years in New York, her ambition to act in films, how much she loved Paris, and her boyfriend, a law student. Eleonora, the makeup artist, who knew her well from having worked with her many times, whispered to me afterwards: 'She talks a lot, she's aware of it'. The meal ended soon after, and Adèle's assistant cleared the table while Vanja prepared to change into the next outfit, helped by María. The outfit had been put together by Mia after lunch, in the way she always worked: she selected items off the rack and laid them out on the floor, trying different combinations according to her inspiration. It was a moment of intense concentration, as she tried to give shape to her vision. For her, this part of her job represented the apex of her creativity. A dressing area was improvised in the loft's dining area. Eleonora arranged her makeup kit on some beautiful acacia wood tables, and Mia told María to wheel over the hanging racks on which dozens of items of clothing were hanging, along with around fifteen pairs of expensive shoes by the most cutting-edge designers. Mia had no trouble getting hold of the clothes; the PR departments of the various labels are always delighted to be given visibility in an independent magazine. Among the clothes on the rack, only a few would be worn by Vanja: these were the pieces chosen by Mia to create her 'looks'. Because the magazine was independent, she had a free hand, and was able to use only the pieces she liked, without having to bend to the imperatives and constraints of advertisers and editors. With María's help, Vanja put on, one by one, the pieces chosen by Mia, who stood watching in silence. She nodded her approval at the final outfit and then added several idiosyncratic touches: she turned the jacket inside out, rolled the trousers up to show Vanja's ankles, buckled several belts one on top of the other, and knotted a shirt over the model's shoulders.

The loft was divided in two by an archway; at the back of the space was where the photographer would be positioned for the shoot. Each wall was painted a different colour: orange, turquoise, acid green, yellow. María told me the assistants had painted them the previous day and that they would paint them white again the next day. As I peered through the archway to look at the set where Vanja was posing with various vintage objects, I noticed two people standing in the shadows, a man and woman in their fifties who hadn't joined the rest of us for lunch. They were the assistants to the set designer, whose idea it had been to paint the walls, and who had chosen the objects that were to be part of the backdrop to the photographs. The two assistants had painted the walls the previous evening and were looking after the objects during the shoot. While I was there, no one spoke a word to them and they didn't come out of the shadows, other than to shift an armchair and a vintage bicycle, as Adèle, the photographer, requested.

The story's theme was 1960s plastic pop art style, which explained Vanja's makeup, the painted walls, the vintage objects, and the panoply of clothes and shoes in vibrant colours. Vanja was waiting in a new multicoloured outfit, with different nail varnish and makeup. Adèle, the photographer, asked her to stand in front of the turquoise wall and told the intern to position a green floor lamp by her. It was not until that moment that I noticed that Adèle was several months pregnant. The session began and Vanja sloped around the lamp, her lips parted, pausing while Adèle, who was standing up, took a series of pictures. Suddenly Adèle stopped and, looking irritated, addressed the intern, who was no more than twenty and was standing five or six feet away from her. 'You have to stay behind me all the time, okay? I might need a chair, or a bottle of water, you have to be behind me all the time.' The bottle and the chair in question were about two feet away from her, practically at the feet of the assistant photographer, who, María whispered to me, was Adèle's boyfriend. The young intern blushed and looked horribly embarrassed by Adèle's reproach to her in front of everyone. She lowered her eyes, muttered a timid apology and shuffled closer to the photographer with the chair and the bottle. Adèle sat down and, under the bemused gaze of her colleagues, sighed theatrically and caressed her pregnant stomach with a dreamy expression. The transition from the tyrannical order addressed to the intern and this image of maternal tenderness was extremely disconcerting. It revealed the power of hierarchies in a context where co-workers only seem to be equal. Adèle confirmed her position of power and only then, once the demonstration of her superior status was made clear, did she pick up her camera again. She took another series of pictures, but tempers were clearly ruffled, with Adèle addressing Vanja politely and the intern and the lighting assistant with antipathy. She used the formal '*vous*' when addressing the lighting assistant and the two assistant set designers, to make it clear that they did not belong to the cast of creatives, who all used the familiar '*tu*' with each other.

Suddenly Vanja looked like she was going to faint. She asked for a coke and sat down in a chair while Mia, María, the makeup artist and the hairdresser fussed around her. She gulped down the coke and ate a piece of apple, and seemed ready to get going again. I took advantage of the break to have a word with the manicurist, Chantal, who was sitting on her own at the makeup table with nothing to do while the rest of the team was working or watching the shoot. Chantal had a lovely open smile, and came across as both discreet and obliging, at no point taking the initiative in conversation. She was from the south of France and had moved to Paris seven months previously. She was happy to be in the capital, but she was living in a tiny 14-square-metre studio in a grim tower block in the 15th arrondissement. She was hoping to be able to move into a council flat, because without a fixed salary or income she couldn't afford 700 euros a month rent.

Around 7.00 pm I slipped away. The shoot wasn't going to finish before 10.00 pm. As I left, I asked María to give me the names of all the people there, apart from the interns and assistants, whose names she didn't know. Later I found out by searching online that Adèle was a renowned photographer who had done work for various major international publications, advertising campaigns for luxury brands, and had held solo exhibitions in highly respected museums and galleries in France and abroad. I also found out that the hairdresser and makeup artist were represented by prestigious agencies; on their personal websites they listed collaborations with international celebrities on publicity campaigns and major fashion magazines like *Vogue*. Vanja was a supermodel and had an exclusive contract with an American luxury label. Chantal, however, had no internet presence.

During the shoot, María told me slightly complacently that no one was paid for the day's work, and added, referring to the set design assistants: 'Those two in the corner, not only are they here today but they spent the whole of yesterday painting the walls and they're coming back tomorrow to paint them white again.'

Working for free in fashion: Modelling

In the previous situation, people worked unpaid to create images for *Mena* because working for such a magazine is respected and valuable to their career progression, in spite of everyone's different status.

Not only is modelling an area of activity that is bound by strict regulations (which merit specific discussion)[2], it is emblematic of attributions of value specific to fashion. Considering the rules that regulate the construction of a model's career is a way of making visible the dynamics and economies, both symbolic and material, that prop up fashion work, as well as of understanding the normalization of unpaid work.

Vanessa is the only model I met first somewhere other than a photo shoot. Thanks to a friend we have in common, she agreed to give me an interview.[3] Originally from eastern France, she had been living in

---

[2]   Modelling is an activity that largely employs women, in which the body and appearance occupy a central place and are at the heart of value production. It also is a job that provokes multiple desires. These elements make the sexual domination that is an inherent aspect of modelling an object of study within different theoretical frameworks. For further discussion, see J. Entwistle, 'The aesthetic economy: The production of value in the field of fashion modelling,' *Journal of Consumer Culture*, vol. 2, no. 3, November 2002; A. Mears, 'Pricing looks: Circuits of value in fashion modeling markets,' in *The Worth of Goods: Valuation and Pricing in the Economy*, Oxford, Oxford University Press, 2011; J. Entwistle, E. Wissinger, *Fashioning Models: Image, Text and Industry*, London, Berg Publishers, 2012; E. Wissinger, *This Year's Model: Fashion, Media, and the Making of Glamor*, New York, NYU Press, 2015. However, despite their undeniable appeal, dealing in-depth with problems related to modelling would have distracted me from the more general issues dealt with in this book, which is why I decided to focus on those aspects of the profession that share characteristics with other jobs in fashion.

[3]   Interviews were often tricky because of language – most models are from Eastern Europe and Russia and often don't speak English. Those who were just at the beginning of their careers were often discreet and taciturn on shoots, and didn't feel comfortable talking in case they were seen as not knowing their place. By contrast, supermodels were usually distant and unapproachable. Whether neophytes or experienced, models are constantly travelling all over the world for castings and shoots.

Paris for several years and was one of the few French models I met in the course of my fieldwork. Most models are from Eastern Europe, Russia or Brazil. She also had a Master's degree in literature, whereas many models haven't even finished high school. She was twenty-three when we met, but looked younger, which meant that she could claim to be eighteen, as her agent had suggested. In spite of her openness, there was something cold and hard about her, another thing that distinguished her from most of the models I met, who seemed to manage under all circumstances to look cheerful, enthusiastic and happy with their lot. I asked her how she had started out. She told me she had come to Paris to study; one day a woman stopped her in the street and asked her if she had ever considered modelling. She had just turned twenty. The woman was a talent scout who worked for a model agency trying to discover future supermodels. There are only two ways into modelling: actively seeking to enter the profession by trying to find an agent or taking part in a beauty contest, or being spotted by a scout. Bearing in mind how strict the physical criteria for becoming a model are, only a tiny number of young women with a very specific 'corporal capital'[4] can seriously hope to enter the profession. Most of the time, therefore, as in Vanessa's case, models are chosen, rather than the other way around. Considering the dream associated with the profession, young women, largely adolescents, rarely turn down the opportunity presented by a scout who suggests they give modelling a go.

After a brief period of hesitation, Vanessa accepted the agency's offer and began going to several castings a day. 'You have your "book", you show up and there are fifty girls waiting; you're one of the fifty, you wait your turn, and it's incredibly disappointing because at the end you don't get anything.' During my research, several of my

---

[4]   L. Wacquant, *Corps et âme: Carnets ethnographiques d'un apprenti boxeur*, Marseille, Agone, 2002.

interviewees spoke of the symbolic violence[5] of these castings, triggered by the constant judgement of their bodies. I was present at one casting, for a fashion show in Paris. During the castings for fashion week, the 'girls', as the models are called, go from one casting to the next for their appearance to be scrutinized by each client. They spend hours standing around in corridors, before being called in to be seen by a stylist or a photographer, who asks them to walk a few metres in high heels, and then to turn around and walk back again. Either before or after this, they have three Polaroids taken of them standing in front of a wall, one face on, in which the girl is holding a white sheet of A4 paper in front of her on which are written her name and the name of her agency or a composite (her photo with her name, her measurements and the name of her agency), then one each of her profile from both sides. The process, which takes only a few minutes and during which the only verbal exchange involves a few spoken instructions and some brief biographical questions, is strangely similar to a police procedure.

Agencies

Agencies, of vital importance in the fashion world, take at least a 30 per cent commission on paid work, although a great deal of modelling work is unpaid. Vanessa's experience bears this out: soon after being signed to the agency she did her first jobs for some fashion magazines, all unpaid, as well as her first paid work, a fashion show for an haute couture label:

Vanessa   I was incredibly disappointed. I did my first job in January, for fashion week. The fashion shows pay almost nothing. I got 200 euros. And then I got some magazine jobs that weren't paid at all.

---

[5]   J.-C. Passeron and P. Bourdieu, *La Reproduction*, Paris, Minuit, 1970.

Giulia   You mean if you're on the cover of *Biba*, for example, you're not paid?

Vanessa   I don't know, maybe *Biba* pays … In general it's unpaid, but some of the big magazines like *Marie-Claire, Elle*, maybe *Biba*, I don't know because I've never done a job for them, they pay what they call a daily fee, you get 100 euros for the day. My first pay cheque was for 200 euros, but I didn't get to see a penny of it. I got a letter from the agency with a payslip, but there was no money with it, and when I asked about the money they said, 'Ah no, you see …'. And that's when I understood: the agency advances money for the models, for every postage stamp or letter that they send in your name … You have to take along a composite to a casting, and that's also invoiced. At the time it was one euro for a composite, and as I was doing lots of castings and I left a composite each time, it ended up being very expensive. I didn't even know. So they pocketed the 200 euros. And when I started I didn't have any photos … so they paid for a photographer to take pictures of me, and naïvely I assumed it was the agency that paid. But no. So in fact I owed them money.

Giulia   They didn't explain any of that to you beforehand?

Vanessa   No. And afterwards they told me that I should have known. They don't tell you anything. Either they think the models are too stupid, or they can't be bothered. So there I was, I realized that not only was I not going to receive my 200 euros, but I actually owed them money.

Such practices turn out to be the norm in the world of modelling. As sociologist Ashley Mears describes in *Pricing Beauty*,[6] most models owe money to their agency. Vanessa always had representation contracts,[7] though most of the young women have a different kind of

---

[6]   A. Mears, *Pricing Beauty: The Making of a Fashion Model*.
[7]   In French law, the representation contract is a contract in which a person, the representative, acts for and in the name of another person. The representative is theoretically neither the person responsible for settling fees, nor an intermediary. In the case of models, a representation contract implies that the agency has not established in advance a credit ceiling for the model.

contract: the agency decides, depending on the value that they attribute to the young woman, at what level it is ready to anticipate the costs and the free services, and draws up a contract for that sum. The sums advanced by the agencies are not limited to postage stamps and a few colour photocopies. Because most of the models are foreign and initially make the move to one of the fashion capitals for a few months to see if they can make it on the local market, or move from place to place for castings and shoots, they live in apartments that are owned or managed by the agencies, who charge them a daily rent. Vanessa experienced this in Milan:

> I was a bit outside it all because I've got a place in Paris. Most of the girls at the beginning are put up by the agencies, so they have an advance payment to make because it's usually something like fifty euros a night ... in the apartments they're sharing a room ... I just stayed five nights. Most of the girls stay for three months in New York, then three months in Paris, then three months in Milan ... There were twelve of us in the apartment.

On top of the cost of the apartment is the cost of a hotel room when the casting or the shoot takes place somewhere the agency doesn't have an apartment, transport costs (plane, taxi, train) and, when necessary, the cost of a visa. Many of the girls find themselves totally dependent on the agencies, caught in a trap that sees them in an endless cycle of working to repay what they owe the agency. For this reason, when Vanessa signed with Elite, a colleague who was better informed suggested that she asked for a representation contract: 'I talked to my friend and she said to me, "If you do that [accept a contract for 70,000 euros], you won't have a life, you'll have to do everything you're offered, you won't be able to turn anything down."' After she signed with Elite,[8] Vanessa left her first agency, whom she

---

[8]   Elite is one of the three biggest model agencies in the world.

had to reimburse for a number of costs, even though she had also signed a representation contract with them:

> When I left I told them, 'I'm leaving, I'm going with another agency'. They tried to persuade me to stay, but I said, 'Look, I've been with you for two years, and nothing's happened. It's not like I'm going to be a model forever, so, you know.' And you know what they said? 'You owe us 500 euros.'

Even though Vanessa had worked unpaid for two years, she was the one who owed her employer money. This is, apparently, the norm in modelling.

The body as capital

Although there isn't a huge amount of socializing among models, and even less of a sense of sisterhood, and although castings are the least propitious occasions for conversation – the 'girls' are, after all, in competition with each other – Vanessa did get to know Kathy, another 'older' (she was twenty-one) French model. Kathy was 'experienced' – she had started modelling at sixteen and now earned an average of 10,000 euros a month. As Vanessa told me, she was a little depressed because she had barely earned anything in two years.[9] Waiting to be seen by a client, the two young women began chatting. Kathy told Vanessa: 'You're worth more than that! You have to leave that agency, it's crap.' Vanessa was at a small agency, and as she said, 'a small agency means small ambition', so she had little hope of her career taking off.

---

[9] Neither Vanessa nor my other interviewees who admitted that they worked unpaid explained to me how they earned money. The way fashion workers talk often creates a fiction of a world that has been liberated from money. People seem to find many solutions: family money, going into debt, being supported by a partner, or finding a part-time job to pay the bills.

Kathy suggested introducing Vanessa to a friend of hers, an Italian man living in Tokyo who happened to be in Paris on business; he knew the heads of some of the biggest agencies in the world. A few days later, the two women met Giovanni for a drink in a five-star hotel. He was middle-aged, one of the ten richest men in Italy. The following day Vanessa and Giovanni met at the Hotel Plaza, where they had a meeting with the head of Elite,[10] a close friend of Giovanni, who immediately fixed a meeting for her to see the bookers – the agents responsible for 'placing girls' in castings – at his agency. Thanks to his contacts, Giovanni was also able to organize meetings with two other prestigious agencies, Next and Major. Vanessa eventually signed with Elite, whose head told Giovanni on the phone that 'We really want her, so much so that we're ready to sign a contract for 70,000 euros'. Even so, mindful of Kathy's warning, she opted for a representation contract. Out of curiosity, I asked her if when she initially accepted Giovanni's help she thought he had an agenda. 'To start with, no, but he did ask me to marry him! What do you expect, he's Italian! Anyway, it wasn't going to happen. Even if he did used to come and pick me up in his Ferrari.'

Several times in the course of our long conversation, I was struck by Vanessa's attitude and the things she said; she seemed inhabited by a contradiction that I couldn't quite put my finger on. She presented herself to me as someone who was passionate about literature and uninterested in fashion, clothes or the glittering world that goes with it; she told me she had landed in this world by chance and agreed to do this kind of work because it's 'more fun than being a waitress'. Her manner – 'cold', 'distant', 'Germanic', as she herself put it – was quite unlike that of the other models I met, which misled me initially, because I thought that she was immune to the seduction of overexposure and the dream. Later I realized that she had gone on

---

[10]   Elite is one of the three largest model agencies in the world.

about the fact that several very wealthy, powerful men tried to seduce her, and that she did in fact often mention the elements of the dream: the Ferrari, the fancy hotels, the luxury labels. When she talked about Giovanni, for example, she told me that once, in a restaurant on the Rue du Faubourg-Saint-Honoré, Donatella Versace had called him on his mobile, as she was interested in buying a building in Shanghai for several tens of millions of euros, and that he had made several million euros on the transaction.

She once spent a whole hour telling me about meeting Antoine, 'the best-paid TV presenter in France, worth a fortune'. The story began when the head of Elite invited Vanessa to a party at Antoine's to celebrate the entry of a writer friend of his into the illustrious Académie Française. Vanessa decided to go on her own. During the evening, bored, she wandered into the library in the sumptuous apartment, a glass of champagne in hand. She was flicking through a book when Antoine came in and offered to lend it to her. A few days later, Vanessa's booker called her to ask if she minded if she gave her phone number to Antoine's secretary. She agreed. 'I told myself he wanted his book back.' Two months later, Antoine sent her a poetic message, telling her that he had booked a flight for her to an island in the Pacific where he owned a house. Vanessa recounted in detail a series of symbols of the dream and overexposure: private dining rooms in Michelin-starred restaurants, after-hours visits to art galleries, an invitation to a garden party at the Elysée Palace to celebrate Bastille Day, for which Antoine bought her an Yves Saint Laurent suit and a pair of Hermès shoes. I wondered why she was telling me all this, and why specifically in this way, without the usual emphasis you'd expect of someone who wanted to point out their place in this world. She didn't tell me about these things with the usual words about 'how lucky she was', or any kind of moral judgement or analysis. I realized later than the point of the story was to highlight all the situations and objects to which she had access, thanks to her corporal capital, even though she always insisted that her interest was in literature. The disparity that I recognized intuitively during the interview but which I couldn't put my finger on was to do with the way she emphasized her cultural capital, in order to conceal the way she drew attention to her appearance.

In her ethnographic analysis of private members' clubs, the sociologist Ashley Mears shows how, for powerful men and men who are seeking power, being seen with models in social spaces increases their prestige and confirms their status.[11] Giovanni and Antoine may not have succeeded in having a romantic relationship with Vanessa, but they nonetheless managed to be 'seen' with her. When Vanessa went to the Elysée Palace with Antoine, she was photographed by a paparazzo on the presenter's arm, and the picture was published in *Gala* with the caption 'summer lovers' and included the fact that she was a model. It was in the interests of Antoine, as a public figure, to be seen in the press with a model, whom he had, incidentally, dressed according to his own tastes: 'I went to his apartment on Tuesday morning, his hairdresser and makeup person were they, they did me up, I looked ghastly . . . And he said to me, "The shoes are Saint Laurent as well", but they weren't my size . . . Honestly, my feet were killing me.'

The caption to the image in which she is shown with Antoine signals that she is a model, not that she is a literary person. It is her status as a model that is immediately visible and socially valorized. Vanessa's cultural capital is a value added to her corporal capital, rather than the other way around: she would never have had access to these networks, these places, these worlds, these luxury items and experiences, without her corporal capital. The body is thus the means by which she was able to access and temporarily experience elite situations. However, although her corporal capital was briefly

[11]　A. Mears, 'Working for free in the VIP relational work and the production of consent', *American Sociological Review*, October 2015. A. Mears, 'Girls as elite distinction: The appropriation of bodily capital', *Poetics*, no. 53, 2015.

appropriated by Giovanni and Antoine in order to affirm their status, Vanessa received no payment, at least in the short term, either financial or symbolic.[12]

If, in modelling, the body is a work tool for valorization and for increasing one's earning potential,[13] in the situations evoked above its capital is appropriated and exploited by men. These types of relationship do not arise from an exception specific to this milieu. In the social world, it is not at all unusual for both women's work and women's capital in the broad sense to be appropriated by men.[14] Despite the particularity of modelling, and the aura of glamour that surrounds the profession, it is part of a broader relationship of sexual and gender-based domination that structures the social world in general.

The rules of the game in fashion economies

Although she was now signed with Elite, Vanessa was still earning very little – on average 1,000 euros a month, not much more than she would have earned as a waitress. Financial reasons did not explain why Vanessa had opted for modelling; if she didn't give it up, it was because she was seduced by the opportunity it gave her to experience the dream of luxury, power and desire. Her financial situation was not out of the ordinary, even if not all models work for free; a few, the ones whose faces are most familiar in the media, have made fortunes, and a few others, like Kathy, earn very well indeed. But these are the minority,

[12]   Various tools for reflecting on the role of the female body in professional and mercantile exchange can be found in the work of Mathieu Trachman and Paola Tabet: M. Trachman, *Le Travail pornographique*, Paris, La Découverte, 2013; P. Tabet and J. Contreras, *La Grande Arnaque: Sexualité des femmes et échange économico-sexuel*, Paris, L'Harmattan, 2005.

[13]   L. Boltanski and A. Esquerre, *Enrichissement: Une critique de la marchandise*, Paris, Gallimard, 2017.

[14]   C. Delphy, M. Blais and I. Courcy, *Pour une théorie générale de l'exploitation: Des différentes formes d'extorsion de travail aujourd'hui*, Paris, Syllepse, 2015.

and no strategy can guarantee attaining that status. There are, however, certain rules to be understood and respected for anyone aspiring to do so:[15] the jobs that bestow the most symbolic value and are most significant for a model's career are unpaid, while the jobs that are well paid often have a negative impact on a model's career. Vanessa did catwalk shows for haute couture houses, the apotheosis of the dream, for which she was paid 200 euros, entirely in line with the norm.[16]

> Then there are the girls who do shows who do really well out of it. They're the ones who've reached the top, they have amazing lives. There are others who do the shows because it's the most prestigious way to get into luxury, you have to do it, but it doesn't work for them. It's not automatic, you know. It's not because you've done a catwalk show that you're going to sign with Dior. And those girls, basically, they do the cool magazines, but there's no money in it. They do the shows, they pay a bit more than the magazines, but not enough, you still have to pay for your own aeroplane ticket . . . New York doesn't pay anything, you're paid in clothes. I know this girl, for a Marc Jacobs show, she got his new perfume and a pair of shoes. That's great, I mean, but it doesn't buy food. In France, for Chanel, they all got a little handbag with some makeup in it.

Not only are the catwalk shows unpaid, but sometimes the models actually have to pay their expenses to get there. The point of doing these shows is not financial:

> The shows count for the big magazines, like *Vogue*, and the really big clients . . . For example if you ever want to do a campaign for Chanel, say, you have to do a Chanel show. Otherwise they'll never use you

---

15 The notion of the 'rules of the game' alludes to the following studies, which use the idea of the rule, or the game, or both: P. Bourdieu, *Les Règles de l'art: Genèse et structure du champ littéraire*, Paris, Le Seuil, 1992; M. Burawoy, *Manufacturing Consent: Changes in the Labor Process Under Monopoly Capitalism*, Chicago, University of Chicago Press, 1979; A. Mears, *Pricing Beauty*.
16 Payment varies from country to country. In the United States, models are paid in clothes. In France it's illegal not to pay the models, but payments vary according to the label's prestige; the higher the prestige, the lower the remuneration.

for an advert. That's how it works. So those girls who do the big campaigns for the big labels, they also do lots of catwalk shows for them, even without being paid. The more you do the shows . . .

The luxury labels' advertising campaigns are the apotheosis of fashion work: extremely well paid and with great symbolic value. However, as Vanessa says, the passage from catwalk show to ad campaign is not automatic. The dream, here, is that of a contract that pays well and offers access to celebrity. The models, like many other fashion workers, agree to work for free because they hope they will get a contract that will change their lives. But how is it possible that models taking part in situations that are symbolically among the most highly valued (haute couture fashion shows, shoots for glossy magazines) are unpaid?

Fashion is governed, in all its spheres of production, by a symbolic hierarchy that places at the top of the prestige ladder work that is considered to be artistic, creative and independent, and at the bottom of the ladder work that is defined as commercial. During the shoot for *Mena* described at the beginning of this chapter, Mia and her colleagues agreed to work for *Mena* without being paid because it is a respected, prestigious independent magazine, and working for it confers prestige and is good for their careers. Independent magazines are, Mia explained, 'magazines where we aren't at the beck and call of the advertisers and editors. They're magazines where we can express ourselves freely, do work that's much more artistic, experimental, thoughtful.' As an independent magazine, *Mena* publishes images and fantasies deemed experimental and cutting-edge, which demand a specific cultural proficiency to be understood and appreciated. In this context, the people on the shoot are creating images that aren't aimed (directly) at selling products and are not intended for mass consumption. That allows them to highlight the cultural and artistic aspect of their fashion work, which is highly valued and constructed in opposition to its commercial dimension.[17] From an economic perspective, magazines like *Mena* are not financed, or only partially, by advertising, and have a very limited circulation. They have no budget for shoots. Although fashion is an industry predicated on profit, the valorization process specific to fashion disparages financially lucrative arrangements. The artistic and cultural circuit is the most valorized, in terms of prestige, while also being the one within which financial remuneration is the exception. Conversely, the circuit of commerce is very well paid, but does not allow for the accumulation of symbolic capital. For models, the circuit of commerce, destined for the mass market, means taking jobs in showrooms, print and television advertising spots and clothing catalogues, while the editorial circuit consists of advertising campaigns for luxury labels, fashion stories in magazines and catwalk shows. Vanessa, for example, finally started to earn money, after working unpaid for two years, when she began doing commercial jobs, which included mail order catalogues, a poster for Air France and a Christmas catalogue. She earned several thousand euros for these photo shoots, but didn't put them in her portfolio, because they would be damaging for her image. On her page on the Elite website, and in her 'book', she only displays images she has had taken for the artistic circuit, that is, the unpaid jobs she has done.

Notwithstanding the apparent logic of 'the negation of the economy',[18] which claims that unpaid work is valued for its artistic and creative dimension, the ultimate aim for both the agencies and the models, as well as other fashion workers, is to win what Ashley

---

[17] The categories 'independent-editorial' and 'commercial' are applied to publications, jobs in modelling and styling and other areas of fashion, as well as to the models themselves. This binary opposition between 'circuits of commerce' and circuits of art and culture (V. Zelizer, *Economic Lives: How Culture Shapes the Economy*, Princeton, Princeton University Press, 2013) is fundamental to fashion economies. For a more detailed analysis, see A. Mears, *Pricing Looks*; J. Entwistle, *The Aesthetic Economy*; P. Aspers, *Markets in Fashion: A phenomenological approach*, New York, Routledge, 2012.

[18] P. Bourdieu, *Les Règles de l'art*.

Mears terms the 'jackpot',[19] in other words the acme of fashion work. Of course, the jackpot varies according to profession,[20] but the logic for aiming to reach it is the same. In order to be in the running for the jackpot, to be aiming for this double remuneration, both symbolic and economic, it is necessary to understand the rules of the game and to construct one's career in accordance with them. In modelling, for example, a worker who has done too many commercial jobs, and has become part of that circuit, can never hope to reach the jackpot or be cast in fashion shows, another acme of prestige, because her image has become part of the circuit of commerce and thus has lost symbolic value. Vanessa, for example, apart from the haute couture shows she took part in right at the beginning of her career, doesn't do fashion shows. Generally models who take part in fashion week shows are paid in clothes and accessories, and above all in photos which they insert into their books to increase their symbolic capital and help them in their race for the jackpot.[21] In other words, the editorial-artistic circuit pays in prestige. But as Vanessa put it, however cool this prestige is, it doesn't buy food.

The rules of the game apply to all fashion workers. Those who are aiming for the jackpot have to construct their careers by juggling the accumulation of symbolic capital, vital for their reputations if they are hoping to rise to the top of their professions, and economic capital, necessary for survival. All the people I met in the course of my research understood this, and were making professional choices

---

[19] A. Mears, *Pricing Beauty*.

[20] For example, for a photographer as well as for a model, that would mean being taken on for an advertising campaign for a luxury label, with contracts for several million euros and rights over the images; for a makeup artist or hairdresser, that would mean an exclusive contract with a luxury label; for a stylist, that would mean being employed by luxury labels and magazines such as *Vogue*, while for a designer the jackpot means being named artistic director of an haute couture label (like the late Karl Lagerfeld for Chanel or Jean-Paul Gaultier for his eponymous label).

[21] Only the most successful supermodels who are widely known to the general public are paid well for taking part in fashion shows: it is they who bring added value to the label rather than the other way round.

accordingly. Constructing a career in fashion implies an understanding of the rules, and also implies a long-term vision, within which, in order to attain both symbolic and material success, they must accumulate prestige through working for free, even if in the short term that means finding a way of guaranteeing their material survival through taking commercial paid jobs.

Visibility as a form of remuneration?

In late capitalist contemporary society, in which the pre-eminence of visual representation holds sway, visibility has enormous value in the social world. Many sociologists of the media argue that media visibility constitutes a form of social recognition.[22] In *De la visibilité* [On Visibility],[23] sociologist Nathalie Heinrich puts forward the hypothesis that visibility represents a new totalizing social fact that necessitates a rethinking of types of celebrity. However, overexposure, and the enviable social positioning to which it offers access, is also a form of visibility trap.[24] This notion is particularly apposite when it comes to describing fashion work, because it offers a way of 'thinking together' the prestige that stems from visibility in the society of the spectacle[25] with injunctions to control and 'governance' of the self, as well as the normalization of precariousness that is the lot of fashion workers. Model castings are emblematic of this duality: the body is scrutinized, measure and judged, in order to determine if it may or may not be exposed. Modelling demands strict physical discipline, in terms of controlling weight, muscle mass, and hiding the signs of aging. Models live under a regime of constant autosurveillance as well as surveillance

---

[22] M. Boidy, 'Politiques de la visibilité', *La Revue des livres*, no. 14, 2013.
[23] N. Heinich, *De la visibilité*.
[24] M. Foucault, *Surveiller et punir: Naissance de la prison*, Paris, Gallimard, 1975, p. 274.
[25] G. Debord, *La société du spectacle*, Paris, Gallimard, 1996 (1st edn 1967).

by their bookers and the clients. But what is the value attributed to visibility in the construction of a career in fashion?

During a shoot one day, in a break between sessions, a model named Kandaka told me in English how despite how hard her job is, being a model 'is a privilege ... the privilege of being part of the creative process, meeting influential people'. As evidence of this, she told me she had taken part in a photo shoot for a book by the late Karl Lagerfeld, artistic director of Chanel, for which Lagerfeld had cast several models and celebrities. Though the two long days of work were unpaid and she had been obliged to sleep sitting up in a chair so as not to mess up the enormous fabric headpiece she was wearing, what was important was that she was now immortalized in a photo with Lagerfeld, in an image that would be seen all over the world by many thousands of people. The visibility offered by this particular job had given her access that to her was a form of payment.

In fashion, visibility is often obtained in exchange for unpaid work[26] because of pressure from agencies, even though it often means for models a period of structural uncertainty, in other words, precariousness.[27] Visibility is a form of capital,[28] a symbolic capital that can potentially be converted into money. This conversion into economic capital is not automatic, and most workers remain in situations of precariousness, or give up working in fashion for economic reasons; this depends, among other things, on the extent to which a person respects the rules of the game and the structural conditions that one might call, depending on one's theoretical position, 'chance',[29] 'luck', or 'risk'.[30] Kandaka worked for Lagerfeld for

---

[26] M. Simonet, *Le Travail bénévole: Engagement citoyen ou travail gratuit?* Paris, La Dispute, 2010.

[27] P. Cingolani, *La Précarité*, Paris, PUF, 2015.

[28] This does not accord with what Nathalie Heinich argues. She considers that visibility 'possesses all the characteristics of a form of capital in the classic sense' (N. Heinich, *De la visibilité*, p. 46); in other words, is something that can be converted into economic wealth, which does not correspond to what I saw in the course of my research.

[29] P.-M. Menger, *Le Travail créateur: S'accomplir dans l'incertain*, Paris, Gallimard-Seuil, 2009.

[30] U. Beck, *La Société du risque: Sur la voie d'une autre modernité*, Paris, Aubier, 2001.

free because she saw it as a privilege to be photographed with a celebrity, not because she hoped that this visibility would be transformed into money (although one does not necessarily preclude the other). Visibility is the currency of her job, while she herself is the capital that enables her to access the elite of desire.

Fashion work as post-Fordist work

Financial recompense is not the only form of remuneration in the professional sector of fashion, and nor is the logic of 'the negation of the economy'[31] unique to it. Fashion has many analogies with other professional sectors linked to culture, academia and creative work. Gina Neff, Elizabeth Wissinger and Sharon Zukin carried out a comparison between modelling work and people who work in web design, in order to understand the spread of the entrepreneurial model in the 'creative industries' and to highlight the normalization of risk within these professions.[32] They identified the same characteristics that I identified during my research: the cultural value of 'cool', the emphasis on creativity and autonomy, the importance of networking, the investment in and by the self, the emotional component and the risk involved in building a career in these sectors. Far from being specific to fashion and the internet, these aspects are in reality typical of many kinds of work in the post-Fordist era.[33]

[31]   P. Bourdieu, *Les Règles de l'art*.
[32]   G. Nef, E. Wissinger and S. Zukin, 'Entrepreneurial labor among cultural producers: "Cool" jobs in "hot" industries', *Social Semiotics*, vol. 15, no. 3, December 2005.
[33]   A. Corsani, M. Lazzarato and A. Negri, *Le Bassin de travail immaterial dans la métropole parisienne*. Schematically, in the 1970s, the Regulation school (see particularly M. Aglietta, *Régulation et crises du capitalisme: L'expérience des États-Unis*, Paris, Calmann-Lévy, 1976) named this 'new era' of capitalism 'post-Fordism' in order to mark the rupture with the previous era, which lasted from the 1940s to the end of the 1960s. According to this theory, Fordism denoted a society of employees, with a guarantee of social and legal protection by the state, as well as regulations guaranteeing a balance between mass production and mass consumption, and a regulation of the means of production based on institutional mediation and reconciliation of social forces.

In the 1980s, during the transition that took place in wealthy countries from industrial to service economies, capitalism began to appropriate 'Bohemian' lifestyles,[34] first promoted by the anti-establishment movements of the 1960s. Hippies in the sixties rejected the monetarization of everyday life and the alienation brought about by salaried work, instead promoting artistic expression, self-actualization and autonomy. These ideas were then injected into the entrepreneurial model and combined into the founding principles of neoliberalism, which pushed the value of risk taking, identification with one's work, and the individual's responsibility for their own success or failure. With the rise of the New Economy in the 1990s and the interlinking of management, marketing and sociology,[35] capitalism began to value the figure of the artist – previously a marginal figure – as a model, making the artist a pioneering figure of the worker of tomorrow.[36]

The sociologists David Hesmondhalgh and Sarah Baker[37] have defined the elements that are characteristic of these professionals: low salaries, flexible working hours, insecurity and uncertainty, the importance of networking and social capital, isolation and a strong tendency to self-exploitation. This dynamic of working for free or for a symbolic payment is a central element of production in contemporary capitalism. Work in the fashion industry fits into the framework of post-Fordist labour, in spite of fashion's apparent singularity in terms of the dream sheen that coats it. The idea of the 'jackpot', introduced

[34] R. Lloyd, *Neo-Bohemia: Art and Commerce in the Postindustrial City,* 2nd edn, New York, Routledge, 2010; R. Gill, 'Technobohemians or the New Cybertariat? New media work in Amsterdam a decade after the web', *Network Notebooks,* Amsterdam, Institute of Network Cultures, 2007.

[35] C. Leadbeater, *Living on Thin Air*; R. L. Florida, *The Rise of the Creative Class.*

[36] P.-M. Menger, *Portrait de l'artiste en travailleur: Métamorphoses du capitalisme,* Paris, Le Seuil, 2003.

[37] D. Hesmondhalgh and S. Baker, 'A very complicated version of freedom: Conditions and experiences of creative labour in three cultural industries', *Poetics,* vol. 38, no. 1, February 2010.

by Ashley Mears, provides an excellent illustration of the relationship between work in fashion and the neoliberal political project.[38] The jackpot is emblematic of the way uncertainty and the normalization of a 'lottery' dynamic[39] serve to maintain the symbolic asymmetrical pyramid of symbolic and economic capital. In a documentary about haute couture, Karl Lagerfeld had this to say about skilled fashion occupations: 'These are the epitome of skilled jobs, fashion and cinema. It's totally unjust; it's not because you want to do something that you're going to succeed, and when it does work out it's for inexplicable reasons. It's totally unjust, that's how it is, it's as simple as that.'[40]

Lagerfeld's words imply that injustice is inevitable in some professional spheres. However, this line of reasoning, which articulates an idea of injustice linked to 'inexplicable' reasons, conceals the real injustice of fashion, which is that of the asymmetric distribution of wealth. Fashion is an industry that generates vast profits, and in which money is distributed in an astonishingly unequal way. A tiny minority, including Lagerfeld himself, own fortunes and are paid staggering amounts of money, while the majority of fashion workers – the people who literally make fashion – are in precarious situations or even working for free. Arguing that this injustice is to do with 'risk' or 'luck', without combatting or even criticizing it, is itself an instrument for maintaining these asymmetries. At the same time, by working for free and omitting the issue of money from their discourse, the fashion workers I interviewed showed that they adhered to Lagerfeld's vision; the structural inequality of the industry is not discussed by those who work in it in terms of injustice or exploitation, but in terms of luck and risk, notions that depoliticize inequality, inscribing it on an

---

[38]   See M. Hilgers, 'Embodying neoliberalism: Thoughts and responses to critics,' *Social Anthropology*, vol. 21, no. 1, February 2013.
[39]   P.-M. Menger, *Le Travail créateur*.
[40]   From *Le Jour d'avant*, Loïc Prigent.

individual level as an element in an individual's career trajectory. Injustice becomes a risk to be taken in order to achieve the dream, or a fragment of it, in order to join the race for the jackpot (itself a dream of prestige and wealth), while profiting in the interim from the overexposure.

The notion of risk is eminently neoliberal; it is a fundamental characteristic of financial capitalism, from the high stakes of the stock exchange to the entrepreneurial model. Rooted in the worlds of finance and business, the spirit that values risk and individual responsibility[41] has been extended to many professional sectors, particularly those linked to artistic creation and culture, and has been assimilated by workers in those sectors. It's precisely by virtue of this incorporation of risk and the logic of the demonetization of labour that these professional sectors have been elevated as models for capitalism, or as prophetic images of the future of work. To conceive of labour (or make people conceive of it) through the valorization of risk is a way of concealing the inequalities that capitalism needs to be maintained, by reducing these inequalities to an issue for the individual. Leaving aside overexposure, it becomes obvious that working in fashion is no different to working in any other professional domain; it is governed by the same rules, above all by the exacerbation of the inequalities and asymmetries that are its organizing principle, and which are intrinsic to capitalism.

---

[41] L. Boltanski and E. Chiapello, *Le Nouvel Esprit du capitalisme.*

6

Prestige and Precariousness: Symbolic and Material Geographies

Mia at home

A lilac ostrich feather Gucci coat was slung over the screen that served to separate the kitchen-living room area from the sleeping area in the apartment shared by Mia and Jaime. They had just returned home from visiting yet another apartment; they were looking for a new place where Mia could have her own bedroom. They had liked the latest apartment but had once again been turned down for the same reason as always: Mia didn't have a regular income. The landlord would have been happy to close his eyes to that if she'd had 17,000 euros in her current account for a guarantee, but she didn't have that kind of money. Mia was upset. She threw her handbag on the table that served as both desk and dinner table. The handbag, worth 2,500 euros, had been given to her as payment for a week's work for a large fashion house. For creating a series of 'looks' and helping dress various celebrities for a fashion show, she received a voucher worth 5,000 euros to spend at one of the label's flagship stores. Theatrically, she took the coat that the Gucci press officer had lent her for a fashion story and threw it on the bed. 'He wants cash? He can have this, the asshole, it's worth 18,000 euros.'

Jaime and Mia's apartment was 46 metres square. A small counter separated the kitchen area from the rest of the living space. On it sat an empty yoghurt pot and a Prada bracelet made of plastic flowers and crystal beads, given to Mia by Angelo to celebration her signing with the Wiew agency.[1] The fridge was almost empty; it contained just a box of fancy pastries and a withered head of broccoli from the supermarket Franprix. On the floor, next to a pair of shoes, some dirty clothes, a supermarket bag and a half-unpacked suitcase, was a pile of expensive clothes that would be transformed into objects of desire for thousands of women when the story appeared in a few weeks' time in whatever fashion magazine Mia's next shoot was for.

Mia's career trajectory is emblematic of the tension, typical of fashion work, between the accumulation of prestige and material needs. I first met her before I started my research, through Jaime. They'd originally met when they were both renting a room in a spacious, elegant apartment in the 10th arrondissement of Paris. It was an ideal setup for Mia – who had just arrived from Milan, knew no one and didn't have a job – because the landlord didn't ask for salary slips, a guarantee or a deposit. Jaime was fascinated by this eccentric Italian woman who worked in fashion, who would leave the apartment in the morning to go for a coffee in the café down the street, wearing a pair of large black sunglasses and a long coat over her pyjamas, and who always had a cigarette hanging out of her mouth. He used to tell me, with a mixture of sympathy, fascination and surprise, about her periods of depression, her uncertainty about her professional horizons, and her need to build a network of professional connections and earn money.

Mia had decided to come to Paris after Angelo, a powerful, successful, internationally renowned stylist, with whom she'd worked on several occasions in Milan, promised her that if she came to France he would give her regular work as his assistant. Mia had been counting on this professional relationship to earn some money and gain experience while building up a network in the city. But the relationship with Angelo was complicated; he was curt and controlling, and when they did paid jobs together he was always late paying her, even though he

---

[1]   Not the agency's real name.

was well aware of her delicate financial situation. Nonetheless, Mia was grateful and considered him as a mentor; it was thanks to him that she had gained experience working on advertising campaigns for major brands. Thanks to him she had also discovered the world of luxury; though she never knew when or how much she would be paid, or whether it would be in cash or in kind (in money or in clothes), she at least got to stay in five-star hotels, and all her expenses were covered by Angelo. Their relationship was tempestuous, and it was unclear where the boundary lay between their emotional and their professional lives. The day of her thirtieth birthday, for example, though she was struggling financially because he hadn't paid her for several months, he sent her thirty massive red roses with a romantic message expressing his admiration for her, sending her all his love and hoping that she would have every success. After several years, Mia decided, with difficulty, to break free of this complicated relationship with Angelo. Since then, thanks to her connections and reputation, she had worked regularly as a freelancer for many international magazines, which brought her visibility, and had done many commercial jobs, which earned her money. As we have seen, when a commercial job was too compromising for her image and her career, Mia would work under a pseudonym.[2]

One day she called me, hugely excited, to tell me that she'd been contacted by a headhunter who had invited her for an interview with one of the two most prestigious agencies for fashion workers, Wiew.[3]

---

[2] She used a pseudonym, for example, when she worked on a commercial for a line of slimming products, when she styled images for a chain of hairdressers, and when she was employed as a style adviser for a French R&B singer.

[3] Signing to an agency is an important step in the career of fashion workers. Like models, hairdressers, stylists, photographers, makeup artists, assistant photographers, commercial directors, aestheticians and campaign designers are also represented by agencies that find them work in exchange for a commission on their earnings. Models sign to specialist agencies, while other professionals are grouped together within the same agencies, which play a central role in the legitimizing of the status of fashion professionals: to be signed to a good agency signifies that someone is well regarded and has reached a certain level in their career; this means that they have excellent professional opportunities, to which they would have less access otherwise.

The interview was in New York, at the head offices of the American agency, which now had branches in all the fashion capitals. Unable to pay for her flight out of her own pocket, Mia arranged for the interview to take place at the same time as a shoot for a catalogue that she was doing in New York for a mid-range French brand. Because it was a commercial job, the brand was paying for her flight in business class and a stay in a five-star hotel, on top of a fee of several thousand euros. The interview went well and Mia signed an exclusive contract with Wiew, with representation in the Paris office. The contract stated that Wiew would take a 30 per cent commission on every payment she received, whether or not it was the agency that had procured the work for her. Once she had signed the contract, Mia was full of enthusiasm and optimism for the future, and told me that she hoped that this meant she would finally enjoy some financial stability. The news was so exciting that as soon as Angelo heard that she had signed to Wiew he sent her the Prada bracelet in congratulations. Six months later, Mia called me, suggesting we meet for coffee in the Marais. She was wearing a sky-blue vintage coat and a pair of Prada moccasins. She began to vent:

> I'm done, I'm leaving Paris, I can't stand it any more. I don't know what I'm trying to accomplish. I've been here four years, I've reached the top of what I could ever have hoped to do by signing to this agency, but nothing has changed in six months. I still don't have a penny to my name, I'm bringing them work instead of the other way around, and on top of that I have to pay them, because they take their percentage. They get me jobs on fancy magazines, but they're never paid. What am I trying to achieve? What am I waiting for? Where am I trying to get to?

As for the 'fantastic setup' in the 10th, it hadn't lasted very long in the end – the landlord decided to take back the apartment after only a few years. Jaime and Mia wanted to carry on renting together and began the search for a new place. They soon came up against a whole series of problems related to Mia's lack of stable employment. As an unmarried foreigner, with neither a permanent job nor a guarantor, she wasn't an attractive tenant for most landlords, in spite of the fact that she was earning on average 5,000 euros a month.[4] They eventually took an apartment with a landlord who was ready to 'close his eyes' in exchange for rent that was above the market rate: 1,300 euros a month for two rooms in La Chapelle – not quite what Mia had been imagining. Not only did she regret the lack of privacy, with only a screen between her and the kitchen-living area, but she also recognized the apartment as a concrete sign of her precarious situation. It didn't correspond to the 'place' she wanted to occupy, not only in geographical and professional terms, but from an economic and symbolic perspective. During the three years she lived there Mia always talked about it scornfully, describing it as 'the junkie squat'.

The value of objects

Despite the social prestige from which she benefits because of working in fashion, Mia is not a good candidate for renting an apartment in Paris. In spite of her professional contact with overexposure, her structural situation as a worker without a full-time job remains unchanged. The coexistence of prestige and precariousness translates materially not only into the back-and-forth between luxury hotels all over the world and her apartment in La Chapelle, but also in the juxtapositions of objects from different symbolic and material spheres, representing luxury and 'struggle'. In a world where image and aesthetics are the basis of the economy, luxury objects have a particular value, which varies depending on the context. Within the world of

---

[4]   Faced with the difficulty of finding a place to rent in Paris, tenants develop various not always entirely legal strategies. It's not uncommon, for example, to fake salary slips in order to increase the figures, or to forge employment contracts. Without such tactics, many Parisians would struggle to find a home.

fashion, they serve to confirm the position of workers in the hierarchy and to underline the fact that they belong in that world, as the following incident demonstrates. One day, Mia and I were sitting at the dining table. She was waiting for the delivery of a pair of moccasins from Miu Miu, a subsidiary of Prada. She had just been telling me about her difficult financial situation; she couldn't afford to pay either her mobile phone bill or her rent that month. I asked her if the shoes were a gift for a job she'd worked on. She said she didn't know. A few weeks later I spotted the shoes by her bed:

Giulia   Ah, they arrived. Are you happy with them?

Mia   No, I hate them. I cried because of them.

Giulia   Why did you cry?

Mia   Because I couldn't afford them. I cried because I bought them even though I didn't have any money. So I hate them.

Giulia   They weren't a gift?

Mia   No, I got 20 per cent off. They were 420 euros instead of 500. But I still hate them.

At around the same time, Mia had an interview with the editor of the fashion section of *Glamour*, a large circulation women's magazine. She wore the Miu Miu moccasins for the interview. The editor noticed them and said: 'When I saw those at fashion week I wondered who on earth could get away with wearing them.' This was the point of the shoes: to confirm, in an asymmetrical hierarchical situation, Mia's cultural competence, which had already borne fruit in her earlier work. The choice of this or that item of clothing or accessory is part of a strategy developed as part of her career development. In this situation, fashion capital[5] has been used to testify to a mutually recognized culture and aesthetic taste that is unusual, but shared by

---

[5]   J. Entwistle and A. Rocamora, 'The field of fashion materialized: A study of London Fashion Week', *Sociology*, vol. 40, no. 4, August 2006.

fashion insiders. Within the circuits of the 'aesthetic economy', luxury items like shoes are not accessories, they are crucial, because they bear meaning.

At the same time, within this economy these objects have a value that goes even beyond that: they are a form of remuneration. According to Ashley Mears, 'perks',[6] non-monetary transactions, are crucial, and have a precise symbolic function: they demonstrate that workers are aware of their place in the system and their transactional value. In other words, perks materialize social relationships and hierarchies; when an employer pays 'in kind', he or she is confirming their position of symbolic domination over the worker, who is being remunerated because he or she is 'lucky to be there'. This is how luxury labels get away with paying models in tubes of lipstick, or haute couture houses with vouchers worth 5,000 euros, such as the one Mia received, and which are no use when it comes to paying bills and rent. Fashion confirms its hierarchies with these objects.

Mia's shoes, clothes for shoots, all the items produced by and for fashion, change their status and value according to the context and whose hands they pass through. In the chaos of Mia's apartment, the clothes for a shoot are nothing but a pile of garments in plastic bags. In less than twenty-four hours they might travel through the most fashionable neighbourhoods in Paris, where most of the upmarket labels' PR offices are located, or end up on the floor in an apartment in the city's 13th arrondissement, to be used in a shoot by a production team, most of whom will be paid very little – if at all. Both objects and subjects will be used for the manufacture of the dream. But luxury items also alter the symbolic status of their subjects. Iris, who has had a variety of different jobs in fashion, discusses the way the value of objects changes: 'It's as if you've undergone a kind of transformation:

---

[6]   A. Mears, 'Pricing looks'.

with this handbag, I feel like this, I look like this, I carry myself like this . . . people look at you differently, and treat you differently.'

The fashion system thus produces both the context and the work whose purpose is to 'exceptionalize' objects[7] (as, for example, in the case of haute couture and its subsidiary labels) and the process of 'exceptionalization' of subjects that is operated by these same objects. Invested with a social and cultural value specific to this world, these objects are at once the transactional currency of a market, the trappings that indicate distinction and belonging, and the indicator of lifestyles that are articulated on different symbolic and material levels.

Between luxury and precariousness

The relationship between objects and their circulation delineates a geography of multi-sited existence, divided between luxury and its opposite. But seen from the outside, the same objects have another function: they serve to put up a smokescreen, situating fashion workers where they are not, or even better, where they are not *all the time* – in other words, in the dream. Objects can be the means to gain access – even if only symbolically or intermittently – to other social geographies. Philip, a stylist and teacher at a Belgian fashion school, who has lived in Paris, recognizes this tension:

Philip Apart from a tiny fraction of the population who work in fashion and rake in the contracts, create and employ people, a few celebrities who earn as much money as sports stars, most of the others – sure, they're in this world, they're associated with the image, but economically they aren't at all . . . It's a job that opens lots

---

[7]   For an in-depth analysis of this notion, see A. Jourdain, 'La construction sociale de la singularité: Une stratégie entrepreneuriale des artisans d'art', *Revue française de socio-économie*, no. 6, December 2010.

of doors. You get to wear things that are totally unaffordable. Me too, sometimes, when I think about it, I've often been given things that it would have taken me three months [of salary] if I'd bought them myself. I got them for free, you know, just got given them. So all this maintains a kind of mystery around this world.

Giulia Doesn't it feel like a kind of schizophrenia?

Philip Yeah, totally. But that's the deal, you know.

One of the roles of luxury items is to situate fashion workers in the highest spheres of luxury, making them an elite of desire. They create a smokescreen and produce an odd misperception. Mia said to me one day: 'People see me and think I'm a millionaire when I haven't got two pennies to rub together.' Philip calls this misperception the 'mystery of the fashion world', his way of expressing the disparity between a worker's economic status and their social image. This misperception is an additional form of opacification of the structural inequalities of fashion. The objects that the elite of desire display in the social space give the illusion of a homogenous world within which anyone can have access to luxury. Yet the majority of fashion workers' lives are marked by financial and job insecurity, even if they own objects of desire. In order for the projection of the dream to function and for workers to continue to be part of this elite of desire, the mystery must be maintained and the opacity must remain, a process in which the workers themselves must participate. My meeting with Victor, a Parisian journalist, revealed this mechanism.

We first met in Brussels in October 2012, during a guided tour of several fashion design studios. Victor, a freelance fashion journalist for specialist magazines, is based in Paris, writes in English and travels a lot. He was invited by the organizers of the event. Though I felt a little uncomfortable at the slightly superior attitude he projected, I decided to cross the symbolic threshold that separated us and, after a brief resistance on his part, we began to chat. He stopped in front of the window of an interior design store and mentioned that he was in the middle of doing up his apartment in the 9th arrondissement of Paris, which he described as being a 'very chic' neighbourhood. Because he said he was thinking about buying some large pieces of furniture, I asked him if he lived in a spacious apartment. His spontaneous reaction showed how disconcerted he was; he stammered that his apartment was 15 metres square, but that he didn't need anything bigger because he was constantly travelling and never ate at home. I was surprised: everything he'd told me up until that point suggested that he had a different economic status. Later, when I asked him where he was staying in Brussels, he named a five-star hotel. Because we had established a bit of a bond, he admitted that because the organizers were only paying for his room and no other expenses, he'd had a McDonald's the previous evening, which he ate on his bed while watching a film.[8] He told me he'd travelled to Brussels by coach. 'You know, people think if you work in fashion you're rich, but we eat McDonald's like everyone else, because we're broke, we're all broke, anyway I am, I have to be really careful.' He went on: 'Everyone's starving in fashion, the creatives are starving. But at the same time you've got nice gear, everywhere you go people are drinking champagne, you get to travel to amazing places, stay in fabulous hotels.' After a moment of silence, he continued: 'There's plenty of money, but it's not exactly shared out equally. It's always in the same hands.'

Victor was aware of the inequalities that are widespread throughout the industry, but he criticized this fact without actually challenging it, having interiorized them in much the same way that so many of the fashion workers I met during my research accept the idea that 'total injustice' – in the words of Karl Lagerfeld – is the pre-eminent rule governing fashion. Fashion workers circulate in the world of luxury but

---

[8]   Mia told me a similar story. She was staying in Cannes in one of the city's luxury hotels, working as a stylist for a singer who had been nominated for a music award. Since she didn't have enough money for a decent meal, every evening she got a takeaway from McDonald's and ate it in her hotel room.

have access only intermittently and in small ways to the opulence that they themselves create with their labour, while only a tiny minority actually owns this wealth. They are constantly confronted by the economic power of the fashion industry and the inequality of its distribution. Yet rather than perceiving this asymmetry as evidence of a structural inequality that has to be fought against, it is understood as a sort of rule of the game nourishing the desire for emancipation thanks to the 'jackpot', attesting to their acquiescence to this 'total injustice'.

The path that led from the initial overexposure in which Victor presented himself to his final assertion that 'everyone's starving in fashion' is a powerful allegory of work in this domain. These circulations are the spatial translations of the rules of the game: Victor is at the apex of the symbolic hierarchy of prestige because he only writes for independent magazines and is not part of the circuit of commerce. But this places him in an economically fragile situation, which explains why, when he's not on a job for the industry of the dream, he lives in a 15-square-metre apartment, eats junk food, travels by coach and teaches English to earn money (a detail he omitted to tell me but which I learned later from someone else). The fact that he didn't tell me about what he did to earn money[9] was evidence that his acceptance of the inequalities of the fashion world also took the form of concealing his own precariousness.

Fashion cities

In the lives of fashion workers, luxury and its opposite coexist in the same sites. Nevertheless, every city has its own specificities in terms of

---

[9] Eleanor, a sixty-something photographer and former model, told me at the end of a three-hour interview, after I had turned off my tape recorder and just as we were about to go our separate ways, that in fact she had always worked as a secretary to earn money. 'Everyone had a job on the side, it was the only way to make ends meet.'

the labour market. Philip described the differences between the two cities I focused on in my research, Brussels and Paris:

> I think that here in Brussels, we're a little more protected from the schizophrenic craziness of Paris, for example. Paris is actually pretty unusual, because London's not like that. There's such a lot of snobbery in Paris in fashion circles, which makes it even more inaccessible, even crueller, everything is more, more, more. Here in Belgium we don't have that kind of competitiveness, the same big names. We don't have all those stylists and photographers ... And that's why people who want to go up a gear leave and go to Paris. The fact of being in Paris can often make things easier, even if living there is so much harder; that's true whether you're in fashion, or in anything, actually.

However cosmopolitan the fashion world is, and though it is a globalized industry within which those who are part of its immaterial production are constantly on the move, the fixed points and where these people live make a difference to their lives. For these incursions into the dream take place *outside* and *far away* from home, a distance that is both geographic and symbolic: a luxury hotel in Hong Kong or New York, a Michelin-starred restaurant in Paris, a party at the Ritz. Home, on the other hand, is the place of opacity, the place where people face up to their material conditions: rent and bills to pay, a fridge to fill.

Paris is the symbolic and material centre of the global production of luxury, and the image that the city conveys is one of opulence and elegance. The ostentation of this fantasy world and its spatial proximity to the mechanics of production and sales not only stimulate consumption but also create the illusion that because it's 'right here', it must be 'within reach'. The image of the city, in particular that conveyed by the fashion industry, with its requirements regarding aesthetics and distinction, seems more than anywhere else to lead workers like Victor to portray themselves as having a different economic status than they actually have. Mia said something similar to me:

Mia   Paris is a fake city, because it lives on images of things that don't exist. Here there are rules about the things you have to have, I'm talking specifically about fashion, which means that if you're not dressed a certain way, if you've got the Prada thing but not the other thing, you're written off. I don't know how to explain it. Everything's fake here.

Giulia   More than in other places?

Mia   Definitely. I've lived in Milan, so I can compare, and I think that in Paris there's much more of a focus on fashion, but in everything … It goes without saying, everyone's pretending to be some type of person, the way they live, who they hang out with. That's how it is, there's nothing you can do about it. Here in Paris you feel *fashion*, appearances, really strongly.

Brussels, meanwhile, is protected from the Parisian madness by the small scale of its fashion industry. There's no fashion week and no big couture labels, which explains why the city projects such a different image. Because it is not constantly displaying luxury, it produces less desire, and fashion workers can lead lives whose contradictions are less extreme. On the other hand, of course, Brussels is not a capital of the dream, so people hoping to hit the jackpot, who want to 'go up a gear', have to go to Paris and pay for the 'luck of being there', which comes at a price of material and economic constraints.

The cartography of fashion cities outlined in my research positions Paris at the absolute apex: more snobbery, more of the dream, more emphasis on appearance, more illusion. This hegemonic condition asserts itself in its confrontation with other cities that fashion workers know, such as London, Milan and Brussels. My interviews with Vanessa were key in helping me trace the economic and symbolic geographies of the fashion capitals of the world:

The most important is New York, followed by Milan. Milan is starting to rise, because the big labels that are really successful, like Prada, Versace, are Italian. Paris is good, Paris is…. It's prestigious to do Paris! But you don't make a lot of money. It's prestigious because there's Yves Saint Laurent, Chanel, Dior, Gaultier ... And when you're in New York and you say you've done a Chanel show or a Saint Laurent show, clients are wildly impressed ... It's very prestigious. New York doesn't have any prestigious labels, except maybe Ralph Lauren.

The rules of the game have been translated into geographical space: Paris is the most prestigious city, where workers accumulate the greatest amount of symbolic capital, but it's also where people are paid the least. To earn money you have to move away from the overexposure:

> There are fashion weeks held in cities like Madrid. The shows aren't at all prestigious. The designers aren't well known. But it pays. I did five days of shows in Madrid and made 10,000 euros. Even well-known girls would rather do a week of shows in a country ... you know ... rather than going to Milan where ... They want to make some money. At the end of the day the point is to earn money.

If, from an existential perspective, the lives of fashion workers often straddle luxury and precariousness, regardless of geography, from a professional perspective each city leads to the accumulation of a specific type of capital, symbolic or economic. In keeping with the rules of the game, the city which is at the apex of prestige, Paris, pays the least, and the cities that are outside the circuit of the dream, like Madrid, pay the most, but don't enable workers to accumulate symbolic capital. According to Vanessa, the jackpot city is New York, where it's possible to be in the dream and earn money as well: 'If you want your career to take off you have to go to New York, because in Paris, leaving aside that it is more prestigious, you don't make money. It's only really in New York that you can work every day and earn a bit of money too.' New York is the city where money circulates the most, because most of the advertising campaigns are produced there. The largest market is there, and there are far more options for reconciling the accumulation of prestige and financial remuneration.

Going beyond this spatialization of the accumulation of capital, both symbolic and economic, many of those I spoke to evoked a globalized image of the world in which, leaving aside the specificities of the fashion industry, cities and states are equivalent. However, my research led me to understand that the socio-economic specificities of different places do have an impact on the lives of workers. In Brussels Victor would not be living in such a small apartment, because there is a law against renting studios that are less than 29 metres square. Mia, meanwhile, would not have experienced the same difficulties in finding an apartment if she were living in Brussels, because it is rare for potential landlords to demand salary slips, and even rarer that they ask for guarantors. At the same time, Brussels as a city does not offer the same visibility or career possibilities as Paris, Madrid or New York. Each city in the fashion system has its own specificities, while participating in both symbolic and material economies and the labour market of the fashion system.

Different countries, with their different laws and systems of welfare protection, have an impact on the lives of fashion workers, exacerbating or minimizing the disparity between prestige and instability, and in some cases making financial precariousness even more severe.

The precariousness of those who are caught in between

The rise of creative work and its increasing valorization in contemporary capitalism has been accompanied since the 1990s by a critical reflection on new forms of work, in which the notion of precariousness is central.[10] Far from being a subject dealt with only by

---

[10] A. Corsani, M. Lazzarato and A. Negri, *Le Bassin de travail immaterial dans la métropole parisienne.*

academics, precariousness is at the frontier of critical thinking, radical political writing and sociological research.[11]

This polyphony of uses leads equally to a multitude of empirical and theoretical meanings. In my research, precariousness indicates economic vulnerability, existential uncertainty, professional instability and a lack of horizons. It is, for workers in fashion, both an experience and a condition. But, more than that, precariousness for these workers takes the form of being 'caught in between'.[12] Despite the heterogeneity of salaries and jobs, of professional, economic and social status, of living conditions and biographical details, fashion workers are constantly and structurally caught between two ways of making their way in their profession: the circuit of commerce and the editorial circuit; the accumulation of economic capital and of symbolic capital; the world of luxury and of precariousness; the symbolic status of an elite of desire and the material status of people in unstable jobs. Not only do fashion workers struggle because of their economic precariousness – when it strikes – and a lack of horizons and certainty, a condition shared by an increasing number of workers, they also have to face the violence engendered by being 'caught in between', which demands that one of their ways of living, that of the dream, is not only visible but overexposed, and that the other, that of financial and professional precariousness and of domination, remains opaque, concealed.

---

[11] R. Gill and A. Pratt, 'In the social factory? Immaterial labour, precariousness and cultural work', *Theory, Culture and Society*, vol. 25, no. 7–8, December 2008. For an in-depth analysis of the question of instability, see P. Cingolani, *La Précarité*; E. Armano, A. Bove and A. Murgia, *Mapping Precariousness, Labour Insecurity and Uncertain Livelihoods: Subjectivities and Resistance*, New York, Routledge, 2017.

[12] The notion of 'being caught in between' refers to the role of temporary creative work that is done by many workers in the cultural and creative industries. See L. Jeanpierre and O. Roueff, *La Culture et ses intermédiaires: Dans les arts, le numérique et les industries créatives*, Paris, Archives Contemporaines, 2014.

7

At the Heart of the Dream: The Designer-stylists

Designer-stylists are at the heart of the dream, because they are at the origin of all of the fashion industry's production, both material and immaterial. Without their work designing clothes, there would be no textile industry, no magazines, no models, no fashion shows, no boutiques, and so on. Without them, the empires of fashion would not exist and could not accumulate their fortunes.

Thierry, designer-stylist

Thierry was introduced to me by a couple who run a contemporary art gallery in Paris. 'He spent ten years as Karl Lagerfeld's assistant, then he left and Lagerfeld never forgave him. Now he isn't working. You have to meet him. He'll have lots of things to tell you.' Thierry asked me to meet him at the famous Parisian café Les Deux Magots, specifying that we should meet upstairs so that 'we can talk in peace and quiet'. I was surprised by his appearance. I'd imagined him to be dressed eccentrically, or at least a little outlandishly: the image of Karl Lagerfeld and his unique way of dressing no doubt had something to do with it. But I found myself sitting opposite a sober, elegant, clean-shaven man of around sixty, with short grey hair and unostentatious glasses. I didn't know this small upstairs room. Unlike the noisy, festive atmosphere of the terrace and the ground floor restaurant, here the chairs and banquettes were reserved for professional meetings: 'It's an excellent place to talk, it's where people from the worlds of media, fashion, art and politics like to meet . . . Lagerfeld also used to eat here a lot.' In these intimate surroundings, Thierry's voice rang out louder than those of the other people in the room.

I asked him to tell me about his career. At the age of just eighteen, he'd left his native Switzerland and moved to Paris to work in fashion, against the wishes of his family. He enrolled at the Couture Guild School:

> At the time you didn't say 'designer' or 'stylist', you said '*modéliste*' [which means, roughly, 'pattern-designer']. It really was a different era. I lived through a very unusual period in fashion. I'm one of the only people from that period who's still around. It's true there was a change then, in the 1970s, let's say after 1968 . . . there was Courrèges, the absolute number one, with his own style, and then you found thousands of industrial copies . . . Prêt-à-porter had just begun, it started in 1965 with Sonia Rykiel, Lagerfeld for Chloé, that was the start of it, but they began to have power in the 1970s.

During and after his studies Thierry interned first for Dior then for Yves Saint Laurent, where he worked on the costume designs for Catherine Deneuve in the film *Belle de Jour*. He enjoyed the work a great deal and while he was at Saint Laurent it seemed his career might really take off. But Thierry wasn't good at career politics, and he couldn't bear the anti-Swiss jibes he suffered, so he decided to move to Rome, where *alta moda* was going through a major expansion period. Armed with the little Italian he had learned at school, he left for Rome with his sketches under his arm, where he found 'all the doors wide open'. Almost immediately he found at job with Simonetta and Alberto Fabiani, a famous pair of Italian designers. After two years, he could no longer bear the tedium. He decided to go it alone as an independent designer, just at the time when the Italian fashion capital was shifting to Milan; he moved there, and in the same way and with similar ease he found work with Krizia, Pierre Cardin and several other labels. However, he really didn't like living in Milan, and in 1976 he decided to return to Paris:

It was 1976, 1977. When I arrived I had nothing, I was a bit naïve, but everything was much simpler then and I found a job in the first week. I had a list of the fashion houses, off I went and knocked on the door, 'Hi, there, I'm a designer'. They said 'Great, show us your portfolio, we'll see you for an interview tomorrow!'

Back in Paris, a few days and phone calls later, Thierry had interviews in person with some of the top French couturiers and immediately began working as an independent designer for several different brands and labels, right across the fashion spectrum. He was curious and versatile and loved 'transforming his creative ideas into a work tool', he did 'everything', he had a good income and lots of work, to the point where he began to receive so many offers of work he had to start turning things down. He explained his success as being due to his long and varied experience: he described himself as being like 'a chef who knows all the recipes, who already knows what works'. But he soon began to experience this as something negative, for, in spite of his material comfort, the lack of challenge meant he lost his taste for this work after just a few years: 'It stopped being fun', he said. This dissatisfaction led him to decide on another career change. 'I'd done France, I'd done Italy. I started to think about the US, about working for, say, Donna Karan, and I liked New York, it's my favourite city.'

Thierry and Karl

Thierry went to New York to sniff out possibilities in the world of American fashion, once again without a precise plan but with a full address book and his portfolio of designs. In the US, he began working with Karl Lagerfeld. In fact, this wasn't the first time they had crossed paths: Thierry had been employed three times by different fashion houses to replace the German designer, because their creative visions were so similar. Thierry arrived just at the point when Lagerfeld, who was already very well-known and overwhelmed with projects, apparently no longer to want to be there; 'he was doing a million things, he always said yes to everything, but he really was only interested in Chanel'. In New York Thierry met the owner of a large department store, who told him: 'Your work makes me think of Karl Lagerfeld.' She asked him if he would like to work with Lagerfeld, who was setting up a clothing line under his own name and needed someone to help him. 'He had second lines, licences in Japan, things he didn't want to do, he only wanted to do the main line.'[1]

Back in Paris, Thierry found five messages waiting for him: Lagerfeld's secretary wanted to set up a meeting. Thierry went to the interview, which lasted barely five minutes. Lagerfeld already knew about Thierry and his work. 'He knew everything, he knew exactly who I was and what I did.' Lagerfeld glanced at Thierry's sketches and offered him a job as head of design in his New York office. Thierry accepted and Lagerfeld told him to 'talk to so-and-so about money. Negotiate the terms of your contract. Make sure they pay you well.' And so Thierry found himself a full-time employee for the second time in his life. He moved to New York, where he was employed as design director for Karl Lagerfeld. He lived in a fancy apartment on Park Avenue and earned a handsome salary. However, just two years later, the New York office closed because 'Lagerfeld, too, he's always changing. He wanted to do something else, a men's line.' Thierry returned to Paris, where he began working again for Lagerfeld, this time not as an employee but as an independent, which meant that he could continue to work on other projects too. He was also trying to create a line under his name, with the backing of a wealthy female acquaintance. The project survived for two years, during which he

---

[1]   In ready-to-wear fashion houses, the 'first line' is the most prestigious and luxury, and the most expensive. The 'second lines' are more commercial, and thus less prestigious on a symbolic level, but vital for the brands since they are the only lines that make a profit, because of the more reasonable pricing.

designed four collections, before closing down when his backer decided to withdraw from the business. 'While I was working for Lagerfeld in the 1990s, I worked on my own collections on the Rue du Faubourg-Saint-Honoré with my friend's support, but all of a sudden she dropped me. We lost a lot of money because we were on Faubourg-Saint-Honoré. She got involved to amuse herself I think.'

In spite of the collapse of his own line, Thierry continued to earn a good living with his collaboration with Lagerfeld. But, although they had a good professional relationship, their personal relationship was tense: 'We had a relationship that I am sorry to say was quite difficult, a bit antagonistic', he told me. 'Basically, right from the beginning in New York, our collaboration got off on the wrong footing.' Lagerfeld was late with his own line and asked Thierry, beneath a shroud of secrecy, to design and have made up several pieces that he didn't have time to do himself. These pieces ended up being the most acclaimed of the collection. According to Thierry, Lagerfeld 'wasn't at all happy', and their relationship was badly affected:

> We were always formal with each other. He used the formal *vous* with me, while he used the informal *tu* with everyone else. For example, when he arrived in New York, he'd bring presents for everyone, a watch for this person, a handbag for that person, and never anything for me. It was always, 'Good afternoon Thierry', very cold.

The tricky relationship between the two designers did not, however, have an impact on their professional relationship, which Thierry brought to an end in 1996, after ten years of working together. That New Year's Eve, 'something clicked', and he ended both his collaboration with Lagerfeld and his other projects: 'I said to myself, that's it, I'm fed up with this crazy lifestyle, and I pulled the plug on everything. I wrote to Lagerfeld and told him that I didn't want to work any more, that I was fed up. He took it very badly.'

Thierry after Karl

Thierry gave up his apartment and left Paris to return to New York, his favourite city. He stayed there for two years, during which time he tried to find work, but to no avail. He says this was because his career was too fragmented for the American market, which expects designers to specialize in a particular kind of clothing and range. Having used up all his savings, he had no choice but to return to Paris. This was around the year 2000.[2] Once again, Thierry had no trouble finding work in the French fashion world, and he began a fruitful collaboration with Givenchy, working as a freelance designer for the second line, which guaranteed him a comfortable income. He continued there until 2008, when Givenchy ended the line. He also worked for Hervé Léger, a label that makes evening dresses popular with celebrities, until the design offices were relocated to Los Angeles in order to reduce production costs. He turned down the invitation to continue working in California. Meanwhile, in addition to his work with these two fashion houses, he decided to try once again to set up his own label, which was launched in 2000 and financed by his salary from Givenchy. In creative terms the project was bold, but not very commercial: 'In 2000, while I was still at Givenchy, I set up my own label, Thierry Dupont, but it was a bit of a disaster. I spent all the money I had, I spent a lot of money . . . My idea had been to create an image.'

Although the collection was well received by the fashion press, in the wake of the end of his collaboration with Givenchy Thierry had no more money to develop his brand. He decided to lower his creative ambitions in favour of a more commercial line. For a backer, he turned

[2]   In fact, if he had stopped working with Lagerfeld in 1996 and spent the following two years in New York, this would have been around 1998. Thierry's narrative was full of inconsistencies in terms of dates. It's not clear if this was simply confusion or a desire to conceal his actual age.

to a wealthy French financier, who was living in Bali for tax reasons, whom he'd met on holiday there. But this new adventure came to an end in 2008, when his new investor withdrew from the project because of the banking crisis:

> The buyers weren't coming, it was a disaster. For us it wasn't tragic, but we had to put more money into the business and my investor said 'stop', he'd already lost two million euros. He said: 'I'd rather lose two million euros than put more money in.' He was right. But because of the financial crisis, I couldn't find anyone else to carry on.

Thierry found himself unemployed, struggling financially, and 'completely disgusted with fashion'. His brother suggested he 'come and spend some time at his place in Parma', and so Thierry decided to move to Italy. But he soon tired of Parma and chose to return to Paris to look for a new job in fashion, almost four years after he had last been there. He didn't get a single response, not even from Lagerfeld. 'When we see each other we say hello, but he doesn't want anything beyond that. But I really needed work the last few years. I wrote to him and I know he received my letters because his first assistant gave them to him, but he never replied.'

At the time I met him, Thierry was still looking for a job, he had no salary and was being supported financially by his brother. He was working on a new design project, and was looking for investors.

The arc of Thierry's career: Fifty years of fashion history

Thierry's story distils fifty years of fashion history in the experience of a single individual. In that period alone, the name changes are emblematic not only of the transformations in fashion and its increasing overexposure, but also the coming into existence of the neoliberal paradigm. Thierry's profession can be described using the terms designer, designer-stylist, *créateur, couturier* or *grand couturier*. But each of these terms carries a specific nuance. When I met the head of a major Parisian fashion school, he told me that the more recent terms '"*créateur*", "creative" and "artistic director" set up a misunderstanding, erasing all the technical skills that make up the profession, by making it synonymous with glamour and sequins'. The word '*créateur*', which came into use in the 1980s and 1990s, emphasizes the power of a single, overexposed individual, obscuring the entire cycle of production and the work done by everyone else. The word 'stylist' began to be used to denote all those offering their skills to work for other people.

When Thierry began his working life in the 1960s, his occupation was denoted by the term '*modéliste*', or 'pattern-designer', a very specific area of work. Paris, the world capital of fashion, had only one school to train a few dozen aspirants to the profession, and Thierry's experience shows that, at the time, talent and a diploma were all that was needed to find work with one of the large fashion houses; he found a job just out of fashion school with one of the most established haute couture houses. The 1970s were the years that saw the move towards the industrial production of luxury goods, and the industry began broadening towards the mass market. Thierry began travelling all over the world looking for work in the dream. His many moves for work point to the changes in scale of fashion production and the rise in power of neoliberal globalization. These changes led to the emergence of new hegemonic centres; first Milan and then New York ousted Paris from its traditional supremacy. Nonetheless, in spite of the change in scale, designer-stylists like him remained relatively scarce. Those who worked in design at the time still constituted a true elite. Because of this Thierry could afford to reinvent his working self multiple times, and to satisfy his impulsive desire for professional and geographical change without risking economic precariousness. The transformations that took place in the 1980s and 1990s, the years during which the huge fashion empires were established, along with increasingly bitter competition for a share in the market, did not hamper Thierry's career. With his experience and his accumulated social capital, he still had easy access to good and well-paid jobs. It was not until the first decade of the twenty-first century that the situation changed dramatically. During that period, he lost his three contracts for reasons linked to 'macro-economic issues'; capitalism was experiencing one of its major structural crises, with a consequent rise in unemployment and job insecurity. Givenchy's decision to drop the line Thierry was working on, despite the fact it had a healthy turnover, was due to global market demands, specifically to the increase in social inequality and the consumption of luxury goods that is typical in such periods of economic crisis. The house was basically closing down all its mid-priced ranges in order to focus on luxury goods in new markets, aimed at the wealthiest people on the planet.

> In fashion, it's not like it used to be, when you had one very expensive line that very few people could afford ... Today, with globalization, you'll have one boutique in London, one in Shanghai, one in Milan, one in New York ... They don't need the cheaper diffusion line; people don't even want it. If Prada is selling a handbag for 5,000 euros, people want that one, not the one they can get for 500 euros. I truly believe that luxury will keep going higher. They aren't looking to make things more affordable.

During this recession, the other fashion house Thierry was working for decided to move all its production, both material and immaterial, from Paris to Los Angeles, in order to cut the costs of production. And then his own line collapsed because of the financial crisis of 2008; his intended customer base had less disposable income and the investor refused to inject additional funds into the project. The global financial crisis signified the end of Thierry's career in fashion.

The transformations of Thierry's work

Throughout Thierry's long career he was witness to a series of structural metamorphoses in the fashion industry, which went from being a model of craftsmanship inspired by Taylorism[3] and centralized in Paris, to a tentacular production model, multiform, delocalized and segmented. Capitalism has transformed fashion and the profession, and Thierry was directly confronted by these changes the last time he looked for a job in New York. 'I had an interview with the design director at Calvin Klein ... And there you have the design director, after him there are twenty designers, one designing skirts, another designing shirts, one jackets. It's all segmented.' This division of tasks, particularly in industrial manufacturing, was a legacy of Fordist capitalism. The fashion industry was no exception, and aligned itself with the model that followed, within which work, management and marketing play a central role. Thierry spoke of this last aspect with particular astonishment: 'And now there's this obsession with marketing; every business has thirty people in the marketing department whose job is to analyse if the tight skirt sells better than the A-line skirt, they spend absurd sums of money on it.' This marketing focus is not limited to large companies, it's also visible in the work of independent labels that have to demonstrate their versatility if they want to be competitive; they have to be skilled not only in design but also in management, communication and distribution.

Thierry came up against this paradigm shift in the 2000s, when he launched his eponymous line, manufactured in Bali. Although his turnover was reasonable, he had to deal with the same pressures that all independent designers were now subject to. It was no longer a case

---

[3]   Taylorism is a technical method of organizing industrial work, controlling the time taken to do it, and of deciding how workers are paid. See F. Godart, *Sociologie de la Mode*, p. 32.

of designing clothes and keeping an eye on production with the help of assistants who dealt with seeking out fabrics, patronage, distribution, relationships with the press, accounts and cash flow. For the first time in his career, all these tasks came under his responsibility, and Thierry struggled with all the responsibility. Faced with so many administrative tasks, he felt as if he was losing his way, and no longer recognized his job as a designer: 'I had all these things to deal with that had nothing to do with design. Like fabrication, money, clients who didn't pay, all the challenges of running a business which didn't interest me, and I was no good at it, to be honest. You can't be good at everything.'

Thierry versus Karl: A question of visibility

The decline of Thierry's career was certainly a consequence of the structural crises of capitalism and the paradigm shift in fashion labour, but it was also linked to issues of visibility. During our interview, Thierry repeatedly told me, in a tone that was both gloomy and bitter, that 'fashion has changed', as if behind this objective statement was his incomprehension in the face of the new model. When I asked him to tell me in what period he thought the change had taken place, he answered: 'I'd say it was fifteen or twenty years ago. It started with the era of the supermodel, Claudia Schiffer, and the others . . . Fashion became a star system . . . the way work was organized completely changed . . . Today it's television that creates the image.' The most significant of the changes in fashion, and the reason for Thierry's inability to cope with the current paradigms of the industry, was, according to him, the evolution of overexposure, in other words the principle of 'mediatized visibility'.[4] He explained that in the first

---

4   N. Heinich, *De la visibilité*.

few decades of his career, those who moved in the fashion world were an exclusive elite who were different and marginal, whose lifestyles were differentiated from those of the masses because of their sophistication. The moment when fashion became overexposed, became a dream where its most famous figures were transformed into stars, and it became imperialized, the professional world of fashion began to expand. The industry needed more workers, and at the same time more and more people wanted to participate in the dream. As a result, the elite of exclusivity and sophistication became the elite of desire and visibility: 'Lots of people want to be in fashion because they think it's easy, they see it as job where "you get to drink champagne, hang out with stunning girls and gorgeous boys, have fun", but there's so much work behind it, actually making clothes, doing the research; they just see the glitter'.

The image of fashion as portrayed in the media, which conceals the structures of production and conditions of labour, makes the world of fashion appear highly desirable. When I asked Thierry if, when he was studying, fashion was a desirable world to go into, he said:

> Absolutely not, absolutely not, no, not at all. That's completely new. First of all, when I got my diploma ... there were very few of us. Today, in Paris alone, there are fifty fashion schools, and no work for the people who graduate from them. When I had my own business, the one that closed in 2000, every week I used to get ten letters from people who wanted to come and work for free, without being paid. And we weren't Dior or Chanel. What do they do afterwards? There's no work, because in a company they don't need fifty designers, there's one at the top, and then two or three assistants maximum, that's it. It's become a fashion for fashion.

Indeed, this 'fashion for fashion' is in line with a historic moment of crisis in employment and the capitalization of visibility. Thierry, born in a different generation and having entered the profession in an earlier era, found himself unable to understand that simply being part of the dream could be a form of remuneration in itself. Nonetheless, he was aware of what was at stake professionally when it came to media exposure, and regretted not having dealt with that aspect of his business more effectively:

> I didn't go to all the parties. That was a mistake, because, without wanting to be presumptuous, if I'd gone about things like that, I'd be famous today, because I think as a designer I am very talented. I think I didn't follow the rules of fashion that I needed to for it to work . . . Lagerfeld, for example, his system, when it came to making a name for himself, it was . . . he had this big bag full of gifts, he was always going to the flea market, he knew, you know, you like bracelets so he'd give you one, he knew how to choose, how to give, that's a big part of how he made his reputation. I wasn't like that at all, I don't care about all that.

Thierry attributes his professional decline to his 'poor handling of visibility'. He didn't 'follow the rules' necessary for his line to succeed; one of the rules is to adopt strategies of seduction in order to accumulate social capital and be visible in the media. That is precisely the issue of visibility, which, he believes, was the deciding factor in the difference between his career and that of Karl Lagerfeld, in his eyes the epitome of success – a success based as much on a tactical handling of visibility as on artistic talent.[5] The celebrity designer had a reach far beyond the sphere of fashion, because, as Thierry put it, Lagerfeld was an 'icon':

> He knows very well that the image that he communicates could seem ridiculous, he used to say: 'I'm a marionette.' It's like a garment that he puts on, he has fun with it. He's almost eighty, he's one of the fashion greats . . . he really gets it, he understands everything about how the market works, he's a real fashion grandee, an icon.

---

[5]   Lagerfeld was undoubtedly the most media-savvy of designers. He was the subject of a number of documentaries, was frequently featured on radio and television programmes, and was active on social media – he even created a Twitter account for his cat.

But although Thierry believes that if only he had followed the rules of visibility, he too would have become famous, he is also aware that it's precisely because he was never attracted by the overexposure that he had been able to work for so many years alongside Lagerfeld:

> With him, you had to remain in the shadows; I never made a big deal about the fact that I was designer-director for Karl Lagerfeld. I would still be there if I'd wanted to stay; he's had the same assistants for the last thirty, thirty-five years, all in the shadows, no one knows who they are. I know who they are. They earn lots of mony, as much as they could ever want, but . . .

The rule that had to be respected when working for Lagerfeld was not to encroach upon his status in the media. Lagerfeld 'paid his staff well'[6] on condition that they remain invisible. In documentaries showing him at work behind the scenes,[7] his assistant designers are never to be seen, giving the impression that he was, as the very word 'creator' suggests, at the origin of all his designs and creations. Charlotte, a fashion journalist, explained to me how the mediatization of the most famous designers and the 'invisibilization' of their teams functions: 'You find yourself with designers who are as famous as rock stars. And in fact in the case of some of them, 'all' they do is provide the impetus for their collections. They've got a studio with fifty people doing all the work and no one knows their names.'

Elsa: The work of the designer-stylist today

The 'fear of boredom' that led Thierry to continually change jobs and city is a neat metaphor for the constant urge for renewal in the fashion

---

[6]   As Thierry himself put it, 'He doesn't care, it's not his money, it's Chanel's.'
[7]   R. Marconi, *Lagerfeld Confidential*, 2007, and Loïc Prigent, *Signé Chanel* and *Le Jour d'avant*.

industry. Comparing the beginning and the end of his career enables one to understand many things about the change in status of fashion in society, as well as about capitalism and the kind of labour it creates. Thierry describes the demands of the current job market thus:

> If you haven't worked for Prada, Gucci, or one of the ten labels that are doing well, you can't work, at any rate at a certain level. I've had a ton of assistants, boys and girls, all very talented, who looked for work for six, seven years. I tell them that the only system is to keep on struggling to get there ... They need to get into a big name and stay there a while, two, three years, they might earn a bit less, or nothing at all, but afterwards it's their visiting card that will mean they can find something else, there's no other way of doing it. The problem is how to get in, it's all about having connections ... The system in my day, which was knocking on doors with your sketches, that's over, you can't do that any more. For years and years I was turning down work. I had so, so, many offers.

In this context, of the overproduction of workers in the dream, and the expansion and overexposure of the fashion industry, the job of 'designer-stylist' is very different to what it was when Thierry started out. Thirty-year-old Elsa is a stylist. She studied at one of Europe's top fashion schools and was spotted at her graduation show by the artistic director of a French fashion house, who invited her to join his company. She worked there as an intern for six months, before being given a permanent contract. She worked for the Henry Carat label[8] for four years, until her contract was terminated. During her time working for the label, Elsa did a bit of everything: studio assistant, assistant designer on the label's first line for women, and then, when the men's line was 'taken over' in Italy, where it was manufactured, she became responsible for that as well. The artistic director of the house was Henry Carat himself, and he was also central to the commercial and marketing strategy. He had 'something to say about everything'.

---

[8]   Not the fashion house's real name.

Elsa had a special relationship with him:

> It was one of gratitude, he'd taken me on, introduced me to the profession, taught me the job, I did almost all the things you could … He was half father figure, half mentor … I was doing creative stuff maybe 40 per cent of the time if I was lucky. It depended a lot on the seasons, but I also spent a lot of time being a high-class secretary, a secretary who had studied for five years.

The variety of her different roles meant that she 'really was in Monsieur's personal bubble'. He was the reason Elsa stayed at the label, despite the low salary and the negative effect it had on her professional development.

From her arrival at the label, she was aware of its precarious financial situation:

> When I started, and told people I worked for Carat, people in Paris were like, 'Uh-oh', and they'd give me slightly funny looks. And then a year later we were working with all the stars. In fact we were completely saved because we were super-underground, very, very cool … We had no money at all compared to some of the other houses, but we had results, and I had the good luck to be working with Monsieur and was involved in all the projects.

In spite of its financial problems, the label secured a new prestige and visibility. Elsa was involved in projects that were symbolically rewarding, and had the 'luck' of being close to Henry Carat. On the other hand, all this led to an excess of work and asymmetric relationships with the female heads of the studio and the management. Elsa basically was doing several different jobs at once, working 'like a madwoman', between ten and twelve hours a day, and sometimes weekends too, with no overtime or days off. For a long time she received the minimum wage, which, after some tense negotiations, was increased to 2,000 euros a month. All this makes her believe that she was mistreated by the management:

Normally, once a month, you're meant to have an appraisal, but that never happened. So we asked them to do it and when I had mine they said: 'Why would we give you a raise, when your job is just doing a few sketches?' They really were mistreating me. My hours, which weren't paid as overtime, that was all decided by the head of the studio and the head of the management. And when they put pressure on me to arrive on time but didn't give me the tools I needed to do my job properly . . . that's a kind of abuse too.

In spite of her privileged relationship with Carat, Elsa never discussed her financial problems with him. The fact of working together on an artistic level did not mean that she could be open with him about her income:

> I wasn't going to bother Monsieur with that, obviously . . . The problem was that he was my mentor, but there was never the space to talk . . . When I went to see the management, they were like, 'But it's Monsieur who decides'. But with Monsieur, you couldn't discuss it because you weren't supposed to bother him.

Beyond these strategies of avoidance and the management's refusal to commit to its responsibilities, the refusal to increase her salary was also motivated by an evaluation of her work: 'I'd try to discuss it with the studio director, but she always said: "Oh, but your work isn't that good, you know." I'd say to her: "Really? How come it's just me who does the sketches, then?"' Exhausted after four years during which she felt she'd been 'squeezed like a lemon', knowing that the production budget had been slashed and people were going to lose their jobs, Elsa decided to leave. She negotiated the conditions of her departure with the idea that she would immediately find another job, but she was overwhelmed from the exhaustion of the previous four years: 'And in fact the day I stopped working, just after the shows, I literally collapsed [bitter laugh] . . . Total burn-out.' A year later she summed up her experience thus: 'We were very privileged, and treated very well by him [Henry Carat], but very badly treated by the management; I'm convinced it was intentional, it was a way of keeping people down, so they wouldn't get too big for their boots.'

This strategy of domination, which consisted of reducing the value of the work of designers and of paying them a low wage, is far from being exclusive to the company that employed Elsa and because of its tricky financial situation. Many of those I spoke to described similar experiences at labels that made profits of millions of euros. The emotional aspect of her work, which led Elsa to see her boss as a father figure, is a constant feature of the fashion world. Elsa was aware, from the similar stories of friends and colleagues, that her experience was not unusual. She didn't hesitate to generalize when she described another form of subjugation specific to work in fashion:

> In the fashion world, there's a huge number of interns who aren't paid, or who are paid 300 euros a month. The game is to treat us exactly the same as the interns. So an intern turns up and they're the same level as you. That's totally standard. You don't feel respected or valued at all. After three years, I began to wonder if you had to be an intern to design the collections. I was like, yeah right, but I'm not going to sort it out when it all goes wrong. It's devious, no one treats you badly to your face, they don't beat you, it's all really underhand. You'll be treated very well but … And you realise you're stuck, you can't do anything about it. And then they tell you, 'You're so lucky to be here!'

For designer-stylists, being 'lucky to be here' is an inherent aspect of a regime of domination and exploitation, in spite of the fact that their work is the backbone of the entire fashion industry. Nonetheless, in spite of the wide extent of this model of exploitation, there are companies with an excellent reputation. The absence of transparent criteria in the way salaries are determined has a precise function, as a tool of domination that functions by devaluing and delegitimizing the work of these designers. 'At Vuitton, it's unbelievable, interns are on the minimum wage. We had an intern who'd been at Vuitton before, where she'd been earning the same as I was earning. It's not that you're stupid, they just won't give you the tools you need to do your work properly. Because you're just not credible.'[9]

In addition to all this, there's no such thing as an average salary in the fashion industry, which makes the market value of labour impossible to ascertain, and prevents negotiations taking place during the hiring process. These vagaries are part the 'exceptionalization' of fashion and the consolidation of a vision of the fashion world that is totally subjective and resigned to 'total injustice', in Lagerfeld's words.

There seems to be no norm according to which salaries are set. Yet, in reality, the system of remuneration is determined by one feature: that of asymmetry. This means that the salaries of artistic directors of luxury fashion houses start at several tens of thousands of euros per month, going up to several millions, while, according to several designer-stylists I met, those who actually do the creative work are often paid the minimum wage.

The rules of the game for designer-stylists

Wage disparities do not exist only among designer-stylists. Unlike jobs linked to the creative arts, professionals working in management, administration and marketing benefit from excellent employment conditions. 'At Henry Carat, the commercial director was very well paid, the head of the studio was very well paid, Monsieur Carat was very well paid . . . and us lot, in the studio, new employees were on the minimum wage, and even the top earning staff were on 3,000 euros a month.'

The dynamic of attribution of value for the work described is a translation of the rule that Elsa describes thus: 'Often the more creative

---

9   Vuitton belongs to LVMH. Within the group, salaries vary widely for the same work; in other luxury labels belonging to the group, designers are on minimum wage.

someone is, the less they earn.' She adds: 'It's not remotely logical, because the creative person is the one making the product.' She emphasizes the inequality between the remuneration for jobs described as 'creative' and for those that are not. Nonetheless, she doesn't challenge the way the dichotomy itself is constructed, which indicates that she also accepts the value placed on creative work in the neoliberal economy. Furthermore, this dichotomy shows not only that wages are set according to the symbolic and social value of a profession, but also that the most valued jobs are the least well paid. Elsa found herself impacted by this dichotomy when she left Carat and began to work on a variety of smaller projects, with the aim of remaining active in the workforce and earning a little to supplement her unemployment benefit. She worked in the circuit of commerce and earned money, but wasn't proud of doing these kinds of jobs which didn't seem to her to be valuable on a symbolic level. The rule applies to designers too: designing clothes for the circuit of commerce is not considered 'creative' and is as a result decently paid, whereas work in high fashion, considered as art or even a kind of 'genius', highly valued in terms of prestige, is extremely badly paid. For designers, no less than other fashion 'creatives', 'the problem is finding the balance between creativity and money', as Elsa put it.

Marguerite: The itinerary of a freelancer

Marguerite is French, a thirty-year-old alumna of two state-funded Paris fashion schools. Since graduating she has gained broad professional experience in several fashion houses in the French capital. Fresh out of college, she was offered two opportunities: a 'photocopying internship' in a well-known fashion house, or a paid job as an assistant designer for a commercial brand. She chose the latter, and subsequently took on further jobs with similar brands, with the intention of gaining experience before joining a major fashion house. This was the point at which she realized that her choice to focus on gaining experience rather than prestige was harming her career: 'I was trying to do something more upmarket but everyone said: "Ah, no, you have no experience with Givenchy, Chloé, Saint Laurent." It turns out that employers have the same obsession with CVs and labels.' Marguerite was 'desperate' to work for one particular fashion house, and she managed to set up several meetings with the label's director, who told her: 'What you're doing is great, but I can't show your work [to the artistic director] because you've not got any experience with Chloé or Vuitton, you haven't worked for any of the big fashion houses.' Marguerite was 'completely disillusioned', because she realized that though she had spent years studying fashion, 'they don't teach you the rules of the game, it's up to you to figure it out. There are so many unofficial rules.' Having managed to save up a little money thanks to her various jobs on the circuit of commerce, she decided to enrich her CV with work experience at a major fashion house. Her first experience in luxury haute couture, working with a design team on the Rue du Faubourg-Saint-Honoré, was, she told me, a 'nightmare':

> No one was paid until the 15th of the month, which meant that for ten days my colleagues didn't eat lunch. He spent every evening at Le Costes,[10] he'd invite everybody but he never paid the bill ... He didn't really have any money either, but on the side he organized fashion shows at the Louvre with supermodels he persuaded to take part who weren't paid either. It was awful, awful, a nightmare!

After this experience she found a job through a recruitment agency as a designer for Marie Elle,[11] a successful upmarket ready-to-wear label with a large turnover. They paid well, and promptly, but the

---

[10] Le Costes is a famous Parisian restaurant very popular with the fashion crowd.
[11] Not the real name of the brand.

power relationships were even more extreme. The difference between the fantasy image of the brand and the reality of its production was shocking: 'Its image was gentle, feminine, sophisticated, glamorous, light, but the reality was unbelievably violent.' The violence was not related to money but to exploitation, bullying and psychological and material control over the lives of the designers. Marie Elle was helmed by a 'terrifying' studio director who would pit the designers against each other and spread rumours about the workers to the management in order to create conflict. Violence was also manifested in the way the staff's time was controlled:

> On Friday evening we still didn't know if we were going to have to come into work over the weekend. So if we had a wedding, say, we wouldn't be able to accept or turn down the invitation . . . It was the same for holidays, we couldn't make plans to go away in the summer. You were robbed of your free time.

Despite the conditions, Marguerite stayed on until the end of her six-month trial period, hoping she would be given a permanent contract, as she had been led to believe she would be when she was first taken on. However, after her sixth month on a temporary contract, she discovered that the company was only offering to take her on as a freelancer. It was by chance that Marguerite learned of her professional destiny a week before the end of the trial period, rather than on the very last day, as Marie Elle had been planning. Returning to head office to see if she could find out more, she bumped into a colleague who was waiting with her portfolio. Naïvely, the young woman told her she was interviewing for Marguerite's job. Furious, Marguerite marched into her boss's office, slammed the door behind her and demanded an explanation: 'And she just goes, "Don't you speak to me like that. Get out of my office!" She wouldn't give me an answer.' A few hours later she was summoned back by Marie Elle, who informed her that she was 'prepared to take her on as a freelancer', adding, 'You're lucky I'm telling you this a week in advance'. The other woman had not been given the job after her interview, whose real purpose was to get hold of her designs for free. Marie Elle had basically asked her to do some sketches on a specific theme, half of which were then used as the basis of the next collection without her knowledge.

After Marie Elle, Marguerite finally landed a job at a large luxury fashion house, where she worked as an assistant on the second line. She was happy in the job, the work was stimulating and the label prestigious, but her relationship with another designer, a woman of her age who was clearly threatened by her, was very difficult; the young woman was strategically undermining her, and Marguerite left after nine months. 'I don't know if I found the strength to leave, or if I lacked the strength to stay.'

After these negative experiences, Marguerite branched out into one-off freelance collaborations which, in spite of the fact that this meant less job security, freed her from the psychological power play and increased her control over her free time: 'Gradually, by becoming a freelancer, I began to keep my distance. Being freelance keeps you in a capsule, you're a satellite, moving from one label to another.' She designed pieces for several luxury and upmarket fashion brands. Despite the advantages, being freelance inevitably meant precariousness: work was sometimes paid by the day, she had no social security benefits, and a collaboration could be terminated from one day to the next. But Marguerite had learned from her past experiences and now knew how to play the game:

> As a freelancer, you establish a balance. It's very unstable, but ultimately you establish a power balance too; yes, they can end the working relationship at any moment, but so can you. It's very interesting. And then, if you're clever, you can negotiate an excellent day rate. It's a bit like a game of poker, you really have to negotiate strategically. But at some point you have to do it.

This proved to be a winning strategy for Marguerite, and she was now getting to the end of each month with money in her account. For a couple of years she worked on average for three companies simultaneously, moving from office to office each day, and learning to organize her working day in terms of the due dates for each project. This period of 'satellite' working ended after an experience that made her realize how insecure freelance work can be. 'I was ripped off by someone, a huge French company', which stole forty designs from her:

> As a freelancer, it's incredible insecure, you have no contract, you're not protected, they can get rid of you from one day to the next, they can steal your designs. It's so violent! So the only security is to get them to pay you an advance; he [the head of the company] didn't pay me, but I trusted him, I'd worked for him seven years before. But actually he didn't want to pay me, and in the end, after fighting for two months, he said to me, 'Okay, I'll pay you a bit'.

After this episode, with ten years' experience under her belt, Marguerite decided to stop working for other labels and to launch her own label, which she was working on when I met her.

Reconstructing a framework

As Elsa said, in spite of terrible professional conditions and all the different forms of exploitation and power play, the fact of working right in the heart of the dream is considered by employers to be a stroke of luck – 'you're lucky to be here'. As for the workers, they prove themselves to be quite tough when faced with these unequal situations, for multiple reasons: ambition and status, means and types of production, or because of subjugation. Those who do choose to stay on in luxury businesses that exploit, bully and create inequality make the strategic decision for the advancement of their careers. Marguerite, speaking of high fashion houses, told me: 'If you do manage to hang in there, as first assistant to so-and-so, maybe one day it'll be your turn ... But there aren't a lot of ways in.'

Those who aspire to the jackpot have to brave precariousness and accept the risks that are inherent to the post-Fordist work culture. When it comes to prestige, the relationship that Elsa had with Henry Carat shows that it is possible to 'cope' because one is fascinated, in thrall to the person's charisma. Indirect participation in the world in which the dresses circulate is also an advantage – Beyoncé and Lady Gaga have both worn dresses designed by Elsa. Moreover, working in high fashion houses also signifies being able to move in luxury circles: 'It's true there's also a 'party' element, these are the kinds of jobs where you get to go to extraordinary parties. I was invited once to a party in the Louvre, to drink champagne. There were so many diamonds everywhere!'

On top of the valorization of the individual through their work is the accumulation of social prestige. Referring to the working conditions at some of the most famous fashion labels, Marguerite said: 'These are places you mustn't work, we all say it to each other. You have no life there. For two months before the shows you work every day till 10.00 pm, you work all weekend ... You work so hard, and for a tiny salary. But people accept it because of the prestige.' She told me about a friend of hers:

> She worked for years for Dior, and it was so violent. She couldn't believe that people stayed there, it was so hard, but at the same time when you say you work at Dior everyone's like, wow, amazing. So it's worth it socially. It's a thing where they get away with it because you're wowed in the same way. But it really was insane working for Dior, everyone's there, holding tight and suffering.

In addition to the fascination for labels, the mechanics of domination also play a part in keeping workers in line: 'There are people who stay there for years, because they've lost confidence in themselves, they are destroyed by the machine.' Based on her own experiences and what she has observed, Marguerite explains:

> They make you work so hard that afterwards you're exhausted, mentally, physically, psychologically, which keeps you from leaving . . . They break you, you have no energy left. It's happened to a bunch of my friends, they end up kind of wasting away. And they all say: 'I can't bring myself to leave. I don't have the time to do my CV, I don't have time to look around, I've got no energy left.' . . . I think that their bosses have deliberately pushed this frantic rhythm so that they don't have time to lift their eyes from their work.

Commenting on the deterioration of work conditions, not only in fashion, but in work in general, Elsa said to me:

> All those suicides of people working for La Poste [the state run postal service]. I think it's because they applied the working conditions of fashion to La Poste, that's all. They keep you down, so they don't have to pay you, because if they valued what you were doing they'd have to pay you. So they're constantly undervaluing you, telling you how lucky you are to have work, saying, 'You're creative, you're so lucky.'

The strategies that keep designers in an acutely asymmetric power balance are deployed in different ways: physical exhaustion which makes it impossible for the employee to find either the time or the energy to look for another job; psychologically violent belittling and undervaluing their work; and the repetition of the discourse of luck. This is articulated on different levels: the luck to have a job in a context of high unemployment, the luck 'to be there' working in the heart of the dream, and the luck to be working in a creative occupation.

My research also revealed that creativity is one of the reasons why designers stay in their jobs. Thanks to their infrastructure, their financial means and their exceptional artistry, the high fashion houses allow designers a wide margin of experimentation and creativity. Marguerite admitted this:

When I was working at this mid-range brand, I had a good quality of life, I could leave work early, I had time to see my friends, take driving lessons, I did stuff, had weekends off. Then after that, I was working for some fancy designer labels, and I didn't have a life at all, I'd get home and I'd still be worrying, I couldn't sleep, I suffered. But the problem was that at the really fancy labels, you do really exciting stuff, the kind of stuff you'd never be able to do on your own. You get to work with extraordinary fabrics, embroidery, you can develop crazy ideas, from a creative point of view, so it's also to do with intellectual stimulation ... At the smaller labels, it's true that it's comfortable, but it's not exciting. So I think people also stick it out for the excitement. I went back to those labels for the excitement.

The high fashion industry is exciting because it offers the chance to design exceptional products from both a material and a symbolic point of view. But the exceptional nature of the product goes hand in hand with the 'exceptionalization' of the working conditions. As Marguerite put it, 'The problem is that if you want to make beautiful things you have to work with psychopaths'.

Maintaining opacity

The series of difficulties and negative experiences that marked the professional life of Elsa, and even more so that of Marguerite, might make it seem that they are unusual cases. In fact, in the entire course of my research I didn't hear a single description of an experience of working in the luxury sector that was entirely positive, which certainly suggests that Elsa and Marguerite's experiences were the norm rather than the exception. This is also related to structural aspects of the industry: the specific rhythm of the fashion calendar, with several collections a year, makes overwork inevitable. Without doubt, working as a designer in such conditions means working enormously hard.

Nonetheless, the exploitation and power play described go well beyond being an issue of working hours.

In that case, how to explain that this reality is rendered almost entirely invisible? What are the factors that contribute to maintaining this opacity? First, in many fashion companies, collaborations with designers begin with a contract containing a confidentiality clause that applies not only to products, which is understandable, bearing in mind that the fashion industry is based on innovation and originality, but also, as Marguerite points out, on working conditions: 'If you say anything you're betraying their confidentiality, because according to your contract you aren't allowed to say it's tough . . . You have contracts where you have to keep quiet about everything that takes place internally . . . You aren't allowed to talk about the company at all.' The fashion houses protect this opacity using legal means and even when the working conditions are 'extremely violent' and infringe French labour laws, designer-stylists respect these agreements out of fear. The world of couture and luxury fashion is both very small and very powerful, and they are afraid that anything they say would be used against them and they would not be able to find another job. Elsa, visibly sapped from being unemployed, was clearly torn throughout our conversation between her desire to unveil the truth and her fear of being recognized. Begging me to be extremely discreet, she said: 'I really shouldn't talk about these things. I've never really talked about this before. I shouldn't, it's a question of respect, because that's part of it too.'[12] Marguerite, like Elsa, acknowledged this injunction to remain silent, bitterly concluding that the desire to keep it all a secret is widespread. Shaking with barely suppressed anger, Elsa told me:

> Everyone is a member of the fashion union, it's obligatory, everyone, everyone, everyone. There's the *Chambre Syndicale de la Mode* in

[12] Elsa said she shouldn't talk, both out of fear and also out of respect for Henri Carat; she seemed to want to excuse him for what she had suffered, even though she knew perfectly well that he had the final word on every aspect of the way the company was run.

Paris. If you want to do a fashion show, you have to join … So basically there is no way that the *Syndicat* doesn't know what's going on. There is no way that there's no complaint in their database that they've received from the unemployment office, no way.

Indeed, the unemployment office and recruitment agencies are custodians of these workers' statements. Even when public agencies, like the unemployment office, know the reality of working conditions in the capital of high fashion, the facts do not circulate and certainly do not lead to any action being taken. The fashion industry and its unique rules appear to be more powerful than French labour law. But perhaps the state has an interest in maintaining the situation.

Fashion schools are also involved in maintaining the status quo. The border between teaching and creating fashion is extremely porous, and it is highly unlikely that such educational institutions are unaware of these realities. Many of the teachers are themselves designers or former designers who have experience of working for the fashion houses. Students and former students familiar with internships presumably relate their experiences to their teachers as well. Yet such information is not compiled into a body of evidence that could be used to denounce these practices or improve working conditions. On the contrary, students are sent to do internships or taken on after they graduate by the fashion houses, which guarantees the continuity of these practices in the fashion industry. Fashion schools are thus participating in the normalization of such exploitation. Opacity is an unofficial rule; it's 'up to you to … figure it out', as Marguerite puts it.

On top of all this, the world of designers for luxury fashion houses is small, and job instability means that workers frequently move from one job to another, which means that stories about their reputations also circulate. This combination of factors makes one realize how pertinent Elsa's comments are: perpetuating the opacity is part of a strategy of maintaining a system of oppression, which is vital for guaranteeing the profits of one of the most powerful industries in contemporary capitalism.

The forms of domination described in this chapter are common in many other professional sectors.[13] Nonetheless, they appear even more brutal when they are part of a dream world. As Marguerite says, 'There is already the classic form of workplace abuse, and then on top of it there's the abuse that's inherent to fashion'. This abuse is specific to the industry, a result of the disparity between the production of an elite of desire, with a mediatized element that is overexposed and maintained, and asymmetries and different kinds of exploitation in the production process, concealed and justified by the fact that the workers are 'lucky to be there'.

*

The fantasy of the dream required by fashion to guarantee its profits is based on both the precariousness and the domination that are omnipresent in the organization of work. Does this explain how the system endures? As Iris put it: 'In fashion, there is a real power that attracts people, it's almost like magic! It's like you've been hypnotized.' And indeed, according to Pierre Bourdieu, fashion produces a symbolic power that seems like magic.[14] This magic functions according to the value conferred on the products of the industry, as well as by a process that makes these arbitrary values become values that are socially recognized. In fashion, magic operates like a form of collective belief[15] in its arbitrary values. Basically, the magic cannot be

---

[13]   C. Dejours, *Souffrance en France: La banalisation de l'injustice sociale*, Paris, Le Seuil, 2009.

[14]   Y. Delsaut and P. Bourdieu, 'Le couturier et sa griffe'.

[15]   The notion of collective belief, as developed by Marcel Mauss (H. Hubert and M. Mauss, 'Esquisse d'une théorie générale de la magie', *L'Année sociologique*, vol. 7, 1902) was taken up by Pierre Bourdieu to construct his theory on magic: 'What makes the system work is what Mauss called collective belief. I would say, rather, that it is a collective ignorance. Mauss said, referring to magic: "It's always society that pays itself in the counterfeit money of its dreams . . . In order to play the game, you have to believe in the ideology of creativity"' (P. Bourdieu, *Questions de sociologie*, p. 205).

understood without contemplating the systemic nature of the phenomenon – in other words, in its 'relationship to a total organization that is both mental and social'.[16] The fashion system functions only if all those who contribute to the production of its goods recognize their symbolic value. The word 'value' is interesting, since it refers both to the measurable economic character of an object and to a shared moral universe. It is, incidentally, also commonly used within the fashion world; Iris, in her job training sales assistants, is responsible for transmitting the 'values of the brand'. In reality, Iris's work serves only to consolidate a pre-existing belief, because the sales assistants are already, when they are taken on, proud to work for a high-status brand. This means that they already understand the value that has been socially attributed to it. As Bourdieu put it: 'The prophet offers nothing new, he only preaches to the converted.'[17]

However, if the notion of magic makes it possible to understand the fascination for working in the fashion industry, it doesn't entirely explain how to understand the process that makes workers *remain* in situations of subjugation. The concept of hegemony,[18] as formulated by Antonio Gramsci, is a way of describing the process of complying with the rules of fashion. Fashion is based on the idea of consent as a 'knowing and willing participation of the dominated in their domination'.[19] In fashion, the 'superstructure' – as Gramsci refers to the immaterial productions and beliefs of systems of power – is efficient to the point of making its workers adhere in a way that is not only consensual, but is above all aware of the violence that is inherent to the dream. Though this point seems significant, it makes it impossible to consider the workers other than as completely

[16] F. Keck, 'Les théories de la magie dans les traditions anthropologiques anglaise et française', *Methodos*, no. 2, 2002, p. 4.
[17] P. Bourdieu, *Questions de sociologie*, p. 162.
[18] A. Gramsci (textes sélectionnés et présentés par R. Keucheyan), *Guerre de mouvement et guerre de position*, Paris, La Fabrique, 2012.
[19] M. Burawoy, *Cultural Domination: Gramsci Meets Bourdieu*, p. 8.

subjugated. However, what I observed during my research contradicts such a Manichean vision. The domination experienced in this professional world can be capitalized and transformed into various forms of prestige, which operates on those who are not part of the dream.

Contemporary capitalism has made fashion, the industry of appearance, into a dream. Assistant photographer Mathilde talks very lucidly about this dream and the attractiveness of occupations that are involved in producing images:

> They are worlds of domination, it's a simple as that. Because that's where the images of fashion are constructed, that's where its values are made, in fact. That's why they are fascinating places ... Because this represents money, this represents beauty ... I think that what we've done is construct a form of social domination through beauty.

Fashion is an industry where power, beauty and money are tightly intertwined. Fashion workers not only produce but embody this powerful beauty, and this makes them the elite of desire, in spite of professional realities and unfavourable economics. That is why the appearance of fashion workers, their aesthetic and corporal capital, is also a tool of power. In fashion, the aesthetic is simultaneously a corporeal injunction, an appropriation of the subjectivity of the workers for profitable ends, and a capital mobilized by these same workers in the social world. To understand work in fashion, it is vital to understand the relationship between domination, power and appearance, which together authorize the notion of 'glamour'.

According to the dictionary, the word *glamour*, which comes from the Scottish, means attractiveness, charm, fascination, enchantment, and, in its original meaning, a magic spell. Today, as in the past, glamour is about prestige and magic, power and appearance, which makes it one of the most efficient terms for describing fashion. It is this conjunction of appearance and power – both endured, in the case of the exploitation and precariousness of workers, and performed, in the case of the prestige that is conferred on them in the social world – that creates from fashion the world of glamour, and from its labour 'glamour labour'.[20]

---

[20] The sociologist Elizabeth Wissinger uses the notion of 'glamour labor' to define the work on the body of models and the work of creating a self-image on the internet. It is a form of control over the body and a construction of appearance in both the physical and the virtual dimensions. 'Glamour labor', according to Wissinger, is the conjunction of aesthetic labour and immaterial work. See E. Wissinger, 'Models, glamour labor, and the age of the blink', in J. Davis and N. Jurgenson (eds), *Theorizing the Web 2014, interface*, vol. 1, no. 1, pp. 1–20; and E. Wissinger, *This Year's Model*. My deployment of the notion of glamour labour does not conflict with what Wissinger discusses. I am using it within a larger framework, because it refers to those who work in fashion in general, as well as aspects other than the body and appearance – the mixture of domination and the power to act that results from the prestige conferred by working in fashion.

Part Three

The Dream, and Those Who Work in It

Looking at this kind of research through the 'emergence of the subject'[1] offers a means of analysing the way subjectivities function and are constructed in specific and defined contexts, and thus of arriving at a general understanding, while avoiding opting for identity or category attributions. The 'subject' is not a fixed entity, but a process, always in the process of being made or unmade, the production of interactions, hierarchies and contexts.[2] The notion of the 'subject' thus refers to the idea of an individual whose subjectivity is a constant production depending on different situations, which might be interpersonal relationships or professional situations, or part of the larger framework of the fashion industry, for example.

The productivity of contemporary capitalism is largely based not on the extraction of the physical strength of workers, but on their actual *life*,[3] their emotions, their relationships, their creativity, their sensibilities, their capacity to manage themselves, to be autonomous, to monitor themselves. If the question of subjectivity is thus central to

[1]   M. Agier, 'Penser le sujet, observer la frontière', *L'Homme*, vol. 203–4, no. 3, December 2012.
[2]   This approach refers to the ideas of Michel Foucault, according to whom, as Mathieu Potte-Bonneville summarizes, defining the notion of the 'subject' requires 'looking outside, in other words focusing on institutions and on our relationships with others as well as on the changing historical framework, which contributes to "defining us"'. See M. Potte-Bonneville, *Foucault*, Paris, Ellipses, 2010, p. 23. The notion of the 'subject' is to be understood as a production of subjectivity. See also F. Guattari, 'De la production de subjectiveé', *Chimères*, no. 4, 1987.
[3]   A. Fumagalli and C. Morini, 'Life put to work: Towards a life theory of value', *Ephemera*, vol. 10, 2010.

any analysis of types of contemporary labour, it is particularly visible in the world of fashion, which is animated and structured around the staging of unconventional, different subjectivities, belonging to the exception and to the dream, but which also demands that subjects be ready to alienate themselves in order to be there and to stay there. Above all, understanding ethnographic situations at the scale of the subject enables one to 'revisit and go beyond the opposition, which can be read in all political philosophy, between the subject that acts and the subject that is subjugated'.[4] If it is certainly the case that the political project of neoliberalism fully invests the space of subjectivity, it is not at all certain that every individual inscribed in the modes of production and lifestyles of contemporary capitalism must inevitably be considered to be subjugated. This general observation applies no less to this research, since, if it is certain that the fashion worker requires specific modalities of subjectification (in other words, constructions of subjectivity induced by the mechanisms of power, which are then assimilated by the individual and 'performed' in specific situations), that does not preclude the existence of a form of consent. The workers are not forced to be there, but if they choose to be there and want to stay there, they are forced to 'be' in a specific way.

The notion of 'consent' is fundamental for describing types of domination, hierarchies and inequalities, and also the injunction to maintain a certain self-control, of the body, of one's affects, emotions, time and relationships, without actually making it a matter of subjugated individuals inexorably 'acted upon' by the mechanics of power. According to Michael Burawoy,[5] consent is not a prerequisite condition for the organization of work within a company, but on the contrary it is produced within it, using different strategies. When these strategies offer more autonomy and responsibility to workers,

---

[4]   M. Agier, 'Penser le sujet, observer la frontière', p. 51.
[5]   M. Burawoy, *Manufacturing Consent*.

these strategies 'construct' the workers as 'individuals' and not as 'members of a social class', which allows them to level the structural inequalities that govern these types of organization, while obscuring the power relations between management and workers.

This notion of 'consent' has been used recently in a context closer to the world of fashion. In her book about the luxury hotel industry in the United States, *Class Acts*,[6] the sociologist Rachel Sherman explains why she chose to use the notion of 'consent' rather than that of 'resistance'. Unlike 'resistance', the idea of 'consent' makes it possible to consider workers as using their capacity for agency to participate in labour rather than resist it. She also explains that the notion of consent entails 'taking seriously the reasons that workers like their jobs and the rewards they derive from them, without losing a critical perspective on unequal social relations of appropriation'.[7] During my fieldwork I adopted a similar perspective to that of Sherman: I wanted to understand from within the motivations, desires, expectations and constraints that workers encountered, while locating the situations and rhetoric that I encountered within the framework of contemporary capitalism, with its structural inequalities and mechanisms of power.

If the notions of the 'subject' and the 'subjugated' are complementary, it is because the subject cannot be considered as separate from power. However, here we must make another lexical precision: in labour, 'power' is understood in the sense of 'power relations'.[8] Power is, as Mathieu Potte-Bonneville writes, 'constitutively interactional',[9]

---

[6]   R. Sherman, *Class Acts: Service and Inequality in Luxury Hotels*, Berkeley, University of California Press, 2007.

[7]   Ibid., p. 16. This position echoes the words of Marlène Benquet: 'Rather than claiming that individuals are alienated, one might, at least theoretically, consider that if they are participating and engaging in their work, it is simply because they have good reasons to do so', *Encaisser! Enquête en immersion dans la grande distribution*, Paris, La Découverte, 2013, p. 13.

[8]   M. Foucault, 'Le sujet et le pouvoir', in *Dits et écrits*, vol. 4, 1980–88, Paris, Gallimard, 1994, pp. 222–43.

[9]   M. Potte-Bonneville, *Foucault*, p. 61.

because it can only be exercised on subjects capable of breaking free from it. The contradiction between these two apparently conflicting elements, the subject with agency and the subjugated subject, cannot be resolved; on the contrary, it is to be tested in the analysis of research situations.

8

At Work with an Up-and-coming Fashion Designer

Meeting Franck

Franck is a young independent Belgian designer whom I met through a mutual friend who works in fashion. He was introduced to me as the most talented of the new generation of Belgian designers, 'adorable', but struggling with the inherent uncertainty of his occupation. We met at Franck's suggestion at his studio in Brussels, where he received me along with two women. When I arrived, we kissed each other on the cheek and he invited me to join them at the large table. I shook hands with the two women and introduced myself. They both kissed me on the cheek, mechanically, without looking at me, and told me their first names without seeming to pay attention when I told them mine. I sat down, slightly embarrassed, understanding from their attitude and their manner of speaking that they had power, and that, in spite of the informal nature of the interaction and the situation, Franck and they were not friends. I had the impression that they were taking part in a competition to own the space, the conversation and the attention. Though I was apparently invisible to them, I had the impression that they were taking part in a contest whose purpose was to show me which of the two was closer to the designer. The situation was embarrassing, but eventually they left the room and left Franck and me alone. We began the interview.

Franck was suffering from a bad cold, which he told me he'd caught because of the huge amount of work he had to do to finish his collection. Because he didn't have the cash flow to pay rent on two places, he was sleeping at the studio on the second-hand couch in the middle of the room and he never got a good night's sleep. Franck said he had wanted to be a designer since he was a young boy. He explained: 'When you're interested in international fashion, it's like being part of a clan, even if your ideas are very different.' His vision of fashion is of a community within which everyone seems to be friends, though they aren't really. We were soon talking about his current situation, which he described as 'very, very tough':

> I think very few people realize, you really have to live it to understand how hard it is. . . . Finding investors, feeding the press, managing the studio. It's intense. That's the life I dreamed of. It's the one I have. I always imagined it would be lots of work, but I didn't imagine the psychological burden that went with it . . . At my age, I still don't have any security, that's just tough for me. If you do it on your own, it's always you who has to pick up the pieces. You don't get paid if you're ill. There are times when you tell yourself you can't afford to fall ill. Knowing that I can is important.

In spite of his media success, Franck was still living on unemployment benefits. His collections and the salaries of his staff – when he has them – are paid by patrons, not by public funds. Sales of pieces from his collections barely cover the production costs, and at best make only a marginal profit. Rather than an artist busy working on his creations, he seemed to be more like someone running a business and worrying about the fate of his company. In reality he is both. Despite his soft voice and gentle eyes, despite his open smile and his affable character, he emanated a certain toughness that came from his determination and his total devotion to his work.

The beginning of our collaboration

A year later, after I had completed a number of interviews as well as many situational observations, I was feeling a little frustrated with my research, and I realized I needed to immerse myself completely in work experience in the field. Searching online, I discovered that Franck was looking for an intern to help him with administration and communication. It was an unpaid internship, offering a 'variety of interesting responsibilities, in a very pleasant environment. Meals will be provided.' Although I had none of the skills required, I leapt at the opportunity and sent him an informal email explaining that I wanted to understand fashion from within. I offered to work for him in exchange for observing life in his studio. I sent the email to his personal address, but it wasn't until several days later that I received a very formal response from a woman whose identity and role I didn't know, inviting me to a meeting with her and Franck to agree on the terms of our collaboration.

When I arrived at the studio on the day of the meeting, two fashionably dressed women were smoking in the courtyard. They greeted me and let me in. Franck was no longer sleeping at the studio – he had moved in with his partner, and the large couch had disappeared. There were several computers on the large table. The two young women who had been smoking came inside; one went into the other room, where the clothes were made, and the other sat down in front of one of the computers, alongside a young man. He was a member of Franck's new team of interns and workers. Pilar, the young woman who had written to me, came up and shook my hand with a determined grip. She called Franck over and we sat down at the table, alongside the interns who were working in silence. Franck did not speak; Pilar explained to me in a bossy, confident tone that they were looking for someone to help them with sorting out the final details of the fashion show coming up in Paris the following month as part of fashion week. They needed someone who would be able to go to Paris with them. Pilar suggested that I come to the studio every day from 9.00 am to 6.30 pm, like the other interns, with Wednesday and the weekends off, and then go with them to Paris the week before the show. We shook on it. I was taken on as a kind of factotum.

The first day I arrived at the studio at 8.55 am. No one was there, apart from André, whom I'd seen at my interview with Franck and Pilar. He offered me a cup of the coffee he'd prepared for the whole team, and we started talking. The screensaver on his computer, which was already switched on, was a photo of a young woman with a newborn baby and a young child. This was his girlfriend and their two children. He didn't live with them, because they didn't have enough money to pay rent. André was twenty-five and in his final year of studying accounting. Without any other leads for finding an internship, he had ended up coming to work for Franck, having agreed that he would work unpaid for three months instead of one, as was demanded by his college.[1] He had been there for two and a half months. He told me he always arrived before his boss, to prepare the coffee and have a quiet cigarette before starting his day.

Just after nine, Pilar and the other members of staff arrived. Franck wasn't there – he had a meeting. There were six of us in the studio; sitting around the large table with André and me was Sarah, who was twenty-one and very fashionably dressed. She was studying communications and her job was to design the website that would be the platform for selling the collection. She was in her third month of a five-month internship. Downstairs was twenty-three-year-old Zoé, similarly stylish, who was studying fashion design and doing a six-month internship with Franck. She was an assistant designer, working off the books, while hoping for something 'more official', like Mélanie, the production assistant,[2] who was in the same situation as Zoé, and Manon, an intern who had just graduated from a French fashion school.

---

[1]   French and Belgian law are not aligned here: French law requires that internships lasting longer than two months be paid at least a token sum, while in Belgium this is at the discretion of the employer.

[2]   During my internship with Franck, Mélanie worked on two-dimensional images of the collection for the catalogue. She used a special program to draw the garments in two dimensions, specifying both colour and fabric, and creating a code for each piece. This catalogue, which provided buyers with all the information they needed, would be used for ordering.

The atmosphere was a little tense, because Pilar was bossy and nervy, and acted as though she was running the company – her official role was sales director, but in reality she had several roles. She sat at her desk in the corner, facing the kitchen, near the large table. Since my earlier visit the previous year, two more desks had been placed in the area facing the main space: this was where Franck and Mélanie sat. Pilar told me that during the day she wanted to organize a schedule with me. Then she asked me to help André with the accounts. I reminded her that I had a degree in literature and social sciences and really wasn't qualified to do accounts. Recalling that I spoke several languages, she solemnly announced to Sarah that I would be dealing with communication. She asked André to show me the computer program that I would be using to enter a large number of postal addresses, in order to create a database for sending out invitations to the show, which André, showing enormous patience, did.

Later in the morning, a man popped into the studio, and exclaimed at the sight of so many people, 'Well, it's quite a little business you have here!' I couldn't stop myself thinking sarcastically that it was a business without paid employees, since the majority of the people there were working for free. The man sat down at the table with Franck, without interacting at all with us, though we were no more than a few centimetres away from him. He turned out to be an employee from the large events company that was sponsoring Franck, covering all the expenses of the forthcoming fashion show.

Towards midday, Pilar announced it was time for lunch, and told André to take me down to buy bread, so that I could see where the bakery was. She also gave us a pile of letters to take to the post office. These were invitations to the fashion show, addressed to various celebrities, fashion personalities, boutique managers, ministers, friends and journalists. While we were queuing at the post office, I was struck by the contrast between the places the letters were being sent – addresses indicating luxury and power – and where they were now, in the hands of a young working-class student, from a world of men and women with roots in Morocco, Turkey and sub-Saharan Africa, the most impoverished immigrants in Belgium. André admitted he had never been interested in fashion, but that he was happy to have discovered this world. He told me, frankly but without resentment, that Pilar could be very difficult. When we got back to the studio, the young women were laying the table; the computers had been removed and Pilar was preparing pasta with pesto. On the table were packets of supermarket cheese and ham, butter, and bottles of Coca Cola, diet Coke and fruit juice. Though lunch wasn't ready yet, I saw that Pilar was standing and eating from a Tupperware while she kept an eye on the spaghetti in the pot on the stove. Surprised, I asked:

Giulia   You aren't eating with us?

Pilar   Oh no, I only eat healthy food – quinoa, salad, soup.

The way she openly spoke about the inferior quality of the meal she was making was extraordinary.

As soon as the pasta had been served, she sat down at her desk and continued eating her lunch, while Franck and Heike, a designer helping Franck with the show, sat and ate with us, though continuing to talk only to each other. I understood that the fact that they weren't talking to anyone else was a way of confirming hierarchies in an environment where we all appeared to be equal. When lunch was over, we all cleared the table and put the computers back on the table, while one of the young women did the washing up.

In the afternoon I stuck the stamps we'd bought from the post office onto the envelopes containing the invitations, and wrote out the addresses in my best handwriting. While she ate her healthy lunch, Pilar announced that she was absolutely overwhelmed with work. She told us she was going to book the tickets to Paris: she and Franck would be taking the train, while the interns – myself included, apparently – would be going by coach. The last hours of the day seemed to go by very slowly. I noticed that no one was finishing up any particular tasks, the interns were discreetly playing video games on the computer, but everyone was looking very concentrated, pretending to work. I didn't understand why we didn't just go home, and had the feeling that Pilar was holding us hostage.

The next morning once again no one was there when I arrived, apart from André, who was early, as usual. The doorbell rang and I opened it to a young girl who looked serious and nervous. This was Fatima, a business student, who had come from Liège for an interview with Pilar and Franck for an internship. The entire morning went by; neither Pilar nor Franck appeared, nor did they call to apologize to the young woman for their absence, or to let her know what time they would turn up. This meant that the atmosphere was more relaxed around the large table, where André, Fatima, Sarah, Manon, the design intern, and I were sitting. Sarah was particularly chatty, speculating out loud with Manon about the trip to Paris. She talked excitedly about the studio apartment in the 'incredibly cool' neighbourhood around the Canal Saint-Martin that a friend was lending them. Still on the subject of their stay in Paris, she added: 'And Franck wants me to be with him at the office in the Place Vendôme, he wants me to be there with him the whole time, I'm going to be there with him in this fantastic place, it's so exciting.' Meanwhile Manon said she was hoping to go to an after-show party, one of the exclusive parties that the labels organize after the fashion shows. Sarah told her that because she knew someone who worked for Vivienne Westwood, they could not only go to the after-show, but also to the fashion show itself, that she was dying to see Vivienne Westwood's showroom that was 'to die for' that her friend had told her about. Zoé came in from the other room and warned Sarah: 'If you want to go and out party after work, don't say anything. Pilar doesn't want you to, she'll be very cross, she told me.'

At midday we began preparing lunch. It was important to respect Pilar's rules, even in her absence. The young women explained that she might turn up any minute and would be cross if we hadn't eaten at the appointed time. Pilar decided on the week's menus, so we took a large jar of supermarket sauce out of the fridge for the planned spaghetti bolognaise. Fatima ate with us, but neither she nor André were included in the conversation between Sarah, Manon and Zoé. Unlike Fatima and André, the three young women were wearing very fashionable clothes and had similarly fashionable hairstyles. The different linguistic registers, vocabulary and physical appearance were evidence that one group was part of the young creative elite, and the other from the working classes. I, meanwhile, was in an uncomfortable position, because the 'creative' interns didn't know where to place me in the hierarchy. My age, my studies and the reason I was at the studio would normally place me at management level, but my bearing, the role of pseudo-intern that Pilar had given me, as well as my spatial position and the jobs I was given, made me more like them.

Pilar turned up towards 2.00 pm. She sat and explained to Fatima the advantages of doing an internship at the studio, and what a fantastic opportunity it would be to work in the heart of fashion. She detailed the kinds of jobs she would be expected to do. Though she lived an hour away from Brussels by train, Fatima said she was ready to do the commute at her own expense, emphasizing how keen she was to do the internship. Later, André asked Pilar if, exceptionally, he could leave an hour early. She agreed, but asked him why. He told her that it was for Valentine's Day. Pilar lost her temper, asking him with a mixture of contempt and sarcasm if he was making fun of her. André, disconcerted by her reaction, assured her he wasn't. With a dramatic laugh, she said to him: 'So what, then? Are you going to buy flowers?' André answered almost in a whisper, saying that he had reserved a restaurant. 'Sorry, what? For 6.00 pm?' He answered that it was for 7.00 pm but he lived far away. Everyone in the room was silent. I was stunned by Pilar's aggressiveness, and stole a glance at Sarah, who was sitting opposite me showing no emotion on her face. A few minutes later I got up to go to the toilet. Pilar followed me and stood in my way in front of the staircase. She whispered to me that she couldn't put up with him any longer and she was going to 'fire' André, and that Fatima – whom she had barely met but who was 'very good' – and I would take over his tasks. Obviously, she told me to say nothing because she wasn't going to tell him until the following day. I went and sat down again, dumbfounded and shocked. The idea of sitting next to André and of knowing something that he didn't was unbearable, but I didn't have the means to say anything and wasn't even sure I should.

Half an hour later, André went out to buy some things for the studio. After making sure that he had left the building, Pilar, as though she were sharing an intimate secret with close friends, announced to everyone that she had decided to 'fire' André because she 'couldn't bear him any longer'. Although I assumed that the interns would be on the side of their colleague, Sarah reacted by saying: 'That's so the right thing to do, honestly, if you can't stand him you really did the right thing.' The other women also backed Pilar, giving her credit for her completely subjective decision. I asked if she would sign the internship agreement so that André could validate his internship, and whether he had ever behaved inappropriately. I wanted to understand if there were other reasons than those she had just given to substantiate her decision. She told me she probably would sign the agreement, but would add a negative comment. She explained that she found him pleasant and obliging, but that he was slow, not particularly intelligent, and that it was 'important that he didn't get ideas above his station'. She said that he could find a job at the post office, or the town hall, but not here, and in any case, she 'couldn't put up with him any more'. She added that giving him an internship had been a bad idea, she knew it from the start, but that she'd been looking for someone at that point and hadn't found anyone else; every day at 6.30 (the end of the working day) he was impatient to tidy up and leave.

When André returned, everyone acted as if nothing had happened. He sat down next to me and explained with his usual patience certain details of the program that I was using for the addresses. The situation was intolerable to me. The reasons given for his departure and the fact that everyone but him knew about it put me on edge; I was furious and was having trouble keeping myself from crying.

The next day, after everyone had arrived, Pilar announced to André that his internship was over. Surprised by the news, the young man asked for an explanation. With a patronizing air, she explained to him that he was not sufficiently invested in his work, that he was slow and that she was going to give him some advice: if he wanted to succeed, he needed to make his work his priority. André responded that he had simply been straightforward, told the truth, and had never asked to leave early, and never arrived late. Pilar grew irritated, replying acidly that 'we all have someone in our life. All of us. But we work, because fashion week is coming up.' She told him he was very pleasant but had bad manners.

This discussion took place two metres away from the large table with everyone watching, which made the situation even more difficult. When André asked if she would nonetheless sign his internship agreement, she answered that she would be happy to but that her comment would be negative. I wanted to comfort André, but the setup prevented any private exchange. Later on, when he went to pick up bread for lunch, Pilar told us that 'not to be unkind, but he comes from a very modest background'. She paused, as if realizing that something in that sentence wasn't quite right, and added: 'Like lots of us, but we've all made a huge effort and developed a certain intelligence about life.' She went on to say that she was particularly sorry for André's children, 'who aren't very fortunate, and won't have much of a life'. The next day, André wasn't there, and Fatima was sitting in his place.

André was excluded because, despite his punctuality and his regularity, at no moment had he wanted to make his work his absolute priority. By refusing to accept that fashion week was more important than his life, he had broken one of the first rules of fashion, devotion to one's work – and for reasons that, as far as Pilar was concerned, were not acceptable. André was an intern who had never considered that he was 'lucky to be there'; while remaining unfailingly polite, he had never showed particular deference to Franck and Pilar. He was not remotely seduced by the glamour or the overexposure, and at the end of the day he wanted to get home as quickly as possible to see his family. Such an attitude and system of values are incompatible with the self-sacrifice required to work in fashion. During my time there, the interns worked every weekend, and on several occasions Zoé, considered the best and the most passionate of the team, stayed at the studio until 11.00 pm. On top of that, André made no effort to hide his background, which was unacceptable to Pilar. His ousting served to consolidate the rules of the game and create a kind of complicity with the 'creative' interns, who were able by contrast to emphasize their commitment to their work.

The next part of my 'internship'

The weeks went by and I didn't have a great deal to do apart from updating the database of contacts, sticking stamps on envelopes, writing addresses and answering a few emails regarding the invitations. By contrast Sarah, Zoé, Manon and Mélanie were enormously busy: the delivery date for the collection was approaching and both the website and the collection needed to be ready. In the other area of the studio, interns were busy finishing off the pieces that had been delivered from the production workshop. Every day, although it was apparent that the team was complete, hopeful interns turned up at the studio for interview. One morning when I was alone in the office between 9.00 and 10.00 am, a candidate rang the doorbell. She had

come from Paris especially for this interview. I asked her to wait, and
Sarah arrived not long after. She noticed that there were dirty dishes
in the sink; as soon as she started washing up the candidate stood up
and took over, saying that she 'really enjoyed washing up'. Eventually,
two hours later, Franck turned up; he sat down at the large table and
asked the candidate to tell him about her work experience. He flicked
through her portfolio, which he didn't seem impress by. She reacted to
this, telling him how motivated she was and how much she loved her
work. Then she said:

> **Intern**   What can I do to help you?
>
> **Franck**   I'll make you do boring things. I know, it's a *deal to deal*
> [sic], I'll exploit you and you'll exploit me.
>
> **Intern**   Yes, I know, that's what I want, to do boring things.

Though she made it very obvious that she was prepared to do
anything, Franck didn't take her on, because he didn't think that she
had the skills necessary to make clothes. I was getting the impression
that these interviews for internships were actually disguised job
interviews for unpaid work. The pedagogical aspect of the internship
was never brought up during these conversations. Pilar, who usually
conducted the interviews, always emphasized what a great opportunity
it was to do an internship with an up-and-coming designer, to be
involved in all the different phases of creating a collection. She would
list the tasks that the intern would be doing, the skills they were
expected to have, but she never mentioned the idea that it was
supposed to be a training and an apprenticeship. On top of that, as the
interns told me later, there was a surplus of trainees at the studio
where there wasn't enough for them to do.

One day, during my second week, only the interns, assistants and I
were in for lunch. It was the first time I was able to talk freely with
them. All three were exhausted; Zoé and Manon had spent half the
night fixing glass beads onto some accessories, while Sarah had been

working on the website. After lunch we cleared the table and Sarah suggested that we leave the washing up for later so that we could carry on working. When Pilar arrived and saw the dirty plates in the sink she was furious. The washing up was a task whose function was to confirm the studio hierarchy; neither Franck nor Pilar ever did it. In spite of the horizontal way the space was arranged, and the illusion of informality in the way the staff interacted, the organization was highly structured and hierarchical. Franck was at the very top of the pyramid; his frequent absences and his lack of interest in the internal dynamics of the studio and the people who were involved in the material production and its daily management confirmed his power and his prestige as an artist. His lack of interest regarding anything that wasn't directly to do with his work or its promotion came over as a form of tacit authority. Despite her bossy behaviour, Pilar could not claim to be Franck's equal, because she was working for him and while he could fire her, she of course could not fire him. She had a Smart contract,[3] and was in charge of everything that wasn't to do with the actual design and production of the clothes. People who were brought in to assist production on a temporary basis, and freelancers like Patty, the pattern-cutter, and Nicolas, the head of production, were treated as peers by Pilar and on the whole interacted mainly with Franck, Zoé and Mélanie. Zoé and Mélanie were theoretically no longer interns and were now part of the permanent team, and although the terms of their employment weren't clear from a contractual point of view, they tended to be treated as though they were an integral part of the studio. The accounts and management interns were right at the bottom of the hierarchy, while the creative interns were closer to Franck and thus symbolically more valued.

---

[3]   The Smart is a kind of social fund for artists and creative professionals. Twenty years after it was set up in Belgium, Smart now has around 60,000 members and is present in eight European countries. Most of its members, however, are in Belgium.

Departure for Paris

Pilar had chosen the cheapest coach company for our journey to Paris. Our departure was at 2.00 pm. Zoé was already at the bus station. Sarah was late. It was cold and wet, and the bus was delayed by an hour. It was Sunday; we were leaving Brussels a day early so that we could start work at the showroom the following morning at 9.00 am. The show itself was taking place the following week in a prestigious location in the centre of Paris. Zoé had dyed her hair for the trip; she was now a redhead instead of a blonde. Her cool, quirky look contrasted with her cheerful, unassuming personality. When I asked her why she seemed so tired and was suffering from a bad back, she told me that the previous evening she had stayed at the studio until 11.00 pm packing boxes and then returned at 7.00 am to load up the van. Everything that was needed was being transported to Paris: the clothes, sewing machines for last-minute alterations, printers, and several boxes filled with whatever was necessary for the pop-up office and showroom that were being set up in Paris.

Eventually the coach turned up. I was sitting on my own, while Sarah and Zoé were sitting together behind me. The journey was the first time I had the opportunity to chat freely with them outside the studio. Sarah told us about her love life, and Zoé talked about someone she'd met recently. 'It's going well, but I haven't seen him for a month now, because of work. We'll see if I have a bit more time when we get back.' Sarah was dreamily speculating about the trip to Paris, listing all the things she wanted to do. Zoé also hoped to be able to enjoy some free time in the city. 'I've worked every weekend for the last month and I'd love to have a day to hang out with my brother, who's going to be in Paris too. I haven't seen him for ages, but I don't know if they'll let me go.' The coach dropped us off at a bus station on the edge of the city, and we went our separate ways: Sarah was staying in a studio flat belonging to a friend of hers, along with Manon, Mélanie and Patty, who were sleeping on the floor on inflatable mattresses. Zoé was staying with her aunt in the suburbs, and I was staying with a friend.

The following morning I arrived at the showroom at 9.00 am. Zoé was already there, mopping the floor. Even though we had only arrived the previous evening, I saw that the showroom was already set up and decorated, and that the entire collection had been hung up on racks. Pilar had insisted that Zoé and Sarah unload the van on Sunday evening. Sarah had spent the rest of the night painting the walls white; Franck thought it looked 'grotty' and had asked her to sort it out. She seemed to be in good spirits, in spite of not having slept all night; Franck had come to the studio in the early hours of the morning with some friends on their way home from a nightclub. They drank a couple of bottles of champagne and listened to music while she painted. 'It was so cool', she said. Zoé, still mopping the floor, was clearly suffering from a bad back. I offered to take over from her, and, if she liked, to give her the details of an osteopath. She refused: 'It will be at least 45 euros', which she couldn't afford, and anyway, she didn't have the time.

Later that morning Pilar told Sarah that she'd booked her an appointment at the hairdresser, because she looked 'unpresentable'. Sarah tried to say no, saying she liked her hair as it was, but it was no use. After lunch she returned with her hair styled in a long, straight bob, not unlike the way Pilar wore her hair. Pilar's attitude towards Sarah was markedly condescending. Zoé was like the perfect employee, warding off any potential criticism with her impeccable behaviour, while Sarah, who tended to be more spontaneous and chatty, was the perfect target for Pilar's controlling excesses.

The Paris showroom was in a basement and ground floor duplex facing the street, furnished like a boutique. The windowless basement housed the office and the dressing area for the fitting model (whose job was to model the outfits that clients wanted to see being worn) as well as the toilet and a kitchen area. Apart from a few moments of crisis during client visits, the days went by without any drama: downstairs in the basement Zoé ironed and finalized the collection, Sarah put the finishing touches on the website, and Pilar dealt with invitations and appointments. Upstairs, Tilda, the fitting model, and I spent most of the time sitting at the table where orders were to be taken. Tilda was eighteen and, apart from the brief periods when she modelled outfits for clients, she spent most of the day with her earphones on watching fashion videos on her iPad. She didn't address a word to anyone, and no one spoke to her. She was invisible, to the point that the interns often forgot to bring her lunch. She was being paid around 400 euros a day.

In general Franck was only around for journalists, bloggers, Belgian television units come to film the rising star of Belgian fashion, and above all clients, upon whom the commercial success of the collection depended. It was these clients – owners or employees of the most important multimark boutiques and concept stores in the world – who were the real judges of the designer's work. Being present in a fashion capital is vital, both from a commercial and from a symbolic perspective.

Two days before the show, at about 9.00 am, while we were cleaning the showroom, Louise turned up at the studio. She was very thin, with long straight hair and a heavy fringe. She wore fuchsia lipstick, a tight, bright yellow jumper, a pair of skin-tight trousers, and the latest trainers. She had come for an interview with Pilar for an internship, which took place in the office area in the basement. I was cleaning the toilets and overheard their entire conversation. Unlike most of the other potential interns I'd met, Louise was very self-confident. She was in her final year at one of the many fashion schools in Paris. Pilar began with her usual commercial-style rhetoric, talking up Franck's success, what an opportunity it was to work with him in Paris during fashion week, to meet so many fascinating people, and then, as she usually did, she went through the various tasks that Louise would be expected to do. The young woman interjected with the occasional 'cool' and 'sure, no problem, yeah, I get it'. I understood, from the tone of her voice, that Pilar was satisfied with Louise, who said that she was ready to come to Brussels for the internship. Pilar explained to her that the minimum length of an internship was six months, which Louise was happy about, although her school demanded no more than a three-month internship. She accepted Pilar's invitation to work as a dresser[4] for the fashion show. The interview seemed to be over and they agreed a starting date. Louise was about to get up and leave when she asked, almost in passing, if her expenses would be covered, justifying her request by explaining that her school insisted on it. Pilar was disconcerted by the question and told her that unfortunately that would not be possible: 'It's not that we don't want to, we can't.' She said that Louise could find an evening and weekend job in a bar, like the other interns. She told Louise to 'sort it out' with her school. Louise responded with another 'no problem' and left.

Desirable projections

Despite what she had been promised, Sarah didn't spend a single moment with Franck at Place Vendôme. In fact, he had access to the offices that a press agency had promised to lend him for two weeks for only half a day, when he was casting models for the show. Apart from the hours she spent cleaning and tidying up the showroom with Zoé, or doing a bit of shopping, Sarah spent every day including her lunch break in the basement, and had no contact whatsoever with either journalists or clients. Zoé also spent most of her time in the basement, doing last-minute alterations, ironing and dressing Tilda for fittings.

---

[4]   During the shows, each model has a dresser who helps her in and out of her outfits and with putting on accessories.

None of their hopes and aspirations looked likely to be fulfilled. None of the interns were going to any fashion week parties; they were working at least ten hours a day and, in any case, had no way of getting into these events. Disillusion began to set in, and the dazzling aura of their Paris adventure began to dim. The young women's fatigue and the collapse of their enthusiasm were becoming more and more obvious, and they pinned their final hopes of seeing the dream come true on their last few days in Paris. On the fifth day, at the end of the afternoon, they seemed particularly excited. Just before they left the showroom, Sarah took out her makeup bag and asked me excitedly if I had any eyeliner. She explained that there was a drinks party at Colette, the high fashion concept store on Rue Saint-Honoré. They'd been given permission to wear some pieces from Franck's previous collection, as a way of representing him at this highly sought-after event. The next day I asked them how it had gone. It turned out that they hadn't managed to get in, but they didn't seem particularly disappointed, as if they had somehow filtered out the frustration.

Over the period of several months that I worked at Franck's studio, I got the impression that the lives of the interns and assistants took place in two simultaneous temporalities: the present and a projection towards the future. For members of staff at the bottom of the hierarchy, excitement, enthusiasm and adrenalin didn't seem to be triggered by actual experiences but by projections, by the fleeting impression of a dream that seemed to be within reach, by the fact of imagining themselves as being there. Imagining themselves in an office on Rue Saint-Honoré, at a Vivienne Westwood or Colette after-party – a whole slew of possibilities that gave them the impression that they actually had a place in the dream. Every concrete disappointment was evacuated to leave room for a dream future or a future in the dream. On the one hand, this projection was fundamental for maintaining a sense of excitement and involvement, but on the other, it dispossessed them, preventing them from analysing the present. The fact that the present was not as exciting as they hoped did not present a problem, because it had already been colonized by other projected desires. As if 'being there' required them to race from dream to dream.

The day of the show

The arrival of the day of the fashion show signalled the end of my internship with Franck, as per our agreement. My day began at 9.00 am, while the interns had started at 6.30 am. They had gone to the location of the show at dawn for a first inspection before going to the showroom. Three young women I didn't recognize were already there by the time I arrived; they were former interns Pilar had called on to help. They had come by coach from Belgium and if they didn't have anywhere else to stay they would sleep in the studio where Sarah was staying. The collection, accessories and everything else that was needed were loaded into the van parked outside the showroom. Pilar carried out one small box then lit a cigarette and stood giving orders. Franck was already at the location where the show was taking place, keeping an eye on the decor that was being put up. Zoé wasn't there. Her back was so bad that she had gone to the doctor. Sarah looked exhausted and smelled of alcohol and cigarettes. She had bags under her eyes and her makeup was smudged. She whispered to me that she'd been out the previous evening at a bar in the 18th arrondissement, that she'd been drinking and taking drugs until dawn. She hadn't been home to change.

Once the van was loaded up, Sarah and I walked over to where the show was being held. Sarah was in a good mood because Franck had asked her if she'd like to go back and work for him in September to build another website. 'I love that guy, I'm so happy he asked me back, I'd do anything for him. I adore what he does, and I'll come back in September even if he doesn't pay me, I so want him to succeed, and what if I did too, how amazing would that be.' We arrived at where the show was taking place and I was struck by how well organized everything was, and by the number of technicians, set designers, photographers and all the other people who were there. The events company that was sponsoring Franck's show[5] was one of the best-known in Europe. It also organized fashion shows for major labels. It dealt with every stage of the event, from the conception to the video production and photography. The contrast between the extravagance of the show and Franck's 'domestic' scale of production was striking.

Outside, the catering team that had been brought over from Belgium was setting up, ready to serve prawn fritters and white wine to the guests as they waited for the show to begin. The show was taking place in the evening in a magnificent rococo-style ballroom. A backstage area had been set up in the orchestra pit of a vast auditorium. Tables for the thirty-odd hairdressers and makeup artists had already been set out, along with a long table for all the workers and the area that would be used to put together the models' outfits. The organization was so efficient that we, the small army of interns and assistants, had nothing to do, at least until it was time to start dressing the models. We sat in a corner around a large table. Because each of the fifteen models needed her own dresser, Pilar had asked each of us to find some volunteers. Sarah had asked a couple of her friends, one of whom was studying fashion journalism in Paris, and the other fashion design in Brussels. Louise, the aspiring intern who had come for an interview two days earlier, was also there, sitting at the table with the rest of us. There were nine of us in total, including the current crop of interns, and former and future interns.

---

[5] The company paid for every aspect of the fashion show: vans for transporting the collection, food for the guests, the rental of the space, technicians, models, hairdressers, makeup artists. It was a Belgian society, which explains why it had decided to sponsor the event.

Pilar and Franck were nowhere to be seen, the space was huge, and there was delicious food for us to eat. All this made for a relaxed atmosphere, despite the impending show. Suddenly Louise announced to no one in particular that she would have loved to do the internship but that it wasn't going to work out because they weren't going to pay her expenses. A lively exchange between the interns took place about their various internships, describing scandalous behaviour as well as their rather less frequent positive experiences (three out of a total of ten) – tales of tyrannical and abusive bosses at women's magazines, communications agencies and fashion houses. Everyone was sharing their worst experiences in tones of utter disgust, describing figures that seemed almost like caricatures. I tried to write down as much of these stories as I could. Occasionally I reacted to what I heard, but I felt uncomfortable and not altogether authorized to comment. What was clear from this discussion was that the strategies adopted to deal with these abuses of authority varied. Louise declared she would never accept such 'abuse', not being paid, and would insist on mutual respect. Although she claimed to be 'super-motivated, super-passionate', she also insisted she wasn't 'an idiot': she didn't have 'sucker written on [her] forehead'. Anne, one of Franck's former interns, had found a way to mitigate the power dynamic imposed by Pilar and became, as Pilar herself told me one day, her 'favourite intern'. She explained that at the beginning of her internship she cried every day and was ready to leave because of Pilar's abuse, but that, on the advice of her mother, she began to defer to her:

> I became a bit of a hypocrite, to tell the truth. I'd fake it, saying [in a compliant tone of voice]: 'Sure, thank you so much for your advice', you know? Then when she said something mean I'd just be like, 'Thank you', you know? Totally fake. And I swear to you she cried when I left. Even though she absolutely hated me at the start, or at least she was like, this is never going to work out.

Though it was true that she had managed to turn the situation around so that Pilar spoke normally to her, she still had to feed the meter for Pilar's car, hoover the floor and wash the dishes. There'd been a change in the way they interacted, but not in the tasks she had to do. When I asked her what she thought of Pilar, she said:

> I've not changed my opinion, she's the kind of person I can't stand [said with great emphasis], but she adores me. I managed to make her adore me and frankly it was worth it; I had to do an internship and I stuck it out for three months even though at the beginning I was literally counting the days, and I really thought I was going to quit.

Louise disapproved – 'it's not right that you had to act like that' – and then told us her worst experience as an intern, where her boss was jealous of her, and humiliated her in front of 'the entire open space', talked to her 'like a dog', invented 'absurd things' for her to do, and forced her to work 'impossible' hours. She cried for a month, and then quit. Everyone – former and current interns – said in unison: 'Then you'd better not come and work for Franck!' Anne told them that Franck and Pilar were 'the worst. Not only do they refuse to pay, but they expect the interns to do the cleaning, to stay at the studio even when there's nothing for them to do, and to work all weekend.' Sarah picked up on the last point:

> I work all weekend, every weekend. Since I got to Paris, I haven't stopped. Tomorrow the website is going live, and Wednesday, I don't care what they say, I'm taking it off. I can't stand it any longer, I'm going nuts ... Even if you work all through the weekend, however hard you work, it's never enough, and that's the problem.

Louise turned to Zoé and asked what her job was, but it was Michelle, another former intern, who answered: 'She's so into it, she's really committed, she never stops, she says yes to everything, she'll stay till 11 o'clock at night on a Friday if she has to.' According to Louise, her attitude could be explained by the fact that she'd been promised a job:

'When there's a promise behind it it's completely normal to give it everything you've got.' She told us how astonished she was by Pilar's offer. Pilar had told her to get in touch with her college to 'sort out' an internship agreement so that she could get away without paying her, and to find a job in a bar to make up for the fact that her expenses wouldn't be covered by the studio:[6]

> I'm passionate about fashion too, but I've got a life, I have to eat. I don't want to work twenty-four hours a day. Can you imagine spending six months working twenty-four hours a day? Sure, I'll do my internship then I'll work in a bar! ... At the end of it you're a wreck, you've lost forty kilos.

As the other women talked about how they were being exploited at Franck's studio, Michelle said she was so glad not to be working there any more, it was 'a real weight off her mind'. She said:

> I got the impression that people are passionate and completely driven, they have to really devote themselves body and soul, and that's not me at all. Our teachers, it's the same thing, three weeks before they tell you: 'Okay, you have to hand in twenty designs.' I have no desire to kill myself working to deliver their stupid project! Frankly, I just don't want to. I want to have time to enjoy what I do, otherwise it's just not worth it, it's complete exploitation. It's a lousy system. I've said to myself so many times that I don't want to stay in fashion. Whenever I think about my degree, I wonder why I ever thought of going into it.

In response, Louise said: 'They're looking for people who are psychologically strong, the kind of people who won't let themselves be broken. That's the point, that's the game, to break you to see if you can get up again or not.'

---

[6]   According to European law, only internships lasting less than one month can be unpaid. [AQ: see note 171 which says that internships longer than two months must be paid] This is why some fashion companies, in agreement with fashion schools, break longer stages into several shorter ones.

The conversation was interrupted at around 4.00 pm by Heike, Franck's assistant designer, who marched in to divide up the volunteer dressers who would be helping each model to get changed. We all walked over to another part of the space. Photos taken during the fittings were stuck to the wall, showing the models wearing the outfits they had been designated. Post-its with notes about which accessories were to be used were stuck to each image. Each of us had been given a rail on which all the 'looks' for the model we were dressing were assembled. An identical photograph to the one that was stuck on the wall was also fixed to each hanger, so that we could put together all the accessories correctly. Each 'girl' had at least two changes, and it was vital to be both fast and accurate, as Heike told us all in English.

The models were beginning to arrive; they turned up in waves, because they were coming straight from other shows. They were Brazilian, Dutch, French, Kenyan, American and Russian. I had been assigned to Jo, who, according to a note stuck to the rail, was a sixteen-year old Canadian. Many of the young women were exhausted; Paris Fashion Week is the last fashion week, after New York, London and Milan, and they had done all or some of them already. The army of hairdressers and makeup artists were also beginning to arrive, and in the space of an hour the auditorium was transformed into a gigantic beauty salon, with mirrors everywhere, boxes filled with hair mousse and other products, and the sound of dozens of hairspray canisters and hairdryers blending with music. Each model had two or three people clustered around her. As the show approached, journalists, celebrities and photographers began to arrive backstage. There were people armed with cameras and video cameras, everyone smiling at everyone else. Franck was giving interviews to different television stations.

On the screens we could see hundreds of awkward-looking people waiting at the entrance, sipping drinks they had been offered. The activity backstage suddenly intensified, the atmosphere became electric: the show was about to begin. Technicians were communicating with each other by radio while Heike gave us instructions through a megaphone. She was assisted by a young, androgynous-looking English girl, even bossier than she was. Heike introduced me to Jo who, like the other models, was already made up and with her hair done. We took our places alongside 'our' clothes rail. Jo dropped her backpack to the floor. I spotted a Hello Kitty doll inside it. She looked exhausted. She took off her clothes, visibly reluctant to reveal her body in front of so many people. Although she tried not to show her naked body, I noticed that she was wearing flesh-coloured patches over her nipples, as if she was trying to preserve a few inches of privacy.

The models were lined up in the order they would be going out behind the black curtain that separated the backstage area from the corridor that led to the catwalk. A member of staff from the events agency was waiting for a signal to start. The tension was palpable. On a screen we could see the packed front of house, and we could hear the music. There were film stars sitting in the front row, behind a crowd of dozens of photographers. The models started to move, the show had started. We took our places, ready for the first changes.

Very soon it was over, although I had the impression that it had barely begun. Franck came backstage, triumphant, with a trolley of buckets filled with bottles of champagne. He opened one, to general euphoria and a round of excited applause and shouts of delight. Dozens of cameras were there to immortalize the moment when Franck and the models were toasted. This really was the dream. Film stars rushed up to congratulate him and be photographed with him, as though to confirm that they were part of the same world. Pilar, who had been drinking since early in the afternoon, was visibly tipsy. The interns hung back, standing together with their glasses of champagne. I stood and chatted with a photographer and a journalist who were asking me about my research and giving me their cards so that we could stay in touch. Gradually the frenzy died down, the lights were switched on, the room emptied, the music was turned off. All that remained were a few bottles of champagne, some photographers and journalists, and a handful of people. The show had only been over for twenty minutes when Pilar shouted and clapped her hands at the interns: 'That's it girls! Time to put everything away and load up the van, it's parked outside, hurry up!' Everyone seemed a bit startled by her command and the way she formulated it, but after a brief moment of astonishment, everyone turned back to their conversations. I tried to catch the eyes of the interns, and saw expressions of disappointment and irritation. For them, the dream was over.

Half an hour later, I left. Pilar, Franck and his partner were sitting on the terrace of a bar by the theatre drinking wine with some Belgian pop stars, while the interns were loading up the van a few metres away. I went over to them and saw Zoé in tears. 'It's because of Pilar', Sarah said. By now it was 11.00 pm. The interns were exhausted and furious with Pilar, who had told them to go to the showroom, unload the van and get everything ready for the next day.

I was as shocked as they were, and told them I thought it was an outrageous thing to be expected to do. Increasingly ill at ease, I excused myself for not helping them, explaining that it was not because of a lack of solidarity but in order to make it clear that there are limits. I'd hardly uttered these words than I realized how stupid I sounded, and, confused and embarrassed, I didn't know what else to say. Manon made her resentment clear: 'It's easy for you, but we've got our internship to finish, we're going to be evaluated.' She asked me if I thought that loading the truck was a 'humiliating' thing to be asked to do. I responded that no activity is humiliating *per se*, it wasn't really about that, but once more I felt an embarrassment that was both moral and political,[7] because Manon was absolutely right: I was able

---

[7] This kind of moral and political discomfort is not uncommon in participant observation. See M. Benquet, *Encaisser!* and S. Chauvin, *Les Agences de la précarité: Journaliers à Chicago*, Paris, Le Seuil, 2010.

to make this decision because I wasn't being evaluated, unlike them, who were being evaluated all the time. The young women drove off in the van.

A few minutes later, Thomas, Franck's partner, came over to tell me that the taxi that was taking us to the restaurant where a celebratory dinner was being held had arrived, and that it was out of the question for me not to be there. I hesitated: going to a restaurant while the interns were working seemed wrong. Thomas saw my hesitation, insisted, and assured me that the interns would be coming along later as soon as they'd unloaded the van. I found myself in a taxi with Franck, Thomas and Patty, the pattern-cutter. Franck was talking about the evening, singing the praises of the work of a friend of his, a well-known choreographer who had come from abroad especially to choreograph the show. He then began to go on and on about how sick he was of not having any money; 'it makes me so uncomfortable to ask people to work for free'. I couldn't help thinking that he never seemed uncomfortable regarding all the interns who worked for nothing, dealing with the day-to-day aspects of running the studio. Then he began talking about his next collection, excitedly describing the shapes and forms he was working on. The collection that had just been presented was already in the past, and he was already projecting into the future.

Patty was offended, because Pilar had said in front of her to two young designers: 'If you want to become rich, take Patty on for what she's really worth and then pay her what she thinks she's worth.' Patty found this very insulting. Franck turned to Pilar and said, mischievously: 'Anyway, you're paid the same as she is.' After a beat of silence, he added, in a kind of detached tone, as if it was nothing to do with him: 'Pilar is horrible, she been making the interns cry again, it's her fault if the girls don't come along to the restaurant, she really should have gone to the showroom with them instead of having a drink with us.'

I said that I found it absurd that the girls hadn't come with us to celebrate the success of the show, after all the work they'd put in. Thomas agreed and called Manon on his mobile. She told him that even if they wanted to come they couldn't because it was too late to get the métro. And anyway, Zoé didn't want to see Pilar. Thomas insisted that they come and said he'd pay for a taxi both ways. They took a long time to agree. Manon pointed out that this didn't solve the problem for Zoé, whose aunt lived in the suburbs, and it was impossible for her to take a taxi the whole way there, but she didn't have anywhere to sleep in Paris because there was no room at Sarah's friend's studio. I asked to speak to her and suggested that she sleep over at the place where I was staying, though I pointed out that we would have to share a bed. I wondered if the suggestion was appropriate, but the thought that after all the work she'd put in she wouldn't be able to celebrate seemed outrageously unjust.

We arrived at the restaurant near Bastille. It was just past midnight. Franck had reserved a private dining room on the ground floor. There were about twenty guests, most of whom had already arrived and were sitting around the large table. I went straight over to the smaller table, where no one was sitting, but Thomas took me by the arm and told me to come and sit with them, next to Patty. Franck explained to the guests that he wouldn't be able to pay for dinner, but that he'd cover part of the drinks bill. Thomas ordered two bottles of champagne, which he said that he was paying for to celebrate his partner's success. The guests were a mix of singers, DJs, photographers, choreographers and journalists, who all enthusiastically raised their glasses for a toast.

Patty asked me why the interns weren't there. Because our conversation was covered by the background noise, she confided in me that she'd stopped working full-time for Franck because she couldn't bear to see how he mistreated the interns, couldn't bear to seem them crying all the time and working so hard for no payment. For her, this was pure exploitation. She told me that during the previous fashion week Zoé had slept on the floor of the showroom, 'on the tiles'. At last the interns arrived. I was sitting at the large table, while they all went and sat at the smaller table away from the main party. It was clear that my position as an academic was valued by Thomas and placed me higher up in the hierarchy, and thus in the dining room. Uncomfortable, the interns sat down; they did not exchange a word with the other guests the entire evening. Pilar, who was sitting at the other end of the main table, stood up to make a toast. She was clearly drunk, to the point that she was having trouble standing, and she declared in a loud voice, in English: 'I wanna do a speech: Franck, we all love you, you're the best!' Everyone clapped and smiled.

A few minutes later, she stood up again; this time people were a little embarrassed, and so I took the opportunity to stand up myself and propose, slightly provocatively, a toast to the interns. Patty and Thomas stood, and everyone clapped; the interns looked very embarrassed but were nonetheless clearly pleased. At 2.00 am we were ready to leave. The bill was 30 euros a head, and the interns had to pay for themselves. Franck called a taxi to take him and a few select friends to an exclusive nightclub that was only open to those who came with an introduction, and where the cost of a drink was astronomical.

I waved to Franck, reminding him that I wouldn't be at the showroom the next day. 'It's over?' he asked, looking a bit sad. I told him that our regular collaboration was over, but that I wasn't going to disappear. In the general bustle, Thomas forgot to give the interns money to pay for their taxi. Manon, Zoé and took one together and I told them I'd pay for it. When we arrived at the small studio I'd been lent Zoé was as embarrassed as I was by the forced intimacy and thanked me multiple times for my hospitality. I did my best to put her at ease and we went up to bed on the mezzanine floor. A few hours later Zoé's alarm went off and she got up to get ready to go to the showroom. I let a few days go by before writing to Sarah for news. She wrote back to me:

I'll tell you about it properly, but Pilar's gone too far this time. I'm going to get a terrible report on my internship, she called me a liar and said I was disrespectful, because I didn't go into work on Wednesday, I had a urinary tract infection, on Thursday and Friday too. I got a doctor's note for three days, so I wasn't worried, but she went absolutely insane, insulted me, and then finally she fired me. Fortunately I'd done all my hours by then, but still. I'm really pissed off. I feel completely abused.

Untangling emotions

Both during and after my 'internship', I felt filled with disgust[8] – a feeling of nausea prevented me from continuing my fieldwork in a milieu I couldn't take any longer, as well as a moral and physical disgust towards myself and my body. Worried that this was affecting my capacity for analysis, I tried to push it away. But disgust is a very specific affect, as Christiane Vollaire has shown,[9] creating in the subject a conflict with rational thought. Through its power over and through the body, disgust attacks the supremacy of reason and conscience. Arriving at the journey of reflection that follows research, and acknowledging the disgust, is a way of grasping the power of the emotions experienced during the research, as well as their heuristic value during the analysis of the data.

Emotions and affects play a central role in the production and upholding of hierarchies in fashion. Emotional engagement is vital in order to be able to 'be there': from the earliest days of my internship, Pilar initiated me into the dynamics of complicity, injustice and

---

[8]   In the introduction to the issue of *Ethnologie française* devoted to disgust, it is pointed out that the interest in the subject in question comes from 'a fascination for the opposite of decoration' (D. Memmi *et al*, 'Introduction: La fabrication du dégoût', *Ethnologie française*, vol. 41, no. 1, 2011, pp. 5–16). It is worth noting that in the case of my project, it was actually being behind the scenes of the dream that produced this disgust.

[9]   C. Vollaire, 'Le tabou du dégoût', *Ethnologie française*, vol. 41, no. 1, 2011.

competition, when she fired André. Even though I thought that the fact that I was doing research implied keeping a certain distance, I was immediately 'affected'[10] and deeply 'subjectified' by what I observed. During my 'internship',[11] I suffered – in spite of my conceptual tools and attempts to remain objective – from the modalities of the relationships between the people around me, which had an impact on my body and changed the way I saw myself. For example, I repeatedly suffered from pains in my back and shoulders and frequently had a knot in my stomach. Even though I considered the emphasis on appearance excessive, I couldn't stop myself feeling fat, inelegant, old, ugly and inadequate. Yet I was incapable of realizing that the way I was judging myself had been exacerbated precisely because the brutality of the world I was observing had rubbed off on me.

Being there in the role of anthropologist was a difficult ordeal: in my emotional confusion I was unable to distinguish between 'objective' data and my own feelings. I didn't know what role or status to give to the emotions triggered by the different situations, and which, in spite of myself, overwhelmed me. How should I deal with emotions, and more importantly, *my* emotions?

According to the American anthropologists Catherine Lutz and Lila Abu-Lughod, emotions are 'tied to tropes of interiority and granted ultimate facticity by being located in the natural body' and 'stubbornly retain their place, even in all but the most recent anthropological discussions, as the aspect of human experience least subject to control, least constructed or learned (hence most universal), least public, and therefore least amenable to sociocultural analysis.'[12]

---

[10]   J. Favret-Saada, *Les Mots, la Mort, les Sorts*, Paris, Gallimard, 1977.

[11]   These aspects became more acute during the internship, because of the effect of being immersed in the field. During the previous year, I did occasional fieldwork, but never for more than two days at a time, after which I went back to my normal life.

[12]   C. A. Lutz, 'Introduction: Emotion, discourse and the politics of everyday life', in L. Abu-Lughod and C. A. Lutz (eds), *Language and the Politics of Emotion (Studies in Emotion and Social Interaction)*, Cambridge University Press, 1990 (digital edn, 2000).

During my research, managing my emotions was a process filled with conflict: in spite of the space they took up, I continued to think of them in a 'negative way'. My understanding of the world of fashion took place through a succession of particularly 'harsh' episodes that obliged me to consider situations through a different lens than the one I had originally adopted. Among these 'decentrings' was the one that led me to consider emotions and feelings – beginning with my own – from an entirely unfamiliar perspective.

During my 'internship', a number of situations arose that put me into an awkward position politically, and made me uncomfortable, even shocked. At certain points in my research – when André was fired, or the interns spent the evening after the show loading up the van – the research categories available to me were no longer useful in terms of understanding the situations. Although at first I thought it was my emotions tainting my vision of the situations, I understood later that in fact they were elements illustrating the power of the process of subjectification in fashion.

The anthropologist's mission is to offer a 'total understanding'[13] of the subject being observed through a multiplication of points of view and at different scales. In spite of that, during my internship I became part of the dynamic of the relationships and conflicts, to the point of being incapable of looking at a situation from a different position to the one that Pilar had assigned me. When it came to analysing the data, I realized that my ethnographic material was completely infused by 'subjectification', a result of these relationships, and of the emotions triggered by my research. I found myself, without even realizing it, unable to displace and decentre myself. The anger and hostility I felt towards Pilar prevented me from seeing her other than from the

---

[13] M. Agier, 'Le dire-vrai de l'anthropologue: Réflexions sur l'enquête ethnographique du point de vue de la rencontre, des subjectivités et du savoir', Ethnographiques.org, no. 30, 2015.

perspective of an intern, the position she had assigned me. To a certain extent I experienced, no less than the rest of the staff, injustices and abuse on an individual, subjective level. This stood in the way of me being able to take a more critical perspective or of seeing the entire chain of domination, within which Pilar herself was implicated not only as a bully but also as a victim, for she too was in a structurally precarious position.

The power of subjectification through emotion reduces the effects of domination to the scale of the individual or the interpersonal, thus depoliticizing them. The time that passed between the period of ethnographic research and the period of writing allowed me to consider the 'failure' of the subjectivized gathering of material as an element itself, a specificity of the world that I was describing, a world in which emotions and subjectivity take up so much space that decentring becomes difficult, and in this way, I was able to gain a political perspective on the relationships, domination and structural violence in fashion labour.

This is how, in the professional world, abuses of authority and domination are simultaneously normalized and 'exceptionalized'. If Franck, his team and the interns accepted Pilar's behaviour, even though they recognized it as bullying, it was because this kind of subjectification is not unusual in fashion. *The Devil Wears Prada* is a perfect illustration of the paradoxical phenomenon of the 'normalization' and the 'exceptionalization' of abuses of power: in a comic register, both book and film show the abuses to which the entourage of the editor-in-chief of a fashion magazine are subjected. The protagonist, Miranda Priestly, inspired by Anna Wintour, editor-in-chief of American *Vogue*, is tyrannical, authoritarian and bullying. In the film, power relationships are 'glamourized', accepted as an intrinsic element of the world of luxury and beauty, and thus legitimized as the price to be paid for attending events like Paris Fashion Week or having lavish outfits at one's disposal. In the course of my research I learned that these power relationships are recognized as such, while being normalized because they are understood to be part of the rules of the game, and exceptionalized because they are part of the dream and thus unique, special and extraordinary. When domination is seen in these terms, it is reduced through personification to being subjective and intersubjective. Miranda Priestly, in the film, and Pilar, at Franck's studio, are not seen by workers as embodying a structurally unequal system that legitimizes their behaviour, they are simply perceived as individuals with bullying natures. The interns never considered that Franck was just as responsible for the abuses they were subjected to, even though he never intervened to put a stop to Pilar's excesses and it was he who required them to work so many extra hours in order to meet the production deadlines.

This phenomenon is what sociologist Raquel Sherman calls 'normalization'.[14] Sherman uses this notion to analyse the way in which workers apprehend the structural inequality that distinguishes them from the wealthy guests in luxury hotels. In this context, she writes that inequality also takes the form of the self-subordination required by these workers during their interactions with guests.[15] She also notes, as I found in my research, that these asymmetries and self-subordination are assumed to be assets and that, although there are frequent discussions about them, they are never criticized.

'Being there' – whether 'there' signifies, in the case of *The Devil Wears Prada*, the heart of the production of the fantasy worlds of fashion, close to one of the most powerful figures in that milieu, or 'working with Franck, going to Paris and taking part in fashion week' – is a privilege that implies the normalization of a certain type of domination and the emotional and subjective organization of work relationships. Even when it is recognized as such, domination is

[14]   R. Sherman, *Class Acts*, p. 17.
[15]   Ibid., p. 57.

identified as a characteristic that participates in the construction of the exception that is the world of fashion. The word 'privilege' is rich in meaning, the Latin root meaning 'personal law'[16] or an exclusive right. A right which by definition does not apply to everyone; it is the right of a minority, an elite, that of desire, which also constructs its 'exceptionalism' through the fact of being beyond the rule of law.

[16] From the Latin *privelegium*, from *privus* (private) and *lex*, law, in other words personal advantage allowed by exception to common law.

9

Knowing How to 'Be There': Work Relationships

The Deauville shoot

Mia had been contacted by Ludo, a fashion photographer at the beginning of his career, who had used his connections to get a commission for a fashion story for Italian *Vogue*'s website. Although on paper at least he and Mia were both considered industry insiders, Mia's career, before she was signed to Wiew, along with her accumulated social capital, meant that she had much more experience than Ludo, who had only a few projects under his belt. Aware of her dominant position, she agreed not to charge a fee for the shoot, on condition that she got to select the theme and make the aesthetic decisions, which from the start proved to be a point of contention with Ludo. The hairdresser and makeup artist were also represented by Mia's agency Wiew; Amélie was chosen by Mia because 'she's cool and fun, she livens things up', while Léonard was chosen by Rebeka, the Wiew booker in charge of hair and makeup artists. During negotiations with Ludo, Mia also insisted on my being there during the shoot.

We were told to meet at eight in the morning, at Place de la Nation in Paris. Mia and I were late; we arrived by taxi, loaded down with bags of clothes and accessories for the shoot. Ludo, who was responsible for all the expenses incurred over the weekend, had negotiated two days in the Royal Deluxe Suite and various public areas in the Grand Belvedere Hotel in Deauville[1] for free in exchange for giving the hotel a credit in

---

[1]   Not the hotel's real name.

the magazine. The rest of the team were already waiting by the minibus that Ludo had rented for the occasion. Wearing her usual sunglasses, Mia got out of the taxi and asked those present to help load the boot of the minibus. Steeve, Ludo's assistant, not being francophone, didn't quite understand Mia's instructions, which visibly irritated her. 'Who is this idiot?' she said, loudly enough for everyone to hear. Ludo explained in a conciliatory tone that Steeve was his Australian assistant. Mia muttered something else under her breath and then said, loud enough for everyone to hear: 'I'm the star here, is that clear?' She proceeded to introduce me to the team. I greeted Ludo with a Parisian kiss on both cheeks. He sported a Mohican, a moustache, oversized black clothes and military-style boots. Then I greeted Steeve, who had an athletic physique, long hair and was wearing sports clothes; Amélie, the hairdresser, who was around forty, small, brunette, with broad hips, and who spoke with a pronounced southern French accent; Léonard, the New Zealand-born makeup artist, who was younger than the rest of us and looked very dapper, with his eyebrows carefully drawn in, and who spoke French with a strong accent; and finally the two models, Kandaka and Ayda, who were standing a little apart from everyone else. Kandaka had dark skin and a shaved head; she wore jeans, a shirt, an expensive coat and a pair of designer ankle boots, and had a large leather handbag hanging over her shoulder. Ayda was also dark-skinned, with short, curly hair held back with little hairclips, and though she too had on jeans, a shirt and a jacket, she was wearing a tatty pair of vinyl ballet slippers and the backpack slung over her shoulder gave her the air of a schoolgirl.

We all got into the van: the models sat in the back with Léonard, while Mia, Amélie and I sat in the second row, and Ludo and Steeve, who was driving, sat in the front. The models put on their headphones and dozed off within minutes, while the rest of us chatted.

Mia told Ludo in a condescending tone of voice that his 'look' didn't work at all, his Mohican was 'naff', he needed to cut it and change the way he dressed to improve his image. Ludo listened and thanked her politely for her advice. The combination of his subversive sartorial aesthetic and his obliging manner, which made me think of a sales assistant or someone who worked at a reception desk, was slightly unnerving, creating a kind of dissonance. I asked him to tell me about his professional path. After studying business in Paris, he had moved abroad and found a job with a yacht rental business. After a few years he began to yearn for a 'more bohemian, unconventional' lifestyle. He taught himself fashion photography and, after several local advertising campaigns, he felt that there were no more 'challenges' locally and decided to return to Paris. Ludo ended up in fashion not because he was passionate about it but because he liked the lifestyle; he wanted to distance himself from a conventional way of life:

> It's true that I'm attracted by people who are a bit wild. I love extravagant behaviour, I find it really attractive, people who don't want to get old, who don't want to be out of touch, who don't want to conform. People who are full of life, who sparkle, it's all so attractive and flamboyant. That's the kind of thing you're more likely to find among artists, not among the kinds of people who make investments for capitalist businesses, that kind of thing, you know, it's not very sexy.[2]

When I asked him what he was doing to break into the saturated Parisian market, he answered that you need to be a 'real conquistador': 'You're not a photographer if you're not an entrepreneur. To be a photographer requires an enormous capacity for coming out of your cocoon, seeking out clients, persuading people, finding an agent, showing your work, talking about the shoots you want to do, about ideas, it's about seduction . . . You understand?'

After a few hours' drive we arrived at the large, imposing hotel in Deauville. A valet greeted us, indicating that we should leave the van

---

[2]   The publishing group Condé Nast, which owns *Vogue* and for which Ludo works for free, is the absolute epitome of the category of 'capitalist business'.

in the car park by the immense swimming pool. We then followed him to the lift that took us up to our suite: 85 square metres, 1,250 euros a night in low season. We were shown the meeting room that would serve as the dressing and makeup area. Immediately Léonard and Amélie began rearranging the tables. They took out a vast number of brushes, makeup, tweezers, tongs, hairpieces and straighteners from their suitcases and laid them out. Amélie began styling the wigs that the models would be wearing while Mia started hanging up the mostly black clothes, and selecting pieces to create 'looks'. Meanwhile Steeve was setting up the lights in the suite according to Ludo's instructions. Ayda and Kandaka were sitting in the improvised dressing area, busy with their smartphones and listening to music, not saying a word to anyone.

Once Ayda's makeup was finished, she put on a wig with a fringe and long straight brown hair with coppery highlights. Unlike Kandaka, who had a strong, athletic physique, Ayda was slim and delicate-looking. The sophisticated hairpiece and long, fake eyelashes contrasted strongly with the adolescent jeans and tatty ballet slippers she'd been wearing. She told me she was nineteen, and was born in Paris to Cameroonian parents. She had been working as an usher at the Palais des Congrès[3] in Paris when a talent scout approached her on the street one day. Although her mother and boyfriend – a hairdresser in a Paris suburb – disapproved, she decided to try her luck as a model, in the hope that it might allow her to put some money aside.

It was nearly lunchtime. We'd been given a special menu by the hotel, but even so the cheapest sandwich was 33 euros. Ludo asked Steeve to go to the nearest supermarket and buy some food. Taking orders was complicated, given that everyone had some kind of food

---

[3]   The Palais des Congrès is a large convention centre in Paris, where concerts and musicals are often staged.

allergy or preference: Léonard was on the Paleo diet, so wasn't eating carbohydrates, the models wanted salad without any dressing, Ludo wanted 'something filling', and Amélie something without too many calories, because she was trying to lose weight. Given his limited budget, Steeve came back with some bread, two packets of cheese, some pre-washed salad leaves, a packet of cheap chocolate biscuits, sweets, crisps and Coca Cola. Mia, Léonard and Amélie complained to Steeve about the poor quality of the food, which clearly annoyed him, though he didn't say anything. Once lunch was over, the models put on long evening dresses, heels, hats and fur cuffs, and everyone left the dressing area for the suite.

Immediately there were tensions between Mia and Ludo. Ludo wanted the 'girls' to pose in sexually suggestive positions: 'Kandaka, lie down on the counter, open your legs, put the bottle of whisky between your thighs, and throw me a sexy look.' Mia reacted with horror, blurting out, 'What the hell?' Ludo replied: 'Hey, it's fashionable and glamorous all at the same time.' Mia said: 'Excuse me, but that doesn't mean anything, what you just said, and anyway, that's not glamour, it's just vulgar. If you do that I'm not having my name on the story.' After conferring in private for a few minutes, they came back and the session got going again. Now it was Mia giving instructions to the two young women. Because she didn't know their names she called them 'babe' or 'love', as is not uncommon in fashion.

The agreement with the Belvedere didn't include staying at the hotel, which meant that we had to be out by 8.00 pm, after four or five photo sessions in the suite. We were staying in a two-star hotel, La Pension du Lys. We unpacked our things in the two rooms that Ludo had booked, one for the three men and the other, a duplex, for the five women. Kandaka and Ayda, who had never met before the shoot, were sharing a double bed, while Amélie, Mia and I were sleeping in two single beds. I was sharing one with Mia. The shower room was tiny, with no window or hot water, and the only window in the room looked directly onto a wall. It was in marked contrast to the suite in the Belvedere. We unpacked and then went down to the minibus. Ludo had found a reasonably priced brasserie for dinner. Once we'd all sat down he told us that he would be paying for the food, but asked us not to order anything too expensive. All of us except for the models were expected to pay for our own drinks.

During the meal no one addressed a single word to either the two models or to Steeve. After we'd eaten we went straight back to the hotel because we were getting up early the next morning: we had to make the most of the hours of daylight for the exterior photos that were to be taken on the beach, in the garden and by the pool.

After a quick breakfast, we made our way to the Belvedere. While Ayda was being made up I had a brief conversation with Kandaka, who initially responded to my questions reluctantly, as if it were an obligation, then began to enjoy the conversation, and allowed me to glimpse something genuine in her. In spite of her cut-glass English accent, it turned out that she was half-Sudanese and half-Kenyan. She had grown up in an upscale neighbourhood in Nairobi. She told me about the stereotypes she has to deal with as an African woman, and described the absurd requests she receives from photographers: 'You can't complain, ever, even when they ask you to do things that are objectively impossible. If you do they'll never call you back and you'll get a reputation for being a pain in the neck. If you're not cool, there are hundreds of girls who can replace you.' She told me that despite the drawbacks, working in fashion is a privilege and a fantastic opportunity, because fashion is everywhere, even in Nairobi slums, where residents who don't have running water or electricity nonetheless wear Nike trainers.

The time it took to reposition the spotlights between two photo sessions meant that everyone present had to find some way of passing the time. Mobile phones had a vital role. The workers were constantly sending photos, chatting on various social media platforms, making calls, taking selfies. Ayda and Kandaka talked neither to each other nor to anybody else, while Mia, Léonard and Amélie shared their impressions about various colleagues they'd encountered professionally: 'cool', 'not cool', 'good vibes', 'bad vibes'. Competence and ability were never mentioned, and what came out of these hours of gossip was a taxonomy of behaviour and characters divided up into those who they could bear to work with and those who were just impossible.

Apart from during the photo sessions and the tetchy exchanges between Ludo and Mia, the only moments of real tension were during conversations between the workers and their agents. During the forty-eight hours we spent together, everyone received at least one call from their booker. These phone conversations were usually an occasion to overdo their enthusiasm. When their phones rang, people who usually seemed consumed by boredom were transformed physically: Léonard sat up straight in his chair, a big smile appearing on his face as he told Rebeka, his booker, that it was 'great', and he was having 'an amazing time'. Mia received a call from Angelo. 'My love,' she said, 'I'm adoring the shoot.' At the end of a call, the workers would immediately drop their smiles, and their bodies would immediately slump back into their position of ennui. They slouched with their chins towards their knees, and went back to fiddling with their phones.

The contrast between the enthusiasm they showed during their conversations and their subsequent physical lethargy reached its apogee when Léonard received another call from Rebeka. I heard him say: 'Tomorrow? Sure, brilliant!' He hung up, stopped smiling and yawned loudly as he ran his hands through his hair. He told us he had to leave immediately for New York to assist Hector on a publicity shoot. Hector was the artistic director of a large luxury cosmetics line. He was paid a multimillion-euro salary. The problem for Léonard was not the imminent departure, but 'cotton buds'. He told me that Hector insisted that there be a specific number of cotton buds on his makeup table; they had to be green and laid out in a 20-centimetre square. Every time they worked together Léonard was responsible for the cotton buds, and this time he wasn't going to have time to buy them, which was extremely serious and would put Hector in a 'filthy mood'.

It was time for lunch. Steeve was about to go down to the van buy food from the supermarket, when there was a minor rebellion, led by Amélie. She told the assistant that she refused to eat the same shitty food as the day before. Mia and Léonard agreed and Steeve, though he looked irritated, said nothing except to point out that he'd just followed Ludo's orders. Amélie handed some money to Steeve, saying that she would rather pay out of her own purse than eat the same thing as yesterday. The others did the same. I offered to go with Steeve to Trouville, the neighbouring town, to look for a bakery and some better-quality salads. In the van I finally had a chance to talk to the young man, who angrily told me that he'd known perfectly well the previous day that the food he had bought was awful, but that Ludo had given him twenty euros to feed eight people and he couldn't perform miracles. He told me that was why he hated fashion: 'There's no money in fashion, ever', while on advertising and lifestyle shoots everyone is properly paid, fed and given decent accommodation.

We got back to Deauville and the team was happy with the food we'd purchased from a good bakery. We got back to work quickly, because the owner of the two Afghan hounds who were to pose with Ayda and Kandaka by the pool had already arrived. In both the colour and the style of her hair she bore an uncanny resemblance to her dogs. She wore a belt decorated with metal dogs that only accentuated this odd fusion. The photo session began: Ayda was wearing a black leather skirt, high heels, a cloche hat and a silk scarf, but her upper body was naked. She lay on a chaise longue by the pool, while Kandaka waded into the water up to her thighs in a long gold dress, high-heeled sandals and fishnet stockings. The enthusiastic owner of the two dogs whispered to me that her dogs 'love doing fashion shoots; they've done films, but they prefer fashion'. No one apart from me seemed surprised by this statement.

The tyranny of cool[4]

The distinctive nature of this shoot was in the fact that it came about as a result of Ludo's initiative, and was not commissioned by a client. In addition, all the young workers were of relatively similar socio-professional status, and were all there for the same reason: to accumulate symbolic capital in order to increase their value on the labour market. As Léonard said to me: '*Vogue* is like the fashion Oscars.' This shared motivation, as well as the informal interactions, the acting out of friendship, the familiar way in which everyone addressed one another, the fact that everyone talked to each other in an affectionate register ('darling', 'babe', 'love', 'honey') could make it seem that this kind of work situation is 'horizontal'. However, a deeper analysis reveals that behind these linguistic and relational registers there exists a hierarchy that is interiorized to the point of rendering entirely unnecessary any trace of exterior authority: everyone knows their own and everyone else's place, as well as the expected modes of interaction. During the shoot, the positions of power were held by the photographer and the stylist, because they conceived the artistic dimension of the images produced. In Deauville, since Ludo was a neophyte on the Parisian market, it was Mia who wielded authority: she was the 'star', as she made quite clear when she first met the team, aware of her position of symbolic power – although, since it was not entirely consolidated, she was obliged to pronounce the fact. Steeve acted like all the other studio assistants I've met during my research: his job involved setting up the lighting and any manual work required

[4]   The title of this section is borrowed from the title of a documentary about the rise and power of Apple: Sylvain Bergère, *La Tyrannie du cool*, 2011.

– the carrying out of which brooked no discussion – and accepted criticism, 'invisibilization', and silent forms of abuse. Though Mia called him a 'cretin', he was actually an art school graduate, who held strong opinions and was quite capable of sticking to his guns. But it was vital that such characteristics not be in the forefront of the personality of a studio assistant,[5] which explains why he did what he was told with no protest. During an interview, Mathilde, who used to work as a studio assistant, had this to say about her former job: 'The kinds of people who are chosen to do the job of assistant, they're the kinds of people you describe as "discreet", the kinds of people who don't say anything and who don't push themselves forward.' Both Amélie and Léonard owed their presence at the shoot to their experience as hair and makeup artists, but also to their manner in these kinds of work situations: Amélie was chosen by Mia 'because she's good-natured', and Léonard, who was unknown to anyone on the team because he had only just been signed to the Wiew agency, had proven to be 'cool', as Mia told me, which meant he had earned his place at the shoot.

Working in fashion requires knowing how to 'be there', that is, knowing the registers of subjectivity anticipated according to your professional role and your position in the hierarchy, while also acknowledging the position of others. Modelling, for example, requires, in addition to the aspects linked to the monitoring of her body and her appearance, a kind of 'invisibilization' in work situations, the establishment of a submissive, smiling manner. Generally in fashion, if one is not yet established and hopes to hold on to one's place, it is vital, according to Kandaka, not to complain and to 'stay cool'. The rule applies no less to models than to other workers.

In a saturated job market, *likability capital* is a value that makes all the difference. The reputation constructed through one's

5   B. Holmes, 'The flexible personality, for a new cultural critique', *transversal* (online magazine), January 2002: eipcp.net/transversal/1106/holmes/en/base_edit#_ftnref24.

work[6] means that when it comes down to equal or even inferior skills, it's the person who's 'cool' who is going to find it easier to get a job; as Léonard told me, 'bringing a good vibe to a shoot' counts for a great deal. Someone less endowed with these skills won't find it as easy to get into the profession. It's important to always be cheerful, smiling, motivated, enthusiastic, creative – even when the hours, the stress, the bullying, and the frustration that results from precariousness might well provoke an entirely different attitude.

The sociologist Rosalind Gill has described forms of inequality and precariousness that govern work in the 'cultural industries', despite the socially egalitarian and inclusive dimension often associated with these sectors of activity.[7] In fashion, too, *cool* is inscribed in contexts that are governed by precariousness and strongly defined hierarchies; it is both a cultural quality,[8] an attribution with a symbolic value and a type of personality,[9] that is to say a register of subjectivity that must be 'performed' in order for someone to 'be there'. As the situation described above shows, despite the apparent informality of these 'unconventional' – Ludo's word – professional domains, in reality there is a precise power structure that is manifested in the way some people are bullying (in this case Mia, but in other cases we have seen it has been photographers, designers or studio managers) and others are 'cool'.

Nonetheless, in Deauville, the 'tyranny of cool' was clearly manifested in the interactions between the workers and their agents. Despite the fact that they are all freelancers, people who work in fashion are not only obliged to accept the choices of their agents, but they must in addition remain pleasant, friendly and conciliatory with them, even when they actually disagree. Although the agency makes

---

[6] D. Hesmondhalgh and S. Baker, 'Creative work and emotional labour in the television industry', *Theory, Culture and Society*, vol. 25, no. 7–8, December 2008.

[7] R. Gill, 'Cool, creative and egalitarian: Exploring gender in project-based new media work in Europe', *Information, Communication and Society*, vol. 5, no. 1, 2002.

[8] G. Neff, E. Wissinger and S. Zukin, 'Entrepreneurial labor among cultural producers'.

[9] B. Holmes, 'The flexible personality'.

money through them, the interactions between the workers and their bookers are indicative of the workers' complete subordination to their agencies. They are unable to negotiate, complain, set down limits, or make demands of any kind, because the fact of being seen as someone who isn't 'cool' can have a considerable influence on their future job opportunities. To turn down offers of work, even unpaid, not to be constantly available by phone, not being pleasant enough with one's agent, can all lead to not getting any more work.

The philosopher Brian Holmes has formulated the notion of the 'flexible personality'[10] to describe the forms of subjectification required in post-Fordist employment. He argues that this flexible personality is the fruit of a new form of social control founded on cultural values – in the case of fashion, on the obligation to be 'cool'. But it also involves a system of self-regulation,[11] within which each worker knows her place and the part she must play. In this way, power has no need to be coercive in order to confirm the hierarchy, which is integrated in advance by the workers and subsequently established in the course of their interactions. Unlike the dynamics of power within businesses with salaried workers, when people are freelance, flexible, 'cool', autonomous and self-starting, as is the case in fashion, power relationships do not need to be 'performed' through the exercise of authority and can be concealed by relationships that appear to be egalitarian and affective.

Flexible relationships in cognitive work

The sociologist Pascal Gielen uses the concept of the 'art scene' to explore social organizations that are 'free of obligations but not of

---

10   Ibid.
11   For more on the question of self-regulation, see the afterword regarding societies of control, written in 1990 by Gilles Deleuze, in G. Deleuze, *Pourparlers, 1972–1990*, Paris, Minuit, 1990.

rules'.[12] The same notions can be applied to fashion, a professional world that is strictly regulated, but which appears to be flexible and informal because of the dearth of explicit obligations. As was seen during the Deauville shoot, the performance of a subjectivity corresponding to one's place in the hierarchy, as well as affect display in professional relationships, are fundamental rules for 'being there'. Inspired by the pioneering ideas of Arlie Hochschild,[13] several academics have focused on the role of affect and emotion in labour, proposing a range of forms of emotional labour.[14] But this awareness is also central to the notion of 'cognitive capitalism',[15] which leads to an entirely new kind of subordination, by constantly mobilizing subjectivity in the production process. In cognitive capitalism, subjectivity is the basis of production, which blurs the border between work and non-work. Work extends both temporally and symbolically over all the areas of life. In fashion, work is characterized by different kinds of flexible relationships: the flexible and porous relationship between work time and non-work time; the flexible relationship between equals, characterized by the blurred border between friendship and control; the flexible relationship with hierarchical superiors, which demands an acrobatic flexibility in order to follow the constant alternating between horizontal affectivity and vertical

---

[12] P. Gielen, 'The art scene: A clever working model for economic exploitation?'

[13] A. R. Hochschild, *The Managed Heart: Commercialization of Human Feeling*, Berkeley, University of California Press, 1983.

[14] I prefer the term emotional labour rather than affective labour, because, as Hesmondhalgh and Baker explain, the first is more sociological, while the second is a metaphor rather than an analytical tool ('Creative work and emotional labour in the television industry', p. 115.) For further discussion of this question, see K. Weeks, 'Life within and against work: Affective labor, feminist critique, and post-Fordist politics', *Ephemera*, vol. 7, no. 1, 2007; E. Dowling, 'Producing the dining experience: Measure, subjectivity and the affective artisan', *Ephemera*, vol. 7, no. 1, 2007.

[15] According to Yann Moulier-Boutang, the transformations brought about by cognitive capitalism are at the root of a structural crisis concerning the 'separation of the body/ force of work, the relationship between the active worker and his work tools, the end result of his activity, his own life, his place of work and the type of activity he performs in the type of job', Y. Moulier-Boutang, *Le Capitalisme cognitif: La nouvelle grande transformation*, Paris, Editions Amsterdam, 2007, p. 239.

authority; and the flexible relationship with oneself, which is necessary in order to know in which register of subjectivity one must place oneself depending on the situation.[16] In fashion, the subjectivity of workers is fundamental to the management of the flexible relationship that exists between the rigidity of the hierarchy and the 'informal' nature of personal interactions.

---

[16]   E. Goffman, *The Presentation of Self in Everyday Life*; *Behavior in Public Places: Notes on the Social Organization of Gatherings*.

10

Getting into Fashion, Creating a Persona, Coping in Fashion, Getting out of Fashion

Getting into fashion

I met Philip in a trendy bar in the centre of Brussels, in the heart of a neighbourhood filled with fashion boutiques, where he both lives and works. In his late forties, he used to work for various Parisian fashion houses and as an independent fashion designer, and today he combines teaching with freelance projects, which gives him 'the luxury of having time'. He told me how he first got into fashion:

> I was a kid who needed to express myself, I drew a lot ... I became a trendy teenager, a teenager who didn't want to be like everyone else, I always wanted to be with people who were a bit different. So I was gradually beginning to figure out what I wanted to do and particularly what I didn't want to do. And when I saw people around me who were in fashion and had been for a long time, they often seemed to know, like in other jobs, what they didn't want to do. I definitely didn't want – at the time, anyway – to do some easy, boring degree, get a job that didn't inspire me, like my friends who became social workers or lawyers, or went into business.

Philip's words distil the reasons that are often given by fashion workers when they describe what led them into a career in fashion. In spite of the wide variety of ages, professions, origins and career paths, the same motives that inspired them to break through the barrier separating spectators of the dream from those who create it are repeated again and again. Eleanor, an American fashion photographer and former model now in her sixties, was born in the early 1950s in small-town America: 'My mother always bought *Vogue* magazine, it was like her escape mechanism. My father eventually left, and that was all she had. She didn't like her job, and I think fashion for her was an escape.' Eleanor grew up in a world where fashion, as seen in magazines, represented a dream that allowed her a respite from reality. Mayra, born in a small town in Flemish-speaking Belgium, is a twenty-three-year-old recent graduate of the fashion design school La Cambre in Brussels. When I asked her how she ended up in fashion, she explained that she too had been influenced by magazines:

> It's that thing you say when you're a kid: what do I want to do when I grow up? It makes you want to dream! I think when you're little you see all those advertisements, and you just think, wow. I used to stick them inside my homework notebook, and I'd tell myself, I'd like to be like her … It's a dream world. And in Paris, when you see the clothes, you're just like, oh, if only I had that, maybe I'd have the life that goes with it … It fascinated me, I wanted to find out what went on behind the scenes, how it was made. And over time my relationship with all that changed, I wanted to create fashion more than I wanted to own it.

In the case of Eleanor, Mayra, Thierry, Ludo and many others I spoke to, their desire to work in fashion was guided by a kind of taste for beauty and luxury, as well as by a desire to be part of the dream seen in the fashion press and in advertising, a dream representing an escape from reality or a 'norm' which is experienced as a frustration.[1] Their quest for an aestheticism and sophistication is combined with a rejection of jobs that don't 'inspire' them, as Philip put it, in other words ordinary life, as symbolized by the traditional wage earner. Their dream is thus at the same time a hollow dream: it is not only a question of choosing to enter this world because of what it is, but also

---

[1]   For more on the social construction of the norm, see E. Goffman, *Stigma: Notes on the Management of Spoiled Identity*, New Jersey, Prentice Hall, 1963; H. S. Becker, *Outsiders: Studies in the Sociology of Deviance*, New York, The Free Press of Glencoe, 1985.

for what it is not, as Ludo put it when he explained that he had ended up in fashion because it offered an alternative to a life that is too 'conventional'.

Going into fashion can be seen therefore as a way of avoiding a certain kind of corporate job as well as the life and persona that go with it. Even though working in fashion is not exempt from hierarchies and rules, it benefits from an aura of exceptionalism, highly valued by workers. The exception, the privilege of 'being there', is located in the fact of being outside these imagined 'norms', distinct from the masses and their ways of working.

This hostile relationship to the norm is also an element in the subjectivities of fashion workers, as Marguerite explains:

> Fashion creates a group, brings together people who might have problems, to do with the body, or society, to the other, so you have this group of people who are kind of borderline, but who have this creativity, this fragility; they might be a bit neurotic, but they put it to use in their art. There are lots of fragile people in this milieu.

According to Marguerite, fashion is somewhere 'fragile' subjects can find their place. Claire, a former head of collection, now a consultant and trend hunter, with thirty years' experience in the world of luxury fashion behind her, agrees. During a long conversation, she told me that 'no one ends up in fashion by chance', because it's a world of 'pariahs':

> It's a pariah occupation, because clothes making was traditionally always done by Jews, gays, people who weren't allowed to do other jobs. They're people who are pariahs even in their own families. People end up in fashion because they're gay, they're disapproved of, because they're incredibly sensitive and that's disapproved of, because they're creative and because it's not a proper job.

All these statements evoke an image of a world that is welcoming and offers a coveted place to subjects who are marginalized or discriminated against in the symbolic hierarchies of the norm:

It's a sort of crazy environment, with these people who are looking for social recognition, and recognition from their own families as well, who are carrying out a kind of revenge because they haven't been treated well, because they weren't comfortable in their own families or their own countries, or historically. I think there's always this symbolic idea of tissue, fabric that covers up nudity, and also that allows people to create bonds, to create affect. We talk about muscular tissue, social tissue with this idea of making a community.

What makes fashion workers into an elite of desire, a community of exception, is not only, therefore, the projection of a dream of which they are the object, but also the fact that they are part of a world where conditions and status that would be considered in other contexts to be deviant[2] are here considered the norm.

Creating a persona

Even though it is accepting of those who do not adhere to the norm, fashion imposes its own rules in terms of subjectification, demanding the construction and presentation of personalities that fit into its world.[3] Annie, who gave up her career as a costume designer in the theatre in order to work in fashion, told me that in fashion 'you're forced to find your own image, your own character, and when it works you hang on to it.' Fashion takes over the space of subjectivity not only in terms of the immaterial productions and relationships between workers, but also in terms of the injunction to 'perform'[4] a 'character', to be visible and to stand out. Mia understands this, and explained it to me with a metaphor: in her life outside work, she is a 'bird of the woods', whereas in her professional life she is a 'river bird':

---

[2]   Ibid.
[3]   B. Holmes, *The Flexible Personality*.
[4]   E. Goffman, *The Presentation of Self in Everyday Life*; *Behavior in Public Places: Notes on the Social Organization of Gatherings*.

In my private life, I like extreme simplicity, simple things, going camping, sleeping under canvas. In my professional life, I stay in crazily blingy five or six-star hotels, and eat in super-expensive restaurants. It's fun, I enjoy it, but it's not my real life. It doesn't really interest me, I'd go even further, I despise that kind of thing. I do it because I have to, it's my work, my creativity, it's what I want to do, so it's my life. But I keep my distance, in the sense that in my life outside work I don't go on holiday to Bali, or stay in the Bulgari hotel, I wouldn't even imagine it, do you know what I mean? Even if I had the money I wouldn't do it because I was brought up with different values, with a totally different philosophy and ethos. But obviously, when I'm there I play the game, it's like playing a role. But it's also true that there are people who'd be ready to kill their own mothers if it meant they could go to the parties.

Another time, Mia told me quite explicitly that when she was working she was 'fake, the whole time', which didn't mean that she lied or said the opposite to what she was thinking, but that she was displaying herself, taking on a role she had created for herself. Fashion schools also play an important role in this process of constructing a subjectivity and of individualization. Philip told me, referring to his students: 'I push them to develop their individuality, because it's really important, even if everything is highly codified, to hang on to a kind of extravagant individuality before they really find their place, otherwise they'll end up just a number like everyone else.'

Fashion codes require that one 'creates a persona', in the sense of creating an identity that 'works', shines, is visible, unique and desirable. But 'creating a persona' also implies 'adapting' or 'adjusting' to the norms that this world insists upon. In his reflections on the work of Michel Foucault, Mathieu Potte-Bonneville explains that for the philosopher, the notion of subjectification evokes the interstices between 'creating a persona' in the sense of 'adapting' to an imposed structure and 'creating a persona' in the sense of 'constructing a self' as a subject – this latter operation is made possible by the first. In

Potte-Bonneville's elegant formulation, 'being there', working in fashion, involves 'creating a self by creating one's self'.[5]

Coping

According to Claire, fashion is a world that's 'incredibly tough, because it's incredibly subjective; it's your moment, then it's not your moment, one day you're amazing and the next day you're only good for throwing to the dogs'. The subjectivity described by Claire, understood here in the sense of personal non-rational judgement, is, according to her, at the very basis of the fashion system, as well as of its malfunctioning. She believes that the difficulties inherent in working in fashion stem from the fact that it is a system 'based on hysteria', a hysteria that is performed by theatrical, eccentric and unpredictable subjectivities, but also a hysteria that is linked to the cycles of production:

> Hysteria is also the model of consumption, it's the real motivation in these jobs. With the motivation of hysteria, one needs an object to dominate, but hysteria is also an element of consumption. You kill the thing you loved yesterday, because the point is you're always in the process of doing something, you're never in the present moment. You're always in the process of projecting yourself into the next thing, and the thing after that. These are jobs for mad people.

The question of how to 'cope' with these rhythms of production and these types of relationship with oneself and others is posed in an explicit manner by all fashion workers, each of whom offers a different answer. Two months after the Deauville shoot I met up with Léonard for another interview. He started working as a makeup artist after a

---

[5]   Mathieu Potte-Bonneville discussed this in detail during his talk at a seminar held by Michel Agier at EHESS in Paris, in April 2013.

childhood and adolescence doing ballroom dancing. He became skilled at making up his dance partner during their frequent travels to take part in competitions, and, fascinated by its luminosity and beauty, he decided that cosmetic art was his ideal job. His way of dealing with the feverish rhythms of the various fashion weeks and his constant travels all over the world was to adopt a lifestyle that includes regular yoga, being teetotal, not smoking and eating a carb-free diet. Although this healthy lifestyle helps him cope physically, it doesn't help with the issue of how to cope with professional relationships on an emotional level. During our conversation, he told me that although his collaboration with the Wiew agency was working out well, he'd stopped working as an assistant to Hector, the world-famous makeup artist. With a hint of regret, he said:

> He is an absolute genius. He's not a queen [an expression used to describe effeminate, often extrovert and emotionally effusive gay men], he's extremely introverted, in terms of business, work, even with his assistants. He is super-crazily intellectual, he thinks of a thousand things a second, and everything he does is totally . . . unlike anything else. He really is a genius, I have so much respect for him.

When I asked him whether Hector ever became abusive, he said:

> Totally. When you work with someone as brilliant as he is, there's always a form of abuse, because people like him have such incredible vision, that no one else can understand, and they get really frustrated if what they've thought of doesn't get done. We're there every second trying to predict what he's going to do next. It's so stressful, you can't imagine. There's so much tension, but what is so crazy is that afterwards he'll hug you as if nothing's happened . . . But it was so stressful . . . I was really disappointed I couldn't deal with it; but it was making me ill, I wasn't doing well at all . . . But I do miss it a bit, I'd have liked to push it a bit further . . .

When he described Hector's manner, Léonard became a little uneasy and the conversation began to sound like a confession. Despite his abusive manner, it was not Hector who was at fault, but Léonard, because he couldn't 'cope', he didn't 'stick it out' or 'deal with it', or manage it, or manage himself. He explained that he felt forced to quit his job as Hector's first assistant because he was suffering from regular panic attacks, insomnia and an unbearable level of anxiety. His friends encouraged him to resign and to put his health first. But Léonard was disappointed that he had not had the strength to stay, which was emphasized in the way he praised Hector and legitimized his tyrannical behaviour:

> I just got to the point where I couldn't do it any more, but I have so much respect for him, I don't think that there's another makeup artist as talented as him anywhere in the world. Really, he's such a special guy. It's just that . . . it was so nerve-wracking . . . I still do the occasional fashion show but I'm not his personal assistant any more, I don't have to put away all his kit, his green cotton buds are not my problem, he's mad about his green cotton buds. Everything has to be neatly laid out on the table and the cotton wool for removing makeup has to be a specific brand, if it isn't he throws it on the floor . . . I get it, when you're at that level, it's the bare minimum to do the amazing work he does . . . He can't work with crappy cotton buds, and it's totally understandable . . . but when it lands on you it's just so stressful . . . After a while, I began to see that I wasn't a very good personal assistant.

Léonard's description takes us back to the notion of the neoliberal individual, that is, an individual who is solely responsible for his successes and failures, his disappointments and his joys, his body, his appearance and his ability to 'cope'; all this arises from the neoliberal cult of personal freedom. This notion has the function of normalizing the different forms of domination and of concealing inequalities; it is situated in the inter-individual and subjective sphere of structural and systemic asymmetry. This normalizing and individualistic attitude is shared by the majority of fashion workers, who tend to deal with the inequalities and forms of domination of the fashion world in a spirit of competition. The fashion world becomes a sort of 'glamour jungle' in which workers have to 'cope' in order to 'be there'.

Marguerite explained to me that in spite of the way fashion people present themselves as worldly and sophisticated party animals, one has to be tough to be able to 'handle' this milieu:

> If you go out and party you won't be able to work the next day, you won't be able to handle it, do an amazing sketch, be clearheaded and ready to work hard . . . 'cause we work really hard here! . . . You have to be totally focused, which means you really do have to be able to cope with it all.

Mathilde is a twenty-eight-year-old assistant photographer at the most well-known photography studio in Belgium, which specializes in fashion photography. She works an average of ten hours a day for which she's paid, off the books, between 500 and 700 euros a month. She thought that she would be 'creating images', but in fact she has found herself doing 'menial work' like moving sets around, painting walls and cleaning the studio. She told me that among the people she knows there are different ways of 'coping':

> You lose control because your life is so monopolized by work that even with your friends you go a bit crazy. You hit a wall eventually. People end up doing drugs. I don't, but it's not uncommon. Plenty of people do, I know my boss was doing coke on some of the shoots. And people have the most unhealthy lifestyles imaginable. They drink coke all day, smoke two packets of cigarettes, eat crap. It's horrible, there's something really depressing about it. And now I don't know any more what I want to do. I've started doing lots of sport, because I realized that if I wanted to be able to cope psychologically, I was going to have to really devote myself to something, and sport's ended up being my salvation in a way.

Cocaine is undoubtedly the most popular drug in this milieu, not least for its energizing properties and the fact that it kills the appetite,

ahead of hash and marijuana, which people take to relax and deal
with stress or insomnia. However, drug taking appears to be less
common than adopting a healthy lifestyle. With their years of
experience in fashion, Claire, former head of collection and now a
consultant for various luxury brands, and Thierry, a designer, consider
that the era of excess and ostentatious overindulgence is over. That is
due to the increase in power of the large luxury holdings and the
construction of fashion empires, which has led to a rising number of
self-employed workers who have to perform impeccably in a highly
competitive market. Audrey's experience is typical of the strategies
and modes of subjectification necessary to 'cope' in fashion. I met her
in 2006 when I was giving Italian lessons and she was working as a
sales rep in the pharmaceutical industry. She was at a crossroads in
her career and had just decided to leave her well-paid job to follow her
passion, which was fashion. She applied to one of the most famous
– and expensive – private fashion schools in Paris and completed her
degree in two instead of the usual three years. I saw her doing
brilliantly at her studies while she was destroying herself as she kept
going. She never slept for more than four hours a night over the two
years of her studies, and stayed up every night till dawn to complete
her assignments. She was constantly ill. She consumed at least one
ibuprofen a day, on top of several cups of coffee and dozens of
cigarettes. Not long after she graduated, the school offered her a
teaching job. Audrey now combines teaching with designing her own
line. One evening, at dinner at her house, I asked how the students
cope with the stress of their course; what I really wanted to know was
if her experience was an exception or the norm. According to her,
everyone deals with the stress as best they can, and every year a
number of students give up in the middle of their degree, despite the
high tuition costs. She added that during the last period of exams, one
student who was presenting her collection to the jury threw herself
out of a window. Seeing how shocked I was at this, she told me that it's

not uncommon; 'there are students who just can't cope, can't deal, and it's not always the least talented ones'.[6]

Audrey was familiar with two professional worlds that at first glance appear to be very different to each other: she went from being a sales rep in a multinational pharmaceutical company to working as a fashion designer and teacher. Yet despite the symbolic differences, these two spheres of production offer many analogies in terms of the skills they require and the pressure they exert on workers. In addition to her undeniable talent, Audrey was able to cope with her studies and then find her place in fashion because she already had the principal tools she needed to do so: an entrepreneurial attitude, which in her case was translated into a desire to push herself to her physical limits in order to achieve professional results, and by the assimilation of a 'Darwinian' competitive logic where only the strongest and most motivated are able to 'cope' and 'stick it out'.

Getting out

Beyond the strategies for 'getting into fashion' and 'coping', some workers manage to find a place in fashion that suits them. They manage to free themselves of the restrictions of 'glamour labour' and find a balance between work time and non-work time. They earn a decent and stable living, and have jobs that they enjoy. Whether they are young or experienced, all those who find themselves in this enviable position did it by renouncing a fundamental element of fashion work: the dream. After fifteen years working as a designer for different luxury brands, Philip decided to renounce this exciting world in order to extricate himself from a financial situation that had

6   Audrey told me that there is on average one attempted suicide a year at the school where she teaches. Other people I spoke to told me that suicide is relatively frequent among fashion workers, for reasons usually related to work and employment conditions.

become 'a little wearing over the last few years'. Now, as we have seen, he combines teaching with freelance projects that are not part of the fashion dream but are decently paid, such as designing uniforms for a state-owned company. Despite the lack of glamour, he doesn't regret his choice:

> When you work in high fashion you don't have the time to do what you're good at. And on top of that, your own time is non-existent. For me, my priority was to have my own time back. Time for me, I didn't want to work all weekend any more. I was older, sure, but not working all weekend and enjoying all the things I'd stopped doing, seeing friends, going on holiday ... it's hardly a luxury, but I didn't have it any more. And yet I was working in the world of luxury.

Arnaud didn't need to experience working in luxury fashion to decide to prioritize his personal life. At his graduation from the fashion department at the Royal Academy of Fine Arts in Antwerp, he won a 50,000-euro prize, which he ploughed into his first collection under his own name. He quickly realized that even if he sold every piece from the collection, he wouldn't make a penny. He decided to stop. In spite of the critical success and the many orders he received, he refused to work at a loss. 'I love what I do, but not to the point of paying to do what I want to do. I don't mind if I don't make a profit, but I can't accept paying to work.' He turned to the circuit of commerce, which, while lacking glamour, guaranteed him a stable income and working hours that enabled him to have a life outside work. He did styling for publicity campaigns for lingerie, and then was taken on by a mid-range Belgian brand to overhaul its image: 'It's not super-creative, but I know I'm lucky to have found a job in fashion that pays ... I've always put my private life before my professional life ... It really was my choice, I don't regret it at all because I'm happy where I am.' Arnaud is 'happy where he is', away from the glamour, in other words the prestige (acquired) and the power (to which he was subjected). A similar choice was made by one of Franck's former interns who, traumatized by her experience working for the independent designer – which almost put her off working in fashion – eventually found a job as a designer for a highly successful brand that has its offices in northern France. She told me that the fact of not having to deal with the psychological pressure and endless deadlines for collections, having a salary with social security benefits, a permanent contract, fixed hours, paid overtime and paid holidays, meant that she was now enjoying working again.

Among the independent designers I met during my research, the only ones who were surviving financially were those who had opened a small, local boutique, in either Paris or in Brussels, where they produced and sold their collections outside the circuit of fashion week and the demands of the fashion calendar. Jem falls into this category. After studying design in Paris, she worked initially as an intern and then found paid work with various mid-range brands:

> Honestly, the atmosphere, the hypocrisy, it's inhuman, the designers in those offices are vile. They talk to you no better than if you were a dog. When you're an intern, the stuff you do isn't exactly interesting: you buy toilet paper and do photocopying. Afterwards, when I got a job there, they would steal my designs, they never paid me for them, that really appalled me. So I stopped and got a job in sales because I needed to eat.

After this brief parenthesis in sales, she opened a boutique where she sells her own designs. She works long hours, and has to deal with all the bureaucratic aspects of being a small business owner, but she earns enough for her and her son to live on, and loves what she does:

> Unlike luxury, which is another world, a world I don't know at all, it's never attracted me, what I like is designing and being in direct contact with clients. I like the human side, all the different slices of life, the different body types; you adapt, that's what's interesting. I want to stay small-scale as long as I can. I don't want to grow at all.

Claire also left the world of glamour after twenty years during which she worked 'like crazy', giving total priority to her career and allowing family life and her children to take a back seat. As head of collections for a well-known label, she would work every weekend and was never home before 9.00 pm. She was motivated by the fact that fashion is 'a high-status milieu, directly or indirectly creative, where you rub shoulders with people whose own talent spills over onto you a little . . . You know the kind of thing: being witty and clever at dinner parties, the crazy things people say.' She went on: 'I know people who've always been really unhappy, but they'll never leave because it's like their visiting card.' I asked her if it was difficult to give up the prestige. She replied that she hadn't given it up by choice, but for reasons that were beyond her control:

> I ended up in hospital, and while I was there I start thinking, 'What kind of a life is this?' I began to wonder if this was really what I wanted, why I had this need for recognition. I started trying to analyse it . . . I never saw my children, we had a full-time nanny, my ex-husband said we needed to employ someone to organize our holidays and book theatre tickets . . . All we did was work and show off.

Claire got out of the world of glamour because she couldn't 'cope' with it any more. In the course of my research, workers often told me about colleagues who 'gave up' because they 'couldn't cope'. Most of the people I met when I was writing this book are no longer working in fashion. The reasons they give for this are often very similar: the impossibility of coping financially, the desire to have a social life and a private life, problems related to physical and psychological exhaustion, the moral disgust they began to feel for the abuse and hypocrisy they encountered. As with Claire, 'getting out' was often the result of no longer being able to 'cope'. This was what happened to Elsa, who gave up her job as a designer at a luxury fashion house, burned out after many years of financial precariousness. Though she was happy to have time for life outside work again, she nonetheless told me how hard she found it to be 'on the outside': 'I left my job and was on the dole, it was awful. All of a sudden I was a nobody. From one day to the next people who used to say hallo to you just ignore you. It's brutal.'

Working in fashion endows a social status, but as soon as a person leaves that world they lose that status. Mia had a similar experience. After several months with her agency Wiew, she was offered a job as fashion editor at a French women's magazine. It meant returning to the world of fashion journalism, which she had always enjoyed. It would mean she was no longer in a situation of precariousness, either financial or existential – the job was stable and she would be earning 9,000 euros a month. Even if in some ways it meant compromising in terms of her creative freedom, since the magazine was run on a commercial basis, and even though Céline, her booker, tried to dissuade her, Mia accepted the job. After a trial period she was given a one-year contract, but then the magazine changed hands and she was laid off with no redundancy benefits. Since then she hasn't got any more work through her booker Céline, with whom she used to have a superficial friendship. Now she doesn't even take Mia's calls. Most of the friends and photographers she used to work with do the same. On top of that, for the first time in years, she hasn't received any invitations for the fashion week shows. She has told me many times how hard it is no longer to exist, to get no responses to her emails, text messages and phone calls. She's been living on her savings from when she was working at the magazine, but they're running out. She says she has been psychologically affected by this sudden disaffiliation,[7] but at the same time she can't imagine working in a different area: 'A normal job? No way. I can't. My work is my life.'

---

[7]   R. Castel, *Les Métamorphoses de la question sociale: Une chronique du salariat*, Paris, Fayard, 1995.

Fashion: A place for the exception?

In some ways, fashion is a world of exception: in its symbolic representations, which make it the site of the dream, and thus of desire and an escape from reality; because it is structured according to its own laws; and because it offers a coveted place to those who have had, in their social and family lives, experienced being 'outsiders'.[8] The world of fashion is also a symbolic locus that constructs its power through the presentation of the exception, an exception that consists of being outside the norms, beyond conventional rules and laws. Although the fashion system does not circumvent many of the traits of contemporary capitalism (structural inequalities in the distribution of wealth, differentiated access to globalization and circulation, delocalization, individuation and precariousness, as well as the dynamics of subjectification and subjection specific to the contemporary workplace), it presents itself as, and bases its prestige on, an 'extraterritorial fiction' and on the 'artefact of exception'.[9] A state of exception that is not endured but asserted, because within fashion, prestige results from the fact of being where other people are not, in other words in the dream and in the heart of overexposure.

Foucault, listing the defining principles of heterotopias, explains in his fifth principle that heterotopias are

> [a] system of opening and closing that both isolate and make them penetrable ... [There are spaces which] seem to be pure and simple openings but that generally hide curious exclusions; everyone can enter into the heterotopic sites, but in fact that's only an illusion: we think we enter where we are, but by the very fact that we enter we are excluded.[10]

[8] M. Foucault, P. T. Coat, *La Pensée du dehors*, Saint-Clément-la-Rivière, Fata Morgana, 2009.

[9] M. Agier, 'Le campement urbain comme hétérotopie et comme refuge'.

[10] M. Foucault, 'Des espaces autres', *Architecture/Mouvement/Continuité*, October 1984 ('Des Espaces Autres', March 1967). Translated from the French by Jay Miskowiec.

Fashion is a heterotopia in this sense as well: from the outside it appears to be a homogenous world of sequins and bright lights, but once the threshold is crossed, one enters a space that is heavily structured, functioning on the principle of permanent exclusions that are economic, social and symbolic.

Nonetheless, this world does make space for people who are different. The relationship between the norm and the exception is the fundamental characteristic of the heterotopia, which functions as a 'social, political and ethical mirror'[11] of society. During our conversation, Claire emphasized the fact that despite the strictness of the rules by which it is governed, fashion offers a refuge to those who are different:

> These jobs are an opportunity for social payback for some people. If you've been criticized by your family, you can show what you are capable of by working in fashion, because even if you're gay, black, someone who is massively sensitive, you can succeed. It's like the story of The Little Engine that Could. There's a place where people like you do really well. It's hugely based on affect – 'I like it', 'I don't love it', 'I don't feel like it', 'I feel like it'.

Some subjectivities that outside the heterotopia are considered to be 'deviant',[12] marginal or stigmatized are established norms within. In fashion the normalization of a certain type of exception is such that when workers find themselves outside, having left behind the aesthetic rules and facing 'reality', they find themselves on a completely different wavelength.

The economic, social and professional status of Claire and Mathilde are entirely different: Claire did a degree at a major fashion school and has held high-status, stable and well-paid positions in fashion. Mathilde is a self-taught photographer from a working-class

---

[11] M. Agier, 'Le campement urbain comme hétérotopie et comme refuge'.
[12] H. S. Becker, *Outsiders*.

background and describes herself as being an 'unskilled worker'. When she worked in fashion she was badly paid and professionally precarious. What the two women have in common is their experience of both exploitation and self-exploitation, as well as the feeling of alienation with respect to the outside world, because of overwork. It was only when they left the fashion world that they were able to recognize the exception in which they had been living. 'Now I take the métro', said Mathilde. 'I hang out with normal people, and it's quite weird for me.' When I asked her what meant by 'normal', she answered: 'I think I define everything according to a pre-existing pattern that was imposed, with visual and aesthetic hierarchies, which everything was based on.' These 'visual hierarchies' are emphasized by the fashion system in order to conceal, behind the presentation of a sort of aesthetic community based on shared values linked to appearance, the structural hierarchies that are inherent to capitalism. Once she left fashion, Claire also began to see that she had been living inside a system of exception founded on appearance. She explained how exotic it felt when she went to see her daughter play guitar in a local cultural centre:

> Everyone was so badly dressed, fat, bursting out of their tee shirts, but they were beaming ... And I really understood it then, I thought to myself, 'They're so badly dressed', but they're cool, happy, relaxed, they don't care if they've got a spare tyre or two, they're basking, displaying themselves, but in a really authentic way, and it's beautiful. I went over to talk to this quite overweight woman and told her: 'You sing so beautifully'. It was like I'd rediscovered my humanity, and it felt so good.

Fashion is a heterotopia because the characteristics on which its exception is based, its emancipation from the norm, are in reality merely the mirror image of that norm. In capitalism, heterotopias are necessary and organic; they serve to confirm the rules, rights and constraints to which those who are 'within it' must submit.

*

Despite all these constraints, to be there, in fashion, 'positions you socially straightaway', as Philip put it, and 'positions' people at the heart of the exception which, in Claire's words is 'an elite of display'. Even if the challenge of social inclusion and visibility is an enormous factor in the reasons that motivate workers to enter and above all to stay in this world of the dream – a dream that is only a fantasy – there are other reasons why workers 'cope'. Zoé, whom I met during my 'internship' with Franck, told me that she earned 'a thousand euros a month. It's pointless asking for a raise, in any case they haven't got it. And anyway I love what I do. I could earn more as a waitress, but that doesn't interest me. This is my passion.' Passion plays a major role in the range of reasons that people 'cope' and stay in fashion.

Mayra recently graduated from fashion school and has just started working as a designer. Towards the end of our conversation, she told me about how surprisingly hard she found her work: the thousands of tasks she had to do on top of designing clothes, building relationships, the endless working hours, and the financial instability she faced. The freedom that her occupation offered her was, she said, 'a very stressful freedom! You aren't as free as all that.' She told me that her boyfriend, an actor, faced similar challenges. After saying that in a serious tone of voice, she paused, smiled and said: 'But anyway, let's be positive!' She went on:

> After a while you carry on doing it because you like what you do and you can't live without it. If we could, we'd all be working at the supermarket, doing office jobs, or being lawyers. If you don't have that passion, you can't do it. You have to make so many sacrifices that you can't do it if your heart isn't in it.'

Despite the difference in age and profession, Dominique, a makeup artist, also defines her work as her passion, a passion that is necessary in order to 'cope' during those unavoidable periods between jobs when she's not working. During one work crisis, Mia told me that she'd been working for ten years and still didn't have financial or existential stability: 'It's my passion, but at a certain point it became an obsession.' She thinks of her work as a kind of addiction: 'If you work in fashion, you're definitely predisposed to addiction ... It's a drug. And there are lots of reasons why people use drugs. Because they like it, because it makes them feel different, lets them escape their heads, their thoughts, their problems.' Mia considers her passion for her work as a kind of drug. Working in fashion is addictive and gives her the illusion of being something other than herself, it produces a sort of 'hallucination' that allows her to detach herself from reality, which is another way of saying that it allows her to enter a dream, which, in the case of fashion, is a dream of beauty, creativity, status and power. Ludo also talks about the addictive aspect of his passion for his work: 'Like lots of passions, it fires you up inside, but it also eats you up, sometimes, because you're always ... you need it.'

One of the things that came out of all of these conversations was the notion that inherent in this idea of having a passion for one's work is a dimension of sacrifice and suffering. In fact, the etymology of the word 'passion' can be traced back to the Latin verb *patior,* meaning 'to suffer', 'to endure', and also 'to permit'. It is also associated with the Greek word *pathos,* meaning 'desire' and 'strong emotions', which similarly suggests an element of suffering. Fashion work is emotional work. But the cost of this passion is high, because it includes multiple forms of precariousness, as well as power relationships, and exploitation that is sometimes self-inflicted.

It's useful to consider the etymology of the word passion when it comes to analysing the role of this affect in work,[13] because it hints at

---

[13]   M. Ballatore, M. del Rio Carral and A. Murgia, 'Présentation: Quand passion et précarité se rencontrent dans les métiers du savoir', *Recherches sociologiques et anthropologiques,* no. 45–2, December 2014.

the contradictions inherent in working in fashion. Passion for one's work can mean that the subject acts in accordance with the passion that motivates, nourishes and rewards them, while the same subject can be 'acted upon' by their passion, by giving into it, like a drug addict giving into his addiction. In light of such an observation, is it legitimate, in terms of the mechanisms of consensual dependence as described in this book, to talk of self-exploitation?

Léonard describes himself as being passionate more about being able 'to express himself' than about makeup itself. Rosalind Gill and Andy Pratt have researched forms of precariousness brought on by cultural and immaterial labour.[14] They emphasize in particular the role of affect in these areas of work, where workers describe their jobs using a 'vocabulary of love', who talk in terms of personal fulfilment, pleasure and self-expression. They use this to analyse the characteristics of what they call 'passionate work'. Beyond its empirical utility, Gill and Pratt's analysis is notable for the way it exposes the ambiguity of the emotional element in post-Marxist theories of cultural and immaterial labour. On the one hand, post-Marxism considers (quite rightly) that all human labour is emotional and that this aspect is thus not specific to immaterial labour, but on the other hand, post-Marxists claim that the affective component is the reason that this kind of labour manages to avoid being controlled by capital, attributing this to its intrinsically transgressive and revolutionary nature. By pointing out this implicit contradiction – if all labour is affective, then all labour is revolutionary – Gill and Pratt also show that these theories ignore the negative effects of emotional labour, including exhaustion, precariousness, competitiveness, individuation, compulsion, self-exploitation, in addition to the interiorization and normalization of power relationships and forms of subjectification imposed within this professional world. Gill and Pratt correctly point out the necessity of

---

[14]   R. Gill and A. Pratt, 'In the social factory?'

'thinking together'[15] the pleasure and satisfaction provided by labour alongside the precariousness that the affective component of post-Fordist work entails. Affect, they argue, cannot be considered to be fundamentally autonomous, and therefore to exist outside relationships of power. The 'passion for self-expression', in the sense of pleasure and personal satisfaction, can only be understood in association with 'passion as an addiction', that is the fact of enduring and 'coping' with things that go beyond one's limits, leading to self-exploitation. These two dimensions are inseparable because 'pleasure itself may become a disciplinary technology'.[16]

This analysis considers that the relationship between subject and power is at the heart of the process of domination – sometimes self-inflicted – of post-Fordist capitalism. Nonetheless, as has been said elsewhere, the aim of this book is not to prove that fashion workers are, against their consent, subject to a power that penetrates the deepest recesses of their subjectivity. Rather than to attempt to resolve this tension, I think it is vital to explore, at a different level, the links between passionate work and the precariousness that is effectively accepted as the price that must be paid for a job that is desirable, interesting, creative and fulfilling. The relationship between the normalization of precariousness and self-exploitation is, for Andrea Fumagalli and Cristina Morini, the fundamental characteristic of the way work has been transformed in contemporary capitalism:

> New languages are useful. These are languages in which the word gratuity has a central place. We see there the attempt to radically modify the nature of the employee's relationship to work by conceiving notably new mechanisms of involvement that disregard economic value. Precariousness, as in the loss of the guarantee of continuity of income and rights, renders artificial enthusiasm indispensable, an autosuggestion that is sufficiently strong that it

15 Ibid., p. 16.
16 Ibid., p. 17.

manages to carry the subject to the point where he will agree to sacrifice himself and to work for free.[17]

The processes of subjectification described in this book, and the spread of the 'flexible personality',[18] are signs of a major anthropological transformation, which does see not an increase in labour as a source of economic capital but as the factor that gives meaning to life. Nonetheless, it is important to emphasize that these transformations benefit capital – represented in the context of my research by the fashion industry in all its different forms – which encourages people to work and generate profits without being paid. These practices are widespread in work in all areas of the so-called cultural, artistic and creative industries, but they are particularly striking in the case of fashion: the practice of unpaid labour and self-exploitation described by Fumagalli and Morini is implemented here by the production of one of the most powerful and richest industries in contemporary capitalism. The issue of exploitation is thus made concrete, and it doesn't matter if the potency of labour in fashion is physical, cognitive, emotional, creative, relational or affective, for the fashion industry, in both its material and its immaterial productions, exploits the full range. In his book *Felici e sfruttati* (*Happy and Exploited*), Carlo Formenti points out that the act of psychologizing economic relationships, which reduces the behaviours of social actors to subjective motivations, is the oldest trick in the book,[19] whose purpose is to conceal exploitation. In the case of people who work in the digital industries – the subject of his research – the trick, which also applies to fashion workers and 'immaterial' workers in general, is to construct and diffuse a discourse that promotes the non-monetary benefits of this kind of work. Formenti points out that, despite the transformations

---

[17]   A. Fumagalli and C. Morini, 'Segmentation du travail cognitif et individualisation du salaire', p. 74.

[18]   B. Holmes, 'The flexible personality'.

[19]   C. Formenti, *Felici e sfruttati: Capitalismo digitale ed eclissi del lavoro*, Milan, Egea, 2011.

brought about by post-Fordism, the dynamics of expropriation (in the Marxist sense of dispossessing workers of the potency of work and the products of that potency, both physical and immaterial) are in reality the same throughout the various phases of capitalism, with one important distinction: today, expropriation refers both to resources he calls 'natural'[20] and to social, communication and affective practices. Formenti concludes: 'As the meaning of the word work changes – increasingly overlapping with the meaning of life itself – the meanings of concepts such as exploitation and alienation also change.'[21]

We know that alienation, in the classic Marxist sense, results from the distancing of the worker from the products of his labour, and the transformation of the individual into a machine through physical and repetitive work.[22] What happens to alienation then in a system where subjectivity and affects are at the centre of production and profit? For philosopher Brian Holmes, the new forms of alienation are the consequence of the excessive individuation of labour, and the erasure of the borders between production and consumption, between time spent working and time spent living.[23] Mia said the same thing to me, using different terms, when I asked her if, considering all the difficulties she was facing, she would be ready to 'give up' working in fashion: 'Today no, I couldn't. Because it's such fulfilling work. It fills your life!' Working in fashion 'fills your life' because it takes over a large part of the existence of these workers, and not only in a material sense. It also colonizes the site of interpersonal relations, which are located in an ambiguous area between the personal and the professional. In addition, it encloses the space of the body and subjectivity, since

---

[20] Formenti argues that the expropriation and the accumulation of capital nowadays is less related to 'shared lands and resources'. This is a highly Eurocentric claim, given that on other continents the terms exploitation and expropriation are used more to refer to land and what he calls 'natural' resources.

[21] C. Formenti, *Felici e sfruttati*, p. 99.

[22] K. Marx, *Salaires, prix et profits*, Paris, Le Temps des cerises, 2006.

[23] B. Holmes, 'The flexible personality'.

people have to both 'create their persona' and 'cope', in other words construct themselves as unique individuals while submitting to the rules of the game. In this way, by giving the worker a place in the dream, work in fashion invades the area of social identity, which is directly linked to the world of work.

Working in fashion thus signifies doing work which is 'fulfilling', in the sense that it is a source of pleasure and satisfaction, but also in the sense that it fills all areas of an individual's life, including those which, in the era of Fordist labour, used to belong to the private sphere, in other words the possibility of existing, both in terms of subjectivity and socially, outside the professional sphere. Workers are no longer alienated in terms of their wishes, affects and desires, but they *lose themselves* as individuals (in the sense of being individuals who are part of the body politic), because of their pursuit of the desire to 'be there'.

In short, these new forms of alienation are the consequence of the erasure of the border between subject and labour; as Mia put it, in spite of the addiction, the exploitation and the precariousness, she cannot conceive of being anywhere else but 'there', in fashion, because her work is 'both [her] passion and [her] life'.

Conclusion

'The difficulty of our occupation is compensated for by the beauty of what we create.'[1]

'Everyone wants this. Everyone wants to be us.'[2]

Loosening the knots

As we have seen, there is a considerable gap between the fantasies of the dream, of luxury and of glamour that fashion disseminates and sells through its products, and the often precarious and unpaid work that produces it. The one constant in this world that applies to all its workers is the volume and intensity of work. Interns, designers, in-house designer-stylists, independent designers and even the artistic directors of the biggest luxury houses, as well as journalists, distributors, embroiderers, hairdressers, stylists, buyers and photographers, all work long hours, sleep for correspondingly few, and have little time for life outside work. The condition of access to the world of fashion is total devotion. Despite these significant drawbacks, people nonetheless choose to work in fashion for multiple reasons: because of the value it confers on aesthetics, beauty and luxury, because they want to be creative, and for the visibility and the social status that is bestowed on those work in this domain. In fashion, prestige and precariousness are difficult to disentangle from one another.

---

[1] Designer Narciso Rodriguez, in *Le Jour d'avant*, Loïc Prigent.
[2] Miranda Priestly, *The Devil Wears Prada*.

In some ways, fashion is a place that is 'apart' from the normal order of things, a domain where unique rules and dynamics reign. In order to 'be there', to perform 'glamour labour' in this realm of exception linked to creativity, desire, beauty and luxury, fashion workers give up rights, protections and the safety net guaranteed by being a salaried employee in a company.[3]

But is fashion really the exception, with its irresolvable tensions between social prestige and precariousness, between interesting work that inspires passion and exploitation? And are the symbolic economies and non-financial remunerations described in this book specific only to this world? In other words, are fashion's modes of work intrinsic to contemporary capitalism in all its manifestations or are they specific to fashion? Matthieu Hély's work on work in the social and solidarity economy (SSE) shows how professionals within this milieu – driven by motivations linked to their political and social engagement – accept low salaries and a high volume of work hours, on the principle that they are giving this much of themselves for 'a good cause'.[4] The SSE combines practices inherited from the voluntary sector with financing and hierarchies inherited from business. The possibility of their engagement having an impact appears to be considered by SSE workers to be a form of non-financial remuneration, and is considered a good reason to put up with exploitation and precariousness.

Despite important symbolic and economic differences, a similar logic is practised in the university sector, which has also been transformed and 'worked on' by neoliberal policies. In his book *The Destruction of the French University*, historian Christophe Granger

---

[3] This notion of the exception only applies to workers whose occupations are mediatized and valorized because they are 'creative'. In haute couture houses, the seamstresses and those who are involved in management are not considered part of the dream, and thus are not part of the exception, both from the point of view of symbolic capital and in terms of benefits and protections. They are salaried employees, like those in any company.

[4] M. Hély, *Les Métamorphoses du monde associatif*, Paris, PUF, 2009.

argues that the employment conditions in French universities are a 'social catastrophe'.[5] He draws on a wealth of supporting evidence to show that a quarter of researchers and teachers are on short-term contracts, working off the books, self-employed or unemployed, many on the minimum wage or not paid at all.[6] The majority of what is produced in French universities – teaching and knowledge – is undertaken by workers with unstable jobs.[7] But although their situations are the very definition of precariousness, these workers are no less passionate about what they do,[8] which pushes them to invest deeply in their work in spite of the conditions in which they work. For in spite of the obvious differences, what the worlds of fashion, the social and solidarity economy, and academia share is that they are filled with subjects who are willing to accommodate precariousness, in exchange for passion, engagement and recognition.

Other professional domains share this coexistence of precariousness, symbolic remuneration and social valorization: the art world[9] and more generally what are known as the 'cultural and creative industries',[10] the intellectual world,[11] and professionals such as architects and urban planners.[12]

All the evidence suggests that these 'exceptions' occupy an important place in contemporary capitalism, because they cover a

5 C. Granger, *La Destruction de l'université française*, Paris, La Fabrique, 2015.
6 They number at present around 50,000. See ibid., p. 4.
7 For further discussion of these issues, see E. Armano and A. Murgia, 'The precariousnesses of young knowledge artisans: A subject-oriented approach', *Global Discourse*, vol. 3, no. 3–4, December 2013; Manuela S. Lodovici and R. Semenza (dir.), *Precarious work and high-skilled youth in Europe*, Milan, FrancoAngeli, 2012; PECRES, *Recherche précarisée, recherche atomisée: Production et transmission des savoirs à l'heure de la précarisation*, Paris, Raisons d'agir, 2011.
8 M. Ballatore, M. de Rui Carrak and A. Murgia, 'Présentation: Quand passion et précarité se rencontrent dans les métiers du savoir'.
9 H. S. Becker, *Art Worlds*.
10 D. Hesmondhalgh, 'Cultural and creative industries', in J. Frow and T. Bennett, *The SAGE Handbook of Cultural Analysis*, SAGE, 2008.
11 C. Tasset, *Les Intellectuels précaires: Genèse et réalité d'une figure critique*, doctoral thesis, Paris, EHESS, December 2015.
12 E. Vivant, 'La classe créative existe-t-elle? Discussion de la thèse de Richard Florida', *Les Annales de la recherche urbaine: Économies, connaissances, territoires*, no. 10, May 2007.

significant part of the global economy. Neoliberalism has in effect placed these sectors of activity at the centre of production and has invested the workers in these domains with significant symbolic capital. In his eulogy to the creative class, Richard Florida claims that it is almost impossible to be non-conformist nowadays.[13] Which means that, in a paradoxical way, the exception has become the norm. Indeed, the new spirit of capitalism[14] has established a mechanism of valorization of the individual and of creativity that has led to a society of 'entrepreneurs who are enlightened about their [unique] lives'.[15] Neoliberalism has appropriated 'alternative' modes of living, working and producing. But if the exception is so widespread, what then does it consist of? And if fixed salaries and social protections are not what motivate people to work, what are workers today in search of and what do they project onto their work?

Let's begin by considering the second question. What emerged in my research, and in research conducted by other people as well,[16] is that the choice of entering an occupation that entails significant precariousness might be motivated, among other things, by the rejection of a certain conception of the wage society, in which salaried work – this is a stereotype, because of course creative work can also be salaried – is considered too standard or 'conventional', in the words of Ludo the photographer. However, this rejection of 'standard' work does not always entail the rejection of rules and hierarchies. Thus, while generally speaking academics appear to claim for themselves a kind of marginality[17] through the choice of the most autonomous work possible, fashion workers accept working in organizations that are extremely hierarchical, if informal, with hierarchies based on

---

[13]   R. L. Florida, *The Rise of the Creative Class*, p. 12.
[14]   L. Boltanski and E. Chiapello, *Le Nouvel Esprit du capitalisme*.
[15]   C. Granger, *La Destruction de l'université française*, p. 82.
[16]   D. Hesmondhalgh and S. Baker, 'A very complicated version of freedom'.
[17]   C. Tasset, T. Amosée and M. Grégoire, *Libres ou prolétarisés? Les travailleurs intellectuels précaires en Île-de-France*, Centre d'études de l'emploi, report 82, 2013.

prestige, emotional relationships and symbolic relationships. Generally, what is being rejected is not a hierarchical organization, nor the possibility of submitting to domination, but the idea of labour that does not confer social status, or the possibility of distinguishing oneself as an individual, or meaning to the worker's life. Labour is thus before anything else the space that one invests in order to construct and express one's subjectivity, and where one defines one's social situation.

Now let's return to the first question. The 'exception' allows workers to construct for themselves a subjectivity that is different to the 'norm' and to occupy a place that is an alternative to a certain image of the wage society, with its hierarchies, supervisors, hours, alienation and organization of labour. These 'exceptional' professional worlds allow subjects who 'are there' to think of themselves as being outside their image of the norm. In a certain way, they think of themselves as being heterotopic subjects, subjects who inhabit places different to the norm, for whom precariousness is the price to pay in order to belong to these 'alternative' places. In 1928, the Chicago School sociologist Robert Park introduced the figure of the 'marginal man' to describe the position of migrants caught between multiple places and cultures. The 'marginal man', wrote Park, is characterized by 'his keen intellectual interest ... his idealism ... a man who ranges widely'.[18] 'It is in the mind of the marginal man – where the changes and fusions of culture are going on – that we can best study the processes of civilisation and Progress.'[19] Just like the workers described above, the 'marginal man' is the load-bearing subject of a society in the making and is situated on the margins of the normal order of things. But while the marginal subject is destined to never feel at home anywhere, the heterotopic subject feels entirely at home in these 'alternative' spaces.

[18]   R. E. Park, 'Human migration and the marginal man', *American Journal of Sociology*, vol. 33, no. 6, May 1928, pp. 881–93.
[19]   Ibid.

A space 'outside' the exception does still exist. Non-precarious work still exists, even within the spaces of exception. But 'standard' work tends to concern only those workers who do not benefit from any symbolic capital. This is an important point, because if the neoliberal project continues to progress to its logical conclusion, creative work will become the norm, and the social world will take the form of an archipelago of exceptions inhabited by heterotopic subjects giving up their rights and all social protection, and subjecting themselves, in the name of self-expression and personal fulfilment.

What fashion can teach us

Professional sectors like fashion remain desirable despite the precariousness by which they are structured. With the emergence of neoliberalism, the cultural and creative industries were in the vanguard of the capitalist economy, from both the financial and the symbolic point of view. And yet these sectors can only function because of the multitude of workers who are simultaneously valued symbolically and economically precarious.

Despite maintaining its image of exception, magic and luxury, fashion is an economic, social and professional reality, emblematic of contemporary capitalism. Its exceptional dimension resides not in the logic by which it is ruled, but in the fact that this logic is pushed to the extreme, and is thus more visible than in other domains. Deconstructing the dream of fashion is a way of understanding the ways in which the sector is representative of current types of work, and probably prophetic, in its excesses, of those yet to come.

Despite its excellent financial health, the world of fashion depends to a large extent on unpaid and unstable work, proof, if it were needed, that exploitation and instability are not only to be found in loss-making sectors.[20] The neoliberal project has spearheaded the spread of a conception of non-monetarized work. This is a radical transformation from the wage society, which is based on a compromise between the extraction of the force of labour, remunerated by a wage that provides spending power and welfare state protection. Today, capitalist modes of production underpay and make vulnerable the very same categories of workers that they valorize by setting them up as exemplars. The creative and cultural industries are sites where it is possible to see both the process of 'exceptionalization' and its impact on work and society. Among the domains of exception, fashion occupies a special place, and offers a warning about the way in which new forms of subjugation linked to the mobilization of subjectivity can be monopolized in order to make profits.

Contemporary labour invests subjectivity in a specific way, by placing in the centre not only the processes of production but also the construction of new symbolic elites. Post-Fordist capitalism has led to a new negotiation of the border between worker and subject. The instability of employment[21] and the proliferation of entrepreneurial practices, as well as the broadening of the market of productions requiring creativity, knowledge and networks, has led to capitalism monopolizing spheres of life from which it was excluded under Fordism. The new skills required by post-Fordist work, combined with structural instability due to mass unemployment and flexible employment policies, have pushed workers to individualize themselves and make their subjectivity a product. Structural precariousness is now understood as an issue of personal responsibility and individual evaluation: the individual alone is responsible for his or her failures and successes.

---

[20] This is also demonstrated in Christophe Granger's research into the French university system. See C. Granger, *La Destruction de l'université française*.
[21] A. Corsani and M. Lazzarato, *Intermittents et précaires*, Paris, Editions Amsterdam, 200

This mechanism of individuation is a powerful tool for rendering opaque the structural inequalities and modes of domination specific to capitalism. In 'glamour labour', demands for workplace rights are virtually non-existent,[22] because the absence of a sense of common ground is a fundamental characteristic of a world dedicated to valorizing the individual. Judging by the weakness of collective mobilizations in the cultural industries[23] and the widespread discrediting of social criticism,[24] it seems that neoliberalism's political project of subjugation through precariousness and individualization has achieved its objectives. A political project bringing together all heterotopic subjects in all the archipelagos of exception is yet to be dreamed up. If we are ever to achieve this, it will be necessary first to 'break the spell'[25] of the dream and of glamour.

---

[22] This is with the exception of the modelling industry, in which attempts are now being made to introduce rights and demands, for example with the establishment of the Model Alliance, founded by former model Sara Ziff. On a different scale, in September 2017 French luxury groups LVMH and Kering signed a charter regarding 'work relationships and the wellbeing of models', committing 'not to cast size 32 female models and size 42 male models'.

[23] Apart from the significant mobilizations of people in the acting profession in France, who have made sure that the question of precariousness is at the centre of debate on employment and precariousness.

[24] L. Boltanski and E. Chiapello, *Le Nouvel Esprit du capitalisme*.

[25] P. Pignarre and I. Stengers, *La Sorcellerie capitaliste: Pratiques de désenvoûtement*, Paris, La Découverte, 2005

Index

Page numbers for figures are given in *italics*, and for tables they are given in **bold**. Notes are given as: [page number] n. [note number]